WEBSTER'S NEW WORLD™

American Words of Freedom

Edited and commentary by Stephen F. Rohde

Complete Text + Commentary + Glossary

Hungry Minds™

HUNGRY MINDS, INC.

Best-Selling Books • Digital Downloads • e-Books • Answer Networks • e-Newsletters •

New York, NY • Cleveland, OH • Indianapolis, IN

About the Author

Stephen Rohde has been a constitutional lawyer for over 30 years. A frequent writer and lecturer, he co-authored *Foundations of Freedom* published by the Constitutional Rights Foundation. Most recently he wrote a series of essays for Salem Press on constitutional history, the U.S. Supreme Court, and the American legal system. A graduate of Northwestern University and Columbia Law School, Mr. Rohde is president of the American Civil Liberties Union of Southern California and practices law in Los Angeles with the firm of Rohde & Victoroff.

Publisher's Acknowledgments

Editorial

Project Editor: Kathleen A. Dobie
Acquisitions Editor: Gregory W. Tubach
Copy Editor: Robert Annis
Editorial Manager: Christine Meloy Beck

Production

Proofreader: Bob LaRoche
Hungry Minds Indianapolis Production Services
Cover Illustration: The Design Library, New York, USA/Bridgeman Art Library. Used under license.

Webster's New World™ *American Words of Freedom*

Published by:
Hungry Minds, Inc.
909 Third Avenue
New York, NY 10022
www.hungryminds.com (Hungry Minds, Inc. Web site)

Library of Congress Control Number: 2001097034

ISBN: 0-7645-6638-5

Printed in the United States of America

10 9 8 7 6 5 4 3 2 1

1B/SZ/RQ/QR/IN

Distributed in the United States by Hungry Minds, Inc.

Distributed by CDG Books Canada Inc. for Canada; by Transworld Publishers Limited in the United Kingdom; by IDG Norge Books for Norway; by IDG Sweden Books for Sweden; by IDG Books Australia Publishing Corporation Pty. Ltd. for Australia and New Zealand; by TransQuest Publishers Pte Ltd. for Singapore, Malaysia, Thailand, Indonesia, and Hong Kong; by Gotop Information Inc. for Taiwan; by ICG Muse, Inc. for Japan; by Norma Comunicaciones S.A. for Columbia; by Intersoft for South Africa; by Eyrolles for France; by International Thomson Publishing for Germany, Austria and Switzerland; by Distribuidora Cuspide for Argentina; by LR International for Brazil; by Galileo Libros for Chile; by Ediciones ZETA S.C.R. Ltda. for Peru; by WS Computer Publishing Corporation, Inc., for the Philippines; by Contemporanea de Ediciones for Venezuela; by Express Computer Distributors for the Caribbean and West Indies; by Micronesia Media Distributor, Inc. for Micronesia; by Grupo Editorial Norma S.A. for Guatemala; by Chips Computadoras S.A. de C.V. for Mexico; by Editorial Norma de Panama S.A. for Panama; by American Bookshops for Finland. Authorized Sales Agent: Anthony Rudkin Associates for the Middle East and North Africa.

For general information on Hungry Minds' products and services please contact our Customer Care department; within the U.S. at 800-762-2974, outside the U.S. at 317-572-3993 or fax 317-572-4002.

For sales inquiries and resellers information, including discounts, premium and bulk quantity sales and foreign language translations please contact our Customer Care department at 800-434-3422, fax 317-572-4002 or write to Hungry Minds, Inc., Attn: Customer Care department, 10475 Crosspoint Boulevard, Indianapolis, IN 46256.

For information on licensing foreign or domestic rights, please contact our Sub-Rights Customer Care department at 212-884-5000

For information on using Hungry Minds' products and services in the classroom or for ordering examination copies, please contact our Educational Sales department at 800-434-2086 or fax 317-572-4005.

Please contact our Public Relations department at 212-884-5163 for press review copies or 212-884-5000 for author interviews and other publicity information or fax 212-884-5400.

For authorization to photocopy items for corporate, personal, or educational use, please contact Copyright Clearance Center, 222 Rosewood Drive, Danvers, MA 01923, or fax 978-750-4470.

Hungry Minds· is a trademark of Hungry Minds, Inc.

AMERICAN WORDS OF FREEDOM
CONTENTS AT A GLANCE

Introduction 1

Declaration of Independence 5

The U.S. Constitution 19

The Bill of Rights 69

Subsequent Amendments 109

Review 143

Resources 149

Reading Group Discussion Guide 151

Index 153

Appendix: President George W. Bush
Address to a Joint Session of Congress
and the American People 161

AMERICAN WORDS OF FREEDOM

TABLE OF CONTENTS

Introduction **1**

Declaration of Independence **5**

 The Foundations of Independence 7

 Uniting the Colonies 8

 War Comes to the Colonies 9

 The Declaration's Influence 10

 Declaration of Independence (1776) 11

The U.S. Constitution **19**

 Decision Time 21

 The Articles of Confederation 21

 A Convention Is Called 23

 Slavery and the Constitution 25

 The Ratification Process 27

 Enter the Federalists 27

 State Ratification 30

 The U.S. Constitution 33

 Article I 36

 Article II 48

 Article III 54

 Article IV 59

 Article V 61

 Article VI 63

 Article VII 64

The Bill of Rights 69

A Constitution without a Bill of Rights 71

Ratifying the Bill of Rights 75

First Amendment (1791) 77

Second Amendment (1791) 86

Third Amendment (1791) 88

Fourth Amendment (1791) 89

Fifth Amendment (1791) 92

Sixth Amendment (1791) 97

Seventh Amendment (1791) 100

Eighth Amendment (1791) 101

Ninth Amendment (1791) 103

Tenth Amendment (1791) 105

Subsequent Amendments 109

More Work to be Done 111

Failed Amendments 111

More to Come? 112

Eleventh Amendment (1798) 113

Twelfth Amendment (1804) 114

Thirteenth Amendment (1865) 116

Fourteenth Amendment (1868) 120

Fifteenth Amendment (1870) 123

Sixteenth Amendment (1913) 127

Seventeenth Amendment (1913) 128

Eighteenth Amendment (1919) 129

Nineteenth Amendment (1920) 130

Twentieth Amendment (1933) 132

Twenty-First Amendment (1933) 134

Twenty-Second Amendment (1947) 136

Twenty-Third Amendment (1961) 137

Twenty-Fourth Amendment (1964) 138

Twenty-Fifth Amendment (1967) 139

Twenty-Sixth Amendment (1971) 141

Twenty-Seventh Amendment (1992) 142

Review **143**

Resources **149**

Reading Group Discussion Guide **151**

Index **153**

Appendix: President George W. Bush
Address to a Joint Session of Congress
and the American People **161**

AMERICAN WORDS OF FREEDOM

INTRODUCTION

We know the words, the lyrics of freedom: When in the course of human events; We hold these truths to be self-evident; All men are created equal; Life, Liberty, and the pursuit of Happiness; We the people of the United States in order to form a more perfect Union; secure the Blessings of Liberty; Congress shall pass no law abridging the freedom of speech, or of the press; due process and equal protection of the laws.

The story of freedom in the United States of America is told in a series of key historic documents. The quest for individual rights and personal liberty is engraved for all time in the Declaration of Independence, the United States Constitution, the Bill of Rights (the Constitution's first ten amendments), and the subsequent amendments—particularly the three Civil War Amendments (the Thirteenth, Fourteenth, and Fifteenth) forged out of that bloody conflict.

These documents, crafted over the last 250 years, represent the heritage of American freedom and democracy. They are worthy of study, not only for the rich history they tell of a people striving for independence, struggling to build a new nation, yearning to live up to the ideals of equality and freedom, but also because these documents help chart a path for each new generation to improve upon the past, to learn from earlier mistakes, and to do better than their ancestors in fulfilling their hopes and dreams of America.

The force of America's freedom documents resides in the texts themselves. Every word of each document is presented here without any excisions or deletions. Each document deserves to be read several times, for every one is an heirloom of American democracy. They are like precious paintings or rare books—cherished artifacts which represent the work of the best and the brightest of our country's founders and subsequent political theorists.

Taking the Bitter with the Sweet

The story of America's freedom documents is a bittersweet tale. Bitter because the promise of the Declaration of Independence was not fully kept when the founders wrote the Constitution. Bitter because that Constitution perpetuated the shame of slavery and excluded women and Native Americans. Bitter because even the Bill of Rights failed to cure these pernicious omissions. Bitter because it would take a grueling civil war to cleanse America of the stain of slavery. Bitter because even the Civil War Amendments would leave women behind. And bitter because in the end these documents are nothing more than parchment platitudes unless they are matched by the genuine conviction of all Americans to join in the unfinished task of building a society based on tolerance, compassion, equality, and justice.

Yet the story of these freedom documents is also a sweet tale. Sweet because America had the audacity to declare its independence on the basis of such high ideals. Sweet because the founders courageously memorialized their ambitious goals for all the world to judge. Sweet because the authors designed a plan of government which, though flawed, was equipped to reinvent itself, to adjust its course, and to mend its ways. Sweet because as each of these documents was written, it advanced in the direction of greater freedom, expanded equality, and more liberty and justice for all. Sweet because America has been brave enough to believe that some day all her citizens can realize full equality, regardless of gender, race, religion, national original, sexual orientation, or disability. And sweet because in doing all this and coming so far, America's freedom documents represent a standard for the rest of the world, a beacon to oppressed people everywhere that freedom and democracy offer the best hope for humankind, forever aspiring to achieve peace and justice.

Living History

Written by human beings, these documents are hardly perfect. They so reflect the tenor of their times that they are now easily exposed to our criticism, sometimes even our condemnation. Crafted in the immediacy of the political, social, economic, and philosophical pressures of the time, they reflect the compromises that inevitably result from the clash of deeply held beliefs and prejudices.

Every time one reads the Declaration of Independence, the Constitution, the Bill of Rights, and the later amendments, one is invited to dwell in another place and time, to be transported back to 1776 at the height of the Revolutionary War to meet the brilliant Thomas Jefferson; to sit among the delegates in the sweltering summer of 1787 at the Constitutional Convention in Philadelphia to hear George Mason of Virginia plead with his colleagues to abolish slavery; to observe James Madison in 1789 writing the Bill of Rights in New York City at the First Congress, and to be there over the next 200 years as another 17 amendments are added to the Constitution in the midst of heated debates over the courts, presidential succession, slavery, the right to vote, equal protection, income taxes, the Prohibition of alcoholic beverages, women's suffrage, the District of Columbia, poll taxes, and congressional pay, as each new generation sought to make America a more perfect Union.

What do these documents tell us about freedom in America? To begin with, freedom has meant different things at different times to different people. When the American revolutionaries wrote the Declaration of Independence, freedom was synonymous with independence. It meant freedom from England, freedom from King George III, and freedom from tyranny. Eleven years later in 1787 when the Constitution was written, freedom meant self-government; the freedom to develop democratic institutions reflecting the will of the American people. When the Bill of Rights was written in 1789, freedom meant the protection of individual rights against unwarranted government interference. And over the next 200 years, when the subsequent amendments to the Constitution, particularly the Thirteenth, Fourteenth and Fifteenth Amendments, were adopted, freedom meant empowering the government to enact laws prohibiting discrimination and enforcing due process and equal protection.

As much as the meaning of freedom has evolved over time, at particular historic moments it meant sharply conflicting things depending on one's perspective. The freedom enshrined in the Declaration of Independence was designed for free white males. Indeed, years later, anti-slave advocate Frederick Douglass would proclaim that "this Fourth of July is *yours*, not *mine*." At the time of the Civil War, according to Abraham Lincoln, to some, freedom meant "the liberty of making slaves of other people." For historian Eric Foner, author of *The Story of American Freedom*, freedom has been "both a reality and a mythical ideal—a living truth for millions of Americans; a cruel mockery for others."

Instead of dry and dusty documents suitable for little more than framing, the charters of American freedom when studied against the extraordinary and colorful history that prompted their creation, come alive as a vital part of that history. American history could not be written or understood without these documents. Why were these particular documents written at these particular times? Why do they say what they say? Why do they not say other things? What if they had not been written? Would American history have been altered? Would our lives today be different?

Who wrote these documents? How did they find themselves at that time and place? What were they trying to achieve? Were their motives pure? When they were written, did these documents achieve their intended purpose? What impact did these documents have on America, its friends, its enemies?

These and other intriguing questions are addressed by the documents themselves and by the commentaries that follow.

America's freedom documents are a gift. No other country, save perhaps the one from which we declared independence, possesses such an abundant written record of its origins, creation, development, crises, successes, and failures. The Declaration of Independence, Constitution, Bill of Rights, and subsequent amendments together with contemporaneous accounts of their drafting, adoption, and ratification reveal the history of American political thought. The trajectory of these documents shows a people striving to achieve the ambitious goals they had originally set for themselves.

The Declaration of Independence is the loud cry of an indignant teenager outraged by the humiliations he has had to suffer at the hands of a tyrannical parent, the rebellious youth declaring his own independence, announcing the high ideals which prompted such a decision and recounting in great detail the violations he has been forced to endure during his subjugation.

Having liberated himself, the youth sets out on his own. Naive and unschooled in caring for himself, the youth stumbles at first in building his new life. After one futile attempt fails, the youth resolves to adopt a brand-new plan. Wiser and more experienced, he writes a comprehensive plan in three parts to conduct his affairs. One would make rules, the second would implement the rules, and the third would resolve conflicts over the rules. But in his zeal to draft a new plan, the youth foolishly retains some of his worst habits and neglects to ensure that fundamental rights are protected.

Fortunately, the plan allows for change and adaptation, and the youth quickly makes some key additions and deletions to improve it. Indeed, in the coming years as the youth grows to adulthood, again and again the plan is amended to address new crises and challenges.

Applying the Documents

Few students of America's freedom documents will become justices of the Supreme Court or constitutional scholars or political scientists. But every one will become a participant in the American democracy. These documents are a citizen's handbook, preparing each of us for a lifetime of active citizenship—as a voter—perhaps even a candidate—and always an informed American.

An understanding—a true understanding—of where the American political system came from, how it was designed, and how it works empowers students of any age to guide themselves, their families, their friends, and their co-workers through the endless debates during election years (and in between) over the nature and future of American government.

Citizens who leave to others the study and understanding of America's freedom documents (let alone who leave to others the privilege and duty of voting) have no cause to complain about the officials who are elected or the laws and policies they enact. That America had the good sense to abolish literacy tests as a prerequisite to voting hardly excuses anyone from becoming literate in the Declaration of Independence, the Constitution, and the Bill of Rights. Our founders did not struggle to win independence, write these charters, and pass them down to us—at the cost of many lives—only to have us put them on a shelf unread or rush through them hurriedly with less attention than we give to the sports or entertainment section of the daily newspaper.

As the beneficiaries of the founders, who bequeathed these documents to us, we are obliged to study their work conscientiously to help us understand the past, confront the present, and prepare for the future.

AMERICAN WORDS OF FREEDOM
DECLARATION OF INDEPENDENCE

The Foundations of Independence 7

Uniting the Colonies 8

War Comes to the Colonies 9

The Declaration's Influence 10

Declaration of Independence (1776) 11

The Foundations of Independence

The Declaration of Independence, signed on July 4, 1776, announced to the world why the American Colonies were throwing off the bonds of tyranny and founding a new nation.

Grounded in its own time and place, the Declaration was hardly written in a vacuum, disconnected from the illuminating history so familiar to the men who wrote it. The Declaration is part of a long stream of important historical documents stretching back hundreds of years, first in England and later in America, that address the most fundamental questions facing society.

English Precedents

In the middle of the eighteenth century, when America's founders first conceived of rebelling against the authoritarian rule of King George III, the men who wrote the Declaration of Independence had a rich history to guide them.

In that era, America's history was England's history, and the political struggle that dominated that history was over the proper relationship between the monarchy and the people. In 1215, the feudal barons of England, overwhelmed by King John's inexhaustible demand for money and military defense, forced him to sign the Magna Carta—the Great Charter—guaranteeing that the crown could not arbitrarily deprive them of their property but must instead convene a grand council to deliberate on such matters. The King also promised to refrain from unlawful arrest or seizure, and that "to no one will he sell, deny, or delay right or justice."

The Magna Carta served the twin purposes of establishing a set of laws governing the relations between the ruler and his subjects and also guaranteeing that the King himself was bound by a higher law that imposed limits on his authority. These historic principles provided the foundation for the British Constitution, an unwritten set of common-law precedents, customs, and practices which protected the ruling class and eventually all British citizens.

When King James II aroused widespread popular opposition in 1689, Parliament proclaimed that he had "endeavored to subvert the constitution of the Kingdom by breaking the original contract between King and people." King James fled the country and Parliament offered the British crown to William and Mary of Orange. The offer was accompanied by the Declaration of Rights of 1689, affirming the "true, ancient and indubitable rights of the people of this realm," including the rights to bear arms, to a jury trial, to be free from excessive bail, and to pay no tax without the consent of Parliament.

Thousands of miles away and across the Atlantic Ocean, in parallel, the men and women who settled America likewise saw fit to document their freedoms and their responsibilities to one another.

Forging a New Nation

In 1620, even before they had set foot on the New England coast, the Pilgrims (separatists, having separated from the Church of England), met together aboard the *Mayflower* to agree upon the form of self-government under which they would conduct themselves in their new home. It mattered little to this band of religious heretics that the Mayflower Compact was beyond their lawful authority. The British crown controlled most of the North American continent and only duly appointed officials were empowered to enforce the laws of England.

The Mayflower Compact became a venerated part of American history, with its solemn undertaking to "covenant and combine ourselves together into a civilly body politick, for our better ordering and preservation and furtherance of the ends aforesaid." Here we find the seeds of the American identity and consciousness: A free and independent people, facing an uncertain future, having the courage and audacity to govern themselves, to "enacte, constitute, and frame, from time to time, as shall be thought most meete and convenient for the generall good of the Colonie, unto which we promise all due submission and obedience."

Inhabiting a new land, these new Americans were forced to depend on themselves for their sustenance, their survival, and their progress. They had to make daily decisions for themselves without depending on a distant monarch, whether benevolent or despotic. Americans had to make their own way—together.

As each of the American colonies was settled, they functioned under a written charter granted by the King of England. And in the very first—the Charter of The London Company—under which the Jamestown Colony was founded in 1607, the settlers were guaranteed the same "laws and statutes" as their compatriots in England. In time, all colonial charters would confer on the colonists "all privileges, franchises, and liberties of this our Kingdom of England." From the outset, the colonists were promised that they were not "second class" Englishmen—a promise they would eventually demand be kept by the King and Parliament.

Ironically, unlike British subjects living in England, whose rights and liberties were protected by an *unwritten* constitution, the colonists had grown up with a tradition of having their rights and liberties guaranteed in *writing*. The power of the written word to declare and protect one's rights had thus become woven into the American experience. Consequently, it surprised no one that when, in the course of human events, the American colonists of the mid-eighteenth century—over 150 years after Jamestown—resolved to break their ties with England, they put it in writing.

The idea of an American union predated the idea of American independence. As noted earlier, the Mayflower Compact and the colonial charters were early attempts at self-government. But these efforts had all been directed at organizing smaller, individual communities.

Uniting the Colonies

The first full-scale effort to bring all the disparate American communities together into a newly constituted unified body occurred in 1643, when representatives of the colonies of Massachusetts Bay, Plymouth, New Haven, and Connecticut tried to form a confederation for their mutual defense against the French and their Native American allies. The United Colonies

of New England, also known as the New England Confederation, was a joint advisory council composed of two members from each of the four colonies. The Confederation met annually until 1664 and occasionally thereafter until 1684, when Massachusetts lost its charter over disputes with the British government.

Ironically, one of the precursors of the American union was attempted by Great Britain itself in 1686 when it created the Dominion of New England, composed of all the New England colonies as well as New York and New Jersey. But the Dominion was headed by a royal governor and his handpicked council. In time, the colonists resented the Dominion because it replaced their own colonial legislatures, leaving them even less in control of their own affairs than before. In 1689, when the Glorious Revolution in England replaced the Stuart monarchy with King William and Queen Mary, the new rulers wisely disbanded the Dominion and restored the colonial legislatures.

In 1754, the renewed threat of war with the French and their Native American allies prompted another serious attempt at creating an American union. Delegates from Massachusetts, New Hampshire, New York, Pennsylvania (which then included much of what is now Delaware), Maryland, Rhode Island, and Connecticut met at the Albany Congress and worked out a plan to combine their resources in anticipation of impending war and to regulate their relations with the Native Americans. Benjamin Franklin used the opportunity to design the outlines of a proposed union, the centerpiece of which was a Grand Council composed of two members from each colony chosen by the colonial legislatures for a term of three years, with a president general appointed by the Council.

Franklin's Albany Plan of Union was by far the most comprehensive and detailed effort to unify the colonies attempted up to that point. Yet it was met with resistance and objections from all quarters. Loyalists, faithful to England, saw it (quite correctly) as undermining the authority of the King, while other colonists denounced it as a threat to the authority of the individual colonial assemblies and a further removal of governmental decision-making power away from the people.

From these early experiences the American colonists learned several lessons. They enjoyed conducting their own affairs under the New England Confederation and the Albany Plan, and they despised their powerlessness under the Dominion. Having tasted even limited autonomy, their appetites were whetted for greater independence.

By 1765, the American colonies were struggling under oppressive laws passed by the British Parliament and abusive practices imposed by King George III. Every time the colonies resisted, the King punished them even more severely. Colonial assemblies began passing resolutions denying Parliament the authority to tax Americans without the consent of representatives duly elected by the very people upon whom these taxes would be imposed.

The relations with England became so strained that in September 1774, the First Continental Congress was convened in Philadelphia. On October 14, 1774, the delegates adopted a Declaration of Rights and Grievances, asserting the right of the colonies to tax and to legislate for themselves. The ability of the colonies to overcome regional differences and forge compromises fostered a strong sense of unity and common purpose.

War Comes to the Colonies

On April 18, 1775, war broke out. British troops encircled the Massachusetts towns of Lexington and Concord. By the next day, the British had sustained 273 casualties; the Americans, 95. The American Revolution had begun.

As the War of Independence raged on, leaders spread the word defending their rebellion and seeking wider support. In January 1776, Thomas Paine, an English journalist who had arrived in America little more than a year earlier, wrote an influential pamphlet entitled *Common Sense*, in which he attacked the British monarchy and treated Americans as a distinct people, who deserved to rule themselves. *Common Sense* was phenomenally successful, selling 120,000 copies in barely three months and galvanizing popular support for the war against England.

In April 1776, the Second Continental Congress opened direct trade with every nation in the world except Great Britain and a month later advised the colonies to establish their own state governments.

On June 7, 1776, Richard Henry Lee, delegate from Virginia, offered a bold motion: "That these United Colonies are, and of right ought to be free and independent States, that they are absolved from all allegiance to the British Crown, and that all political connection between them and the State of Great Britain is, and ought to be totally dissolved." Congress postponed a final vote until July, to allow a committee to write a formal declaration of independence.

On June 12, 1776, five men were appointed to the drafting committee: Thomas Jefferson, John Adams, Benjamin Franklin, Roger Sherman, and Robert R. Livingston. This Committee of Five delegated the writing of the first draft to Jefferson. In a matter of a few days, Jefferson prepared his draft, Adams and Franklin made some editorial changes, and they submitted their work to Congress.

The Declaration of Independence was not written to express the abstract ideas of a small group of political theorists. In fact it was the outgrowth of a collaborative effort of people inside and outside the Second Continental Congress reflecting ideas and complaints long held throughout the colonies. Almost one hundred resolutions and instructions were issued between April and July of 1776 by various states, counties, towns, grand juries, and private and quasi-public groups, enumerating the serious injuries visited upon the American colonies and calling for independence from Britain.

Although he later arranged to have his tombstone list him as "author of the Declaration of Independence," it is unlikely that Jefferson himself would have claimed sole authorship of the Declaration at the time. In the eighteenth century, educated people regarded with disdain any striving for novelty or originality, which today is so often valued as a sign of intellectual

Adams and Jefferson writing.
© Everett Collection

preamble to the Declaration of Independence and Jefferson's own preamble to the Virginia Constitution became the catalog of specific accusations against King George found in the body of the Declaration.

As far as the preamble was concerned, the Continental Congress made only a few minor changes. Of 28 lines, the Congress deleted only three. But the Congress exercised greater editorial discretion when it came to the lengthy bill of particulars against King George. Seven of Jefferson's 31 original charges were deleted or altered substantially. Of approximately 100 lines of text, the Congress struck about 40.

The Declaration's Influence

The Declaration of Independence was seldom read publicly in the period immediately following its adoption. Abroad, the first numbered provision of the French Declaration of Rights of 1789—"Men are born and remain free and equal in rights"—was more an echo of George Mason's language than of the American Declaration of Independence.

But by 1826, one observer noted that "everything connected" with the Declaration of Independence "excites deep and acute interest." The Declaration's twin themes of opposing tyranny and upholding equality continue to provide welcome support to groups ranging from workers and farmers to women's rights advocates. In 1848, the delegates to the Seneca Falls Convention, a pivotal event in the women's movement, paraphrased the Declaration with the statement: "We hold these truths to be self-evident that all men and women are created equal."

In 1854, Abraham Lincoln said that he "never had a feeling politically that did not spring from the sentiments embodied in the Declaration of Independence."

brilliance. Many years later, Jefferson told his friend, James Madison, that in drafting the Declaration he "did not consider it part of my charge to invent new ideas altogether, and to offer no sentiment which had ever been expressed before."

In drafting the Declaration of Independence, Jefferson had two inspiring texts to draw from: his own draft of the preamble to the proposed Virginia Constitution and a preliminary version of the Virginia Declaration of Rights written by George Mason, which had been published in the *Pennsylvania Gazette* the very day the Committee of Five was appointed. Any knowledgeable study of the Declaration reveals that Jefferson borrowed heavily from Mason's work. In Jefferson's hands, Mason's Declaration of Rights became the

Declaration of Independence (1776)

The Declaration of Independence documents the reasons why the American colonies were severing their bonds with England and forming a new nation.

THE DECLARATION OF INDEPENDENCE OF THE UNITED STATES OF AMERICA

When in the Course of human events, it becomes necessary for one people to dissolve the political bands which have connected them with another, and to assume, among the Powers of the earth, the separate and equal station to which the Laws of Nature and of Nature's God entitle them, a decent respect to the opinions of mankind requires that they should declare the causes which impel them to the separation.

We hold these truths to be self-evident, that all men are created equal, that they are endowed by their Creator with certain **unalienable** Rights, that among these are Life, Liberty, and the pursuit of Happiness. —That to secure these rights, Governments are instituted among Men, deriving their **just powers** from the consent of the governed, —That whenever any Form of Government becomes destructive of these ends, it is the Right of the People to alter or to abolish it, and to institute new Government, laying its foundation on such principles and organizing its powers in such form, as to them shall seem most likely to effect their Safety and Happiness. Prudence, indeed, will dictate that Governments long established should not be changed for light and transient causes; and accordingly all experience **hath** shown, that mankind are more disposed to suffer, while evils are sufferable, than to right themselves by abolishing the forms to which they are accustomed. But when a long train of abuses and **usurpations**, pursuing invariably the same Object **evinces** a design to reduce them under absolute **Despotism**, it is their right, it is their duty, to throw off such Government, and to provide new Guards for their future security. —Such has been the patient sufferance of **these Colonies**; and such is now the necessity which constrains them to alter their former Systems of Government. The history of the present King of Great Britain is a history of repeated injuries and usurpations, all having in direct object the establishment of an absolute **Tyranny** over these States. To prove this, let Facts be submitted to a candid world.

He has refused his Assent to Laws, the most wholesome and necessary for the public good.

He has forbidden his Governors to pass Laws of immediate and pressing importance, unless suspended in their operation till his Assent should be obtained; and when so suspended, he has utterly neglected to attend to them.

He has refused to pass other Laws for the **accommodation** of large districts of people, unless those people would relinquish the right of

unalienable: alternate spelling for *inalienable,* incapable of being surrendered or transferred.

just powers: legitimate authority.

hath: archaic form of *have.*

usurpations: wrongful seizures.

evinces: openly displays.

Despotism: rule by unlimited and oppressive power.

these Colonies: original American colonies.

Tyranny: abusive exercise of unrestrained power.

accommodation: convenience.

Representation in the Legislature, a right **inestimable** to them and formidable to tyrants only.

He has called together legislative bodies at places unusual, uncomfortable, and distant from the depository of their Public Records, for the sole purpose of fatiguing them into compliance with his measures.

He has dissolved Representative Houses repeatedly, for opposing with manly firmness his invasions on the rights of the people.

He has refused for a long time, after such **dissolutions**, to cause others to be elected; whereby the Legislative Powers, incapable of **Annihilation**, have returned to the People at large for their **exercise**; the State remaining in the mean time exposed to all the dangers of invasion from without, and convulsions within.

He has endeavoured to prevent the population of these States; for that purpose obstructing the Laws of Naturalization of Foreigners; refusing to pass others to encourage their migration hither, and raising the conditions of new Appropriations of Lands.

He has obstructed the Administration of Justice, by refusing his Assent to Laws for establishing Judiciary Powers.

He has made judges dependent on his Will alone, for the tenure of their offices, and the amount and payment of their salaries.

He has erected a multitude of New Offices, and sent hither swarms of Officers to harass our People, and **eat out their substance**.

He has kept among us, in times of peace, Standing Armies without the Consent of our legislatures.

He has affected to render the Military independent of and superior to the Civil Power.

He has combined with others to subject us to a jurisdiction foreign to our constitution, and unacknowledged by our laws; giving his Assent to their Acts of pretended legislation:

For **quartering** large bodies of armed troops among us:

For protecting them, by a mock Trial, from Punishment for any Murders which they should commit on the Inhabitants of these States:

For cutting off our Trade with all parts of the world:

For imposing taxes on us without our Consent:

For depriving us, in many cases, of the benefits of Trial by Jury:

For transporting us **beyond Seas** to be tried for pretended offences:

For abolishing the free **System of English Laws** in a neighbouring Province, establishing therein an Arbitrary government, and enlarging its Boundaries so as to render it at once an example and fit instrument for introducing the same absolute rule into these Colonies:

For taking away our Charters, abolishing our most valuable Laws, and altering fundamentally the Forms of our Governments:

For suspending our own Legislatures, and declaring themselves invested with Power to legislate for us in all cases whatsoever.

inestimable: incapable of being measured or appreciated.

dissolutions: destructions or eliminations.

annihilation: complete elimination.

exercise: use.

eat out their substance: take everything away.

quartering: providing living accommodations.

beyond Seas: away from one's regular residence.

System of English Laws: the statutes and court precedents applicable to all Englishmen.

He has abdicated Government here, by declaring us out of his Protection and waging War against us.

He has plundered our seas, ravaged our Coasts, burnt our towns, and destroyed the lives of our people.

He is at this time transporting large armies of foreign mercenaries to **compleat** the works of death, desolation and tyranny, already begun with circumstances of Cruelty & perfidy scarcely paralleled in the most barbarous ages, and totally unworthy of the Head of a civilized nation.

compleat: archaic form of *complete.*

He has constrained our fellow Citizens taken Captive on the high Seas to bear Arms against their Country, to become the executioners of their friends and Brethren, or to fall themselves by their Hands.

He has excited domestic insurrections amongst us, and has endeavoured to bring on the inhabitants of our frontiers, the merciless Indian Savages, whose known rule of warfare, is an undistinguished destruction of all ages, sexes and conditions.

In every stage of these Oppressions We have Petitioned for Redress in the most humble terms: Our repeated Petitions have been answered only by repeated injury. A Prince, whose character is thus marked by every act which may define a Tyrant, is unfit to be the ruler of a free People.

Nor have We been wanting in attention to our British brethren. We have warned them from time to time of attempts by their legislature to extend an **unwarrantable** jurisdiction over us. We have reminded them of the circumstances of our emigration and settlement here. We have appealed to their native justice and magnanimity, and we have conjured them by the ties of our common kindred to disavow these usurpations, which would inevitably interrupt our connections and correspondence. They too have been deaf to the voice of justice and of **consanguinity**. We must, therefore, acquiesce in the necessity, which denounces our Separation, and hold them, as we hold the rest of mankind, Enemies in War, in Peace Friends.

unwarrantable: inexcusable; unjustified.

consanguinity: being descended from the same people or ancestors.

We, therefore, the Representatives of the United States of America, in General Congress, Assembled, appealing to the Supreme Judge of the world for the rectitude of our intentions, do, in the Name, and by the Authority of the good People of these Colonies, solemnly publish and declare, That these United Colonies are, and of Right ought to be Free and Independent States; that they are Absolved from all Allegiance to the British Crown, and that all political connection between them and the State of Great Britain, is and ought to be totally dissolved; and that as Free and Independent States, they have full Power to levy War, conclude Peace, contract Alliances, establish Commerce, and to do all other Acts and Things which Independent States may of right do. And for the support of this Declaration, with a firm reliance on the Protection of Divine Providence, we mutually pledge to each other our Lives, our Fortunes and our sacred Honor.

COMMENTARY

The Preamble

The Preamble to the Declaration of Independence was intended to explain clearly why the time had finally come for the American colonies to declare their independence from Great Britain. Colonial leaders felt a solemn duty to each other, to future generations, and to history to justify their revolution against the British monarchy by clearly recording what they believed were the powerful reasons justifying this momentous decision.

The Preamble also served to announce to the world that the inhabitants of America considered themselves "one people," who were entitled to the rights enjoyed by their fellow British subjects. This was as much a Declaration of Equality as a Declaration of Independence. Indeed, the document's most famous words declare just that: "We hold these truths to be self-evident, that all men are created equal, that they are endowed by their Creator with certain unalienable Rights that among these are Life, Liberty, and the pursuit of Happiness."

With these words, weaving together the enlightened ideas of British political theorists such as John Locke with fundamental biblical precepts, the Preamble placed beyond debate the essential principle that Americans, as their birthright, possessed the very same rights that every Englishman had long taken for granted.

The Preamble certainly did not mince words. Previewing the detailed accusations to follow, the Preamble charged in strong and uncompromising terms that the King's history of injury and injustice amounted to tyranny. Elsewhere, the Preamble declared that in such cases it is the people's "right, it is their duty, to throw off such Government, and to provide new Guards for their future security."

With utter confidence, the Preamble concludes by promising to "prove" these historic allegations by submitting "Facts . . . to a candid world."

Equality for Some

The hindsight of history calls into serious question the founders' credibility in declaring that "all men are created equal," when in fact all the colonies had slave populations. Northern merchants and southern plantation owners prospered from slavery and every prominent leader from George Washington to Thomas Jefferson owned slaves. Yet in their own time and place few detected any hypocrisy, any more than at several points in our subsequent history vast majorities of freedom-loving Americans have been impervious to widespread patterns of discrimination against women, racial and religious minorities, immigrants, political dissenters, and, most recently, gays, lesbians, bisexuals, and transgendered persons. It is often convenient to look with self-righteous disdain and surprise at the insensitivity of the Founders toward the subjugation of African slaves and their descendants, while remaining conveniently blind to the denial of equal rights which succeeding generations of Americans have tolerated, as if racism, bigotry, and intolerance were purely vestiges of the past.

This is not to say that genuine efforts to abolish slavery as a cleansing step toward true independence were not attempted. In October 1774, the First Continental Congress proposed, and within a year all the colonies had adopted, a Continental Association imposing an economic boycott on British shipping, including the importation of African slaves. And when in 1776 the Second Continental Congress opened all American ports to foreign commerce in direct violation of the British navigation acts, importing slaves remained prohibited.

But given the colonies' economic dependence on slavery and the prominent goal of winning independence, the drafters of the Declaration ignored the reality of slavery and invoked the ideal that "all men are created equal." Unfortunately, when the Revolutionary War ended, some northern merchants and southern planters immediately renewed the African slave trade. Despite the courageous efforts of Quakers, abolitionists, and succeeding generations of Americans, and despite the adoption of three of America's freedom documents—the Declaration of Independence, the U.S. Constitution, and the Bill of Rights—it took almost a hundred years and a bloody civil war before the Thirteenth Amendment finally abolished slavery.

Having cited the equality of all humankind, the Preamble proceeds in only a few sentences to outline the ideal relationship between a free people and its government. According to the Preamble; the government does not control the people, the people control the government. The government is placed at the service of the governed in two fundamental ways. First, governments are instituted to "secure" the rights of the people and secondly, governments derive "their just powers" from "the consent of the governed." It follows that any power exercised by any government without the consent of the people is therefore unjust, and whenever any "Form of Government becomes destructive of these ends," it is "the Right of the People to alter or to abolish it" and to establish a new government.

These were truly bold and revolutionary ideas in 1776. At a time when kings and queens throughout the world ruled by *divine right*—claiming their authority directly from God—it was unprecedented for a group of loyal subjects to take it upon themselves to assert the right to abolish the rule of the monarchy.

The Grievances

Despite the current popularity of the Preamble, to the men who wrote and signed the Declaration of Independence, the list of 28 grievances against King George was the heart of the document. Here, the Declaration reads like a criminal indictment cataloguing a long series of accusations against the British monarchy and the Parliament.

The first group of charges condemns the King for disrupting the colonial legislatures, calling them together and then dissolving them at whim, refusing to assent to laws duly passed, and failing to enforce those he had approved.

Next, the Declaration accuses the King of interferring with immigration and freedom of movement, and with hindering the independence of the judicial process, which Americans wanted to shield from royal interference. There follows an objection to the wasteful habits of the King's officials in spending money on themselves.

Several very important charges assert a preference for a citizen militia with civil control of the military and against a permanent army in times of peace and the practice of housing troops in private homes in times of war.

At the center of the list of grievances is the key accusation that the King had joined with the British Parliament to impose upon the colonies taxation without representation, striking at the fundamental proposition that government must be based on the consent of the governed. It was one thing for colonial legislatures acting through duly elected representatives to levy a tax for the common good, but it was an outrage for the British Parliament, where the colonies had no representation, to do so.

Several charges complain that the right to trial by a jury of one's peers had been repeatedly violated.

The next charge objects to the institution of a Roman system of law in Quebec (then under English control) in place of the common law applied in England and the colonies, and to the westward extension of Quebec into an area where the colonists hoped to later expand.

A group of five grievances lists all the ways the King had made war on the American colonies, in violation of the most essential duty of a ruler to protect the people from foreign and domestic attack.

At this point in the original Declaration as drafted by Jefferson and the Committee of Five, there was a lengthy criticism of the African slave trade, the King's refusal to allow the colonies to prohibit it, and his attempt to turn American slaves against their masters. The Second Continental Congress deleted this charge, no doubt to avoid drawing attention to the colonies' hypocrisy for maintaining slavery while declaring that "all men are created equal."

The final accusation against King George and the concluding paragraph of the Declaration constitute the formal declaration of independence. The document reminds the world that at every stage the Americans had sought redress but they were met with "repeated injury." Furthermore, the colonists had appealed to their fellow "Brittish brethren" for justice, only to be ignored.

Having made the case for independence, the Declaration concludes by stating that the united colonies are, by right, "Free and Independent States."

The Declaration's final words reflect a common bond deeply felt by the signers and by extension all Americans: with "a firm reliance on the protection of divine Providence, we mutually pledge to each other our Lives, our Fortunes and our Sacred Honor."

Notes

Notes

Notes

AMERICAN WORDS OF FREEDOM
THE U.S. CONSTITUTION

Decision Time 21

The Articles of Confederation 21

A Convention Is Called 23

Slavery and the Constitution 25

The Ratification Process 27

Enter the Federalists 27

State Ratification 30

The U.S. Constitution 33

Article I 36

Article II 48

Article III 54

Article IV 59

Article V 61

Article VI 63

Article VII 64

Decision Time

Having declared its independence on July 4, 1776, the United States of America faced a choice. Would it be governed as a loose federation of 13 independent states or would it be a single unified nation, made up of separate but interdependent states?

The Declaration of Independence referred to "these United Colonies" as "Free and Independent States." Consequently, for its first 11 years, from 1776 to 1787, the country functioned as a loose confederation of 13 fiercely independent sovereign states.

In July of 1776, the same month the Declaration of Independence was signed, the Second Continental Congress appointed a committee to draft a new constitution for the emerging nation. Distracted by the demanding work of fighting (and paying for) a war, Congress eventually found the time to approve the first American constitution on November 15, 1777, known as the Articles of Confederation. It still took four more years, until March 1781, for all 13 states to ratify that document, a delay that suggests some were ambivalent about the shape of the new government.

The Articles of Confederation

The Articles of Confederation created a national government that functioned solely through its legislature—a perpetuation of the Continental Congress.

The new Congress was empowered to declare war and make peace, draft men for the army, conduct diplomatic relations with foreign countries, regulate American Indian affairs, coin money, and issue currency. But Congress could not levy taxes and was therefore entirely dependent on the individual states to contribute monies voluntarily to enable Congress to carry out its national duties. Indeed, the Articles left no doubt that the states were supreme over Congress: "Each state retains its sovereignty, freedom, and independence, and every power, jurisdiction, and right which is not by this Confederation expressly delegated to the United States in congress assembled."

Congress could recommend laws to the states, but each state held final authority to pass only such legislation as it saw fit, regardless of any conflicts among the different states. The Articles established no single head of the national government nor did it institute a system of national courts.

The very organization of the new government under the Articles of Confederation fostered a weak, leaderless, and decentralized system. Delegates to Congress were selected annually by state legislatures. No delegate could serve more than three out of every six years, thereby preventing experienced representatives from helping to improve the functioning of the national government on a consistent basis. To add to the lack of continuity, sessions of Congress rotated among Philadelphia, Princeton, Annapolis, and New York City and on many occasions not enough state representatives were present to constitute a *quorum* (the minimum number necessary to conduct a valid session), thereby preventing any business from being accomplished.

Without an executive branch, Congress first had to pass laws and then implement and enforce them, all with delegates who came and went through a revolving door.

Meanwhile, America was still fighting a war with Britain, which did not end until Lord Cornwallis surrendered to George Washington at Yorktown in 1781. Whatever the burdens of financing and conducting the war, at least it had given the delegates to Congress a unifying purpose. But when the war ended, the states no longer had a common enemy, and the delegates resumed their greatest loyalty to their respective states, not to the rather amorphous national Congress. One contemporary observer feared for the future of America, predicting that it seemed destined to dissolve into "thirteen little republics, ripe for endless squabbling, like the republics of ancient Greece and medieval Italy." Disunity was exacerbated by conflicts between small landless states such as Maryland, Delaware, Pennsylvania, Rhode Island, and New Jersey and large landed states like Virginia and Connecticut, which sought to expand their territory westward. Congress was powerless to play any effective role in resolving these conflicts.

In addition, Congress had no authority to address the economic problems facing southern farmers, northern manufacturers, and all the states in the wake

Members of the Constitutional Convention.
© Everett Collection

George Washington wrote to James Madison that "without some alteration in our political creed, the superstructure we have been seven years raising at the expense of so much blood and treasure, must fall. We are fast verging to anarchy and confusion."

John Jay wrote to Washington that, "I am uneasy and apprehensive; more so than during the war . . . we are going and doing wrong, and therefore I look forward to evils and calamities."

The weaknesses of the national government under the Articles of Confederation and the ineffectiveness of the individual states to manage their own affairs came to a head in 1786 in western Massachusetts. While farmers were suffering from low prices and huge mortgages, creditors in eastern Massachusetts, eager to protect their investments, convinced the state legislature to reject measures to protect farmers from foreclosure.

The farmers, led by Captain Daniel Shays, a hero of the Revolutionary War, took the law into their own hands. Shays and 2,000 armed men forcibly closed various county courthouses to block foreclosure proceedings. In February 1787, Shays and his men marched on a federal arsenal in Springfield but were stopped by the state militia.

Shays' Rebellion sent a shock wave through the entire country. The Massachusetts state legislature had utterly failed to resolve the conflict between farmers and creditors, prompting an outbreak of armed conflict. If the state government could not maintain peace among its citizens, was anarchy not far behind? If it could happen in Massachusetts, leaders elsewhere feared it could happen in their states. What was the future of the new nation? Even before Shays had taken

of the Revolutionary War, which had seriously disrupted commercial activity and created unbearable debt. Efforts in 1781 and 1783 to grant Congress the power to impose a 5 percent duty on imported products to help pay the national debt were rejected by the state legislatures, which jealously guarded their exclusive power to tax.

Under the Articles, each state was free to conduct its own trade with foreign nations, leading to confusion and disruptive competition: While Massachusetts, Rhode Island, and New Hampshire imposed restraints on British trade to extract concessions from Parliament, Connecticut willingly allowed unrestricted trade with England but imposed a tax on imports from Massachusetts.

There was even serious talk about dividing the states up into three entirely separate confederations, one for the New England states, one for the middle states, and one for the Southern states.

For the men who had valiantly fought a war to establish a new nation, the situation was intolerable.

up arms, a group of Virginians, fearful of the drift and disunity in the country, had called upon the Congress to convene a meeting of state delegations to consider adopting a uniform system of commercial regulations.

A Convention Is Called

Eventually, delegates from five states gathered in Annapolis, Maryland in September 1786 and called for a full-scale meeting in Philadelphia, which the Congress approved, for the "express purpose of revising the Articles of Confederation."

On May 14, 1787, 55 delegates from all the states except Rhode Island met at the Philadelphia State House for what became known as the Constitutional Convention. These were men of considerable experience in government, politics, and law. One-third were veterans of the Revolutionary War and 34 were lawyers. They all attended out of a deep concern for the future of their new nation.

By the time the Constitutional Convention opened, the founding generation had become quite skilled in drafting constitutions. Between 1776 and 1780, every state had written its own constitution. Even before the Declaration of Independence was signed, New Hampshire, South Carolina, Virginia, and New Jersey (in that order) had adopted provisional constitutions, and Rhode Island had converted its original colonial charter to the equivalent of a constitution by removing all references to Great Britain and King George III. By the end of 1776, Delaware, Pennsylvania, Maryland, and North Carolina (in that order) had adopted constitutions, and Connecticut had also revised its charter to delete references to Great Britain and the King. In 1777, Georgia, New York, and Vermont followed suit and in June of 1780 the Massachusetts constitutional convention ratified its state constitution.

This was a thrilling period of constitution building. No two state constitutions were identical. Each state developed different mechanisms to conduct its affairs, but leaders in all the states were engaged in the ambitious enterprise of implementing self-government by creating structures designed to make representative democracy work. No one questioned that each state should have its own written constitution specifying the powers and responsibilities of state government. These written instruments reflected principles of government that their authors saw as fixed and immutable, superior to statutes or regulations that any temporary legislature might pass and then later modify or repeal. These were *constitutions*—blueprints for the foundation of state government. To be sure they could be amended, but only through carefully designed procedures which discouraged frequent or idle revisions.

Scores of colonial leaders, legislators, and lawyers were involved in the time-consuming task of drafting, debating, approving, and ratifying each of these state constitutions. Invigorated by the challenge and humbled by the responsibility, the founding generation rose to the occasion with the knowledge that they were engaged in vitally important work of historic proportions.

Never before had so many citizens been directly involved in crafting democracy. Drawing on published works concerning political theory and philosophy and their own personal and diverse experiences, the drafters understood that the state constitutions should provide the requisite stability and structure to allow their local governments to function during the war with England and thereafter. Indeed, the state constitutions proved that the independence and autonomy the inhabitants of the colonies were boldly demanding were in fact their birthright. These documents told the world—and particularly King George and the British Parliament—that Americans were fully capable of governing themselves.

The state constitutions gave great solace to the men and women fighting for independence. These documents were concrete proof that their leaders were equipped to discharge the duties and responsibilities of government to protect its citizens, provide for the common defense, and establish an ordered society.

For the average farmer, merchant, mother, and father, the War for Independence was a staggering undertaking. Up to that point, all of them had seen themselves as loyal subjects of the King—as English. The very notion that the American colonies would presume to challenge and eventually defeat the most powerful nation in the world was simply astonishing. It required an extraordinary leap of faith. And it required the colonists' utmost trust and confidence in their emerging leaders. The fact that these leaders had the courage, wisdom, and intelligence to draft brand new state constitutions was reassuring to the people. Having a vision of what the nature and structure of government would look like *after* independence strengthened the likelihood that it would be won.

Madison Takes the Forefront

Despite the fact that the mandate for the Constitutional Convention was for the express purpose of revising the Articles of Confederation, the delegates promptly ignored the limitation, cast aside the existing Articles, and drafted an entirely new plan of government. From the outset, the debates were shaped by a shy, academic man from Virginia. James Madison, 36 years old, was short and not particularly charismatic. But he was a brilliant political thinker and exceedingly well-read. He was a student of the Enlightenment and deeply committed to building a strong national government. (The detailed notes Madison took throughout the Convention were not published until 1840, four years after his death. His notes proved to be far more complete than the official journal kept by William Jackson and published in 1818.)

Madison arrived at the Constitutional Convention with a thoughtful and comprehensive plan for establishing a national republic. His Virginia Plan, presented by fellow Virginian Edmund Randolph, proposed a central federal government with three branches: legislative, executive, and judicial. Congress would be *bicameral*—with a lower house elected directly by the people and an upper house chosen by the lower house from nominations made by the state legislatures. Representatives in both houses of Congress would be apportioned based on the population of each state, unlike the system under the Articles in which each state—large or small—had a single vote in Congress. Under Madison's plan, Congress would have the power to veto state legislation.

Fearing the power that the more populated states would obtain under the Virginia Plan, the smaller states offered the New Jersey Plan, under which there would be a one-house Congress, with each state having one vote. But since the New Jersey Plan was no different than the existing structure under the Articles, the delegates saw it as nothing more than the status quo and quickly rejected it.

Beyond the conflict between larger and smaller states, there was the equally intractable conflict between northern and southern states. Although the populations in the North and South were relatively equal, there were more northern states, which could threaten southern interests, particularly when it came to the question of slavery.

Consequently, the Convention was stalled on the issue of representation. Indeed the impasse threatened to abort the entire enterprise. William Paterson, who offered the New Jersey Plan, reminded his colleagues that the convention had been convened only to strengthen the Articles of Confederation, not to draft a brand new constitution. He warned that he would lead a small-state secession unless the larger states compromised on the issue of representation.

On June 27, Luther Martin of Maryland spoke for three hours in favor of equal representation for large and small states, at which point Madison's notes indicate, Martin "was too much exhausted he said to finish his remarks, and reminded the House that he should tomorrow, resume them."

On July 2, a committee headed by Benjamin Franklin, the 81-year-old avuncular Philadelphian, proposed a compromise that Madison enthusiastically supported. In the upper house, each state would have two senators, appointed by the state legislature, with six-year terms, while in the lower house, which would introduce bills involving the expenditure of money, representation would be apportioned according to population. The executive branch would be headed by a president with a four-year term, chosen not by direct vote but by an Electoral College, with each state's total number of senators and representatives added together to determine the number of its electoral votes. The president would be commander of the armed forces, would nominate judges and government officials, and would have the power to veto bills passed by Congress. The federal judiciary would serve as the third independent branch of the new government, with the authority to decide disputes between the states and between citizens of different states.

Under this new plan, the individual states were asked to do something unprecedented: willingly relinquish a significant portion of their authority to a higher political power. Thus, just as John Locke had conceived of individuals existing "equally free and independent" in an original "state of nature" willingly giving up some of their freedom in return for the protection and benefits of an ordered society, so too were the 13 "equally free and independent" states asked to relinquish some of their sovereignty in return for the protection and benefits of a federal government.

In the end, Madison got almost everything he wanted, except that Congress would not be given the power to veto state legislation. Instead, the Constitution and the laws passed by Congress were declared the "supreme Law of the land."

How to Amend and Ratify

Pleased with what they had created, the delegates were eager to ensure that the new Constitution would be difficult to change. Amendments could be proposed only by a two-thirds vote of both houses of Congress or at another constitutional convention requested by two-thirds of the state legislatures. Either way, all amendments would require ratification by three-quarters of the states.

On the other hand, to enhance the chances of the Constitution itself being ratified, the Convention decided that only 9 of the 13 states needed to approve it. The framers decided on this standard even though

the slightest revision of the existing Articles, let alone a radical new plan of government, required the approval of *all* of the states.

Slavery and the Constitution

At the time of the Constitutional Convention, every state except Massachusetts had slave populations, although states from Pennsylvania northward had fewer slaves than the southern states and slavery was far less important to the economics of the northern states. Despite the principles of equality and freedom that animated the Declaration of Independence and despite the devotion of all the delegates to these abstract ideals, at no point did the Convention officially consider the abolition of slavery. As in 1776, an opportunity to remove the stain of slavery was squandered.

One unsuccessful attempt was made to bring the issue before the Convention. On June 2, 1787 the Pennsylvania Abolition Society presented a petition calling for an end to the slave trade to Benjamin Franklin, a delegate to the Convention, who also happened to be president of the Society. But another representative of the Society, Tench Coxe, privately cautioned Franklin *against* submitting the petition, and Franklin agreed. Coxe said he feared "that the memorial, in the beginning of the deliberations of the Convention, might alarm some of the Southern states, and thereby defeat the wishes of the enemies of the African Trade."

Neither Franklin, nor any other enemy of slavery ever introduced the petition. That is not to say that some of the delegates did not speak out against slavery. On August 22, 1787, George Mason, who, like Washington and Jefferson, owned slaves, gave a speech decrying slavery in which he said that slaves " . . . produce the most pernicious effect on manners. Every master of slaves is born a petty tyrant. They bring the judgment of heaven on a Country." He concluded that it was "essential in every point of view that the General Government should have power to prevent the increase of slavery."

Meanwhile, most of the delegates at the Convention, far from supporting the abolition of slavery, were in favor of institutionalizing it. Since the population of the individual states was emerging as the method of apportioning representation in at least one of the houses of Congress, the status of slaves had to be addressed. The northern states did not want slaves counted at all, while the southern states wanted all slaves to be counted. The impasse was resolved with an ignominious compromise using the *federal ratio* which counted three-fifths of the slaves for both representation and direct taxation.

The federal ratio first came up in 1783 as an amendment to the Articles of Confederation when Congress was considering apportioning federal expenses among the states using total population. A congressional committee recommended that "two blacks be rated as equal to one freeman." Northerners moved for a 4-to-3 ratio, while Southerners favored the 2-to-1 or even a 4-to-1 ratio. As a compromise, James Madison proposed a 5-to-3 ratio which was finally accepted. However, amendments to the Articles required the unanimous approval of all state

James Madison, author and president.
© Bettmann/CORBIS

legislatures and when New Hampshire and Rhode Island rejected the federal ratio, it failed. Despite the rejection, Congress used the formula in 1786, so it was familiar to many of the delegates at the Constitutional Convention held the following year.

The shameful mark that slavery left on the Constitution was not confined to the Three-Fifths Clause in Article I Section 2. Slavery (never, of course, bearing its ugly name) is prominently referred to in three more provisions in the Constitution and indirectly in several others. Article I, Section 9 prevents Congress from prohibiting the importation of slaves until 1808 and limits the tax to ten dollars per slave. Under Article IV, Section 2, runaway slaves must be returned to their masters "on demand" and may not be emancipated. And under Article V, no Amendment prohibiting the slave trade could be adopted before 1808.

Some of the indirect references to slavery found elsewhere in the Constitution include (a) authorizing Congress to call forth the militia to suppress domestic insurrections (such as slave uprisings); (b) prohibiting both federal and state governments from levying export duties, thereby guaranteeing that the products of a slave economy (tobacco, indigo plants, rice, etc.) would not be taxed; (c) providing for the indirect election of the President through elections based on representation in Congress, which, because of the Three-Fifths clause, inflated the influence of the white Southern vote; (d) requiring a three-fourths approval of the states to adopt amendments, thereby giving the South a veto power over any potential amendments affecting slavery and (e) limiting the privileges and immunities clause to citizens—thus denying these protections to slaves and in some cases to free blacks.

On September 17, 1787, after the final draft of the Constitution was read to the delegates, Benjamin Franklin made an impassioned plea to any who had reservations about the document to overcome their objections and join in unanimously supporting it. Franklin confessed that "there are several parts of this Constitution which I do not at present approve," but having lived so long he said he had learned "to pay more respect to the judgment of others." He observed that most men "think themselves in possession of all truth," which, he said, was like a certain French lady, who in a dispute with her sister, said "I don't know how it happens, Sister, but I meet with no body but myself that's always in the right." Describing the Constitution as "so near to perfection," Franklin voiced the wish "that every member of the Convention who may still have objections to it, would with me, on this occasion doubt a little of his own infallibility, and to make manifest our unanimity, put his name to this instrument."

The elder statesman did not get his wish for unanimous approval. On September 17, 1787, of the 42 remaining delegates, 39 signed the Constitution but George Mason, Edmund Randolph, and Elbridge Gerry, citing among other things the lack of a Bill of Rights, did not.

The Ratification Process

That the Constitution had been approved at the Philadelphia Convention hardly meant that it would be ratified by the requisite 9 of 13 states.

Having toiled in secret from May to September 1787 (the shutters of the Pennsylvania State House had been nailed shut to guarantee the privacy of the deliberations), the delegates to the Constitutional Convention had no idea how their handiwork would be received by the public at large.

For the next nine months one of the most thrilling, contentious, and illuminating political debates took place throughout America. In state legislatures and ratifying conventions, in an endless array of newspaper editorials and political pamphlets, and on street corners and in taverns, the American people argued about nothing less than the future of their country. Rarely if ever have the people and their elected representatives engaged in such a feisty argument over the very foundations of democratic governance.

Anticipating hostility from state legislators and governors, who would likely see the new Constitution as a threat to their sovereignty (not to mention their jobs), the framers purposely left them out of the ratifying process. Instead, Article VII established a four-stage procedure for ratification. First, the Constitution would be transmitted to the Confederation Congress (which remained in effect under the existing Articles of Confederation); next, Congress would transmit the Constitution to each of the 13 state legislatures, which in turn would transmit it to special ratifying conventions in each state, with delegates chosen by special elections. The delegates would deliberate and then vote on the proposed Constitution. Finally, upon the ratification by nine of the ratifying conventions, the Constitution would take effect.

This very process differed markedly from the amendment process under the Articles of Confederation, which was, after all, still the law of the land. Under the Articles, any amendment had to be approved first by Congress and then by *all* 13 state legislatures. While the process under Article VII of the proposed Constitution had reduced the requirement of unanimity to a three-fourths vote, some concluded that the framers were bypassing existing law intentionally. Supporters of ratification were gambling that if the new Constitution was ratified by at least 9, and hopefully all 13 states, it would become effective, superseding the Articles of Confederation in all respects.

Enter the Federalists

Advocates for ratification of the Constitution became known as *Federalists*, while opponents were characterized as *Anti-Federalists*. Early precursors of political parties, neither of these groups had the organization, discipline, or influence of later political parties. Nonetheless, these two factions helped frame the debate and constituted loose coalitions that exchanged information and plotted strategy from state to state.

The Federalists were pleased with their name since it evoked the notion of unity and an improvement over the disorganization experienced under the Articles of Confederation. By contrast, most Anti-Federalists resented the title imposed upon them by their opponents. To begin with, their name immediately implied that they were *against* something rather than in *favor* of something. Many leaders who were labeled Anti-Federalists felt deeply that their side was in *favor* of state sovereignty and in *favor* of individual liberties, both of which they believed were threatened by the new Constitution. Indeed, given that the term "federalism" refers to the structured dispersion of power among many centers, each of which cooperates under a constitution for the common good, the Anti-Federalists claimed as much right to the title "Federalists" as the Federalists did.

Nevertheless, the labels stuck and any doubt was soon eliminated when Federalists Alexander Hamilton, James Madison, and John Jay published a series of 85 highly influential essays supporting the new Constitution. Collectively, these essays became known as *The Federalist* (sometimes called *The Federalist Papers*). Considered the single most authoritative exposition of the new charter of government, *The Federalist* quickly became the debater's handbook for supporters of the Constitution.

The Federalist was prompted by the pamphlet wars in New York City and elsewhere, which were sparked by the decision of Congress on September 28, 1787, to submit the Constitution to the people of the several states. Most of the nation's almost 100 newspapers had already printed the complete text of the Constitution shortly after September 17. Almost immediately newspapers in Philadelphia, Boston, and New York (then the capital of the United States) weighed in with essays generally supporting the Constitution and denouncing Anti-Federalists as selfish *placemen* (state office holders).

Hamilton quickly realized that the campaign to ratify the Constitution had to be elevated above such common political squabbling. He conceived of a series of essays to be published in daily newspapers and later collected in book form to present a comprehensive defense of the Constitution and a detailed refutation of Anti-Federalist arguments.

With no shortage of egotism, even Hamilton realized that he did not have sufficient time to write all the essays necessary to cover every provision of the Constitution and all the Anti-Federalist claims he could anticipate. Consequently, he invited four other prominent Federalists to co-author the work. Gouverneur Morris declined and William Duer was asked to withdraw after Hamilton judged his initial essays as unsuitable to the important task at hand. Fortunately, John Jay and James Madison joined the enterprise.

Suffering from painful bouts of rheumatism, Jay completed only five essays (Numbers 2 through 5 and 64), thus denying his contemporaries and history of the benefit of his lucid and persuasive prose. Where Hamilton was uncompromising in belittling his opponents, Jay wrote with a welcoming pen, bringing people to his side by appeals to their better selves.

In the style of the times, *The Federalist* was published under a pen name, or pseudonym. While some writers used pen names to conceal their opinions or protect themselves from repercussions, many used them because it was customary in such political tracts to direct attention to one's arguments rather than one's personality. Consequently, throughout the ratification debate, pamphlets and newspaper essays were signed "The Federal Farmer" or "An Old Soldier" or "A Son of Liberty." Most writers preferred to invoke the aura of classical Greece and the Roman Republic with pen-names such as "Cato" and "Caesar," while still others invented their own classical-sounding pseudonyms, such as "Republicus," "Brutus, Jr." or "Philadelphienis."

For *The Federalist*, Hamilton had no need to make up a fictitious classic name. Instead, he selected Publius Valerius, the great Roman leader who established a just and benevolent republican government after the revolutionary overthrow of Tarquin, the last king of Rome. Publius, whom the people of Rome called Publicola or "people-lover," was an ideal choice, symbolizing the Federalists' devotion to republicanism and constitutional democracy.

The Federalist essays first began appearing in the *Independent Journal*, published in New York City on October 27, 1787, less than a month after Congress had sent the Constitution to the states for ratification. Soon the essays were being simultaneously published in three other newspapers—the *New York Packet*, the *Daily Advertiser* and even the Anti-Federalist *New York Journal*. As the essays, addressed to "the People of the State of New York," began to roll off the presses, Publius appeared twice a week in four of the city's five newspapers. *The Federalist* also began appearing in newspapers elsewhere in New York State, as in well as the pivotal states of Pennsylvania, Virginia, and several New England states. However, it was not carried in any newspapers in Connecticut, New Jersey, Delaware, Maryland, North Carolina, South Carolina, or Georgia.

As *The Federalist* expanded beyond newspaper essays and simple pamphlets, Hamilton arranged with printers John and Andrew McLean to publish the essays in first one and then two bound volumes. As the pace of the ratification debate quickened, Hamilton and Madison were under pressure to generate cogent, thoughtful essays on an almost daily schedule. At the time, Madison was living in New York City as a representative to the Congress. He worked feverishly to complete his writing, the burden of which increased when Jay's illness prevented him from carrying his load. In later years, Madison reminisced that it "frequently happened that whilst the printer was putting into type parts of a number, the following parts were under the pen, & to be furnished in time for the press."

The speed at which Hamilton and Madison wrote, with little time for consultation or collaboration, has lead to some confusion over who actually wrote each of the essays. Hamilton claimed that he authored two-thirds of them, but Madison took credit for 15 of the essays Hamilton also claimed. Today, through painstaking research and computer-assisted textual analysis, we know that Hamilton wrote 52 essays, Madison 29, and Jay 5.

While today we recognize Hamilton, Madison, and Jay as the authors of *The Federalist*, their identities were not made public until five years later, in 1792, when a French translation was published. Subsequently, and especially as new democracies have emerged, *The Federalist* has been published in Italian, German, Spanish, Portuguese, Arabic, Bengali, Assamese, Korean, Vietnamese, and Japanese, confirming its enduring value as "the best commentary on the principles of government which ever was written," according to Jefferson.

In *The Federalist*, Hamilton achieved all that he had set out to do. In *Federalist* No. 1, he made the case for the "utility of the UNION," the "insufficiency of the present Confederation to preserve that Union," the "necessity of a government at least equally energetic with the one proposed," the "conformity of the proposed Constitution to the five principles of republican government," and the "additional security which its adoption will afford to the preservation of that species of government, to liberty, and to property."

This was a tall order, but the combined intellect and experience of Hamilton, Madison, and Jay were fully up to the task.

Doubtless, *The Federalist* helped persuade many Americans to support the new Constitution. It also reassured leaders in many states not only by demonstrating the sound theoretical foundation upon which the proposed national government would be built, but by showcasing the intelligence and vision of men like Hamilton, Madison, and Jay, all of whom were expected to play key roles in that new government.

In *Federalist* No. 10 Madison may have achieved what most historians and political scientists now regard as the greatest single American contribution to political theory. In this one essay, Madison challenged two previously unassailable political principles that the Anti-Federalists seized on in opposing the Constitution: First, that according to French political philosopher Montesquieu (1689–1755) and others, only small republics could enjoy the benefits of democracy based on patriotic citizens governing themselves, and second, that, according to Aristotle and others, *factionalism*—the tendency of people to divide into groups to pursue their own selfish and narrow agendas—was the enemy of republican government and individual liberties. In a brilliant turnabout,

Madison argued that factionalism was precisely what would allow constitutional democracy to succeed in a large nation like the United States. The very diversity of a large country as opposed to the insular parochialism of a small nation would make it far less likely that any one single group could command a majority of voters and oppress others. In other words, the very instinct of people to ally themselves with like-minded people into various factions (or interest groups, as we call them today) creates a check on the aggregation of power into any single group. Furthermore, Madison argued that elections in a larger republic attract a wider span of "fit characters" to serve in office.

State Ratification

On December 7, 1787, six weeks after the first essays from *The Federalist* appeared in the midst of scores of other newspaper essays and pamphlets, Delaware became the first state to ratify the Constitution by a vote of 30–0. In Pennsylvania, the Federalists were so eager to push an election bill calling for a ratifying convention that they convened before representatives from the western part of the state, most of whom were expected to oppose ratification, could get to Philadelphia to participate in the debate. When a few of the Anti-Federalists who were present realized what was happening, they stormed out of the chamber, thereby depriving the General Assembly of a quorum. Incensed, Speaker Thomas Fitzsimmons, himself a signer of the Constitution, ordered the sergeant-at-arms to drag the Anti-Federalists back to their seats, so that the Assembly could pass the election bill. A few days later, on December 12, Pennsylvania voted 46–23 to ratify the Constitution. In short order, on December 18, Georgia (26–0) and on January 9, 1788, Connecticut (128–40) voted in favor of the Constitution.

Along the road to victory, the Federalists encountered some obstacles as they turned their attention to the rest of the states. The Anti-Federalists—especially in Virginia and New York, two very important states, began to make headway by suggesting that ratification should be conditioned on the adoption of certain amendments to the Constitution to cure the defects identified by the Anti-Federalists. And no defect was more glaring than the omission of a Bill of Rights. George Mason, a leading Anti-Federalist in Virginia and a delegate to the Constitutional Convention, had refused to sign the new Constitution because it had no Bill of Rights. Anti-Federalists made a persuasive case that not only did the framers of the Constitution establish a dangerously powerful central government, but they refused to ensure the protection of individual rights by including a Bill of Rights.

In the states that had yet to ratify, demands for amendments became louder. Madison and his Federalist allies feared that if the remaining states ratified *conditionally*, that is, only if specified amendments were approved, there would be no clear mandate in favor of the new Constitution. There was no telling what would happen if these amendments were open to debate. Other amendments could then be raised, essentially re-opening the entire Constitutional Convention. The Federalists wanted ratification with no strings attached.

Sensing where the political winds were blowing, Madison and his allies offered *recommendatory* amendments to overcome a demand for *conditional* amendments. In other words, states were urged to ratify the Constitution unconditionally, but to submit to the new Congress *recommended* amendments to address the Anti-Federalists' concerns. In Virginia, where Anti-Federalists George Mason and Patrick Henry (who had refused to be a delegate to the Constitutional Convention in the first place because he said he "smelt a rat") were gaining support, Madison made an astute promise: "ratify the Constitution, elect me to the First Congress, and I will get you that Bill of Rights."

The Federalists' strategy was working. On February 6, 1788, Massachusetts ratified the Constitution with recommendatory amendments (197–168). In New Hampshire, unsure whether they had the necessary votes, the Federalists got a postponement in hopes of building momentum for ratification, especially if other states fell in line. Maryland ratified on April 28 (63–11), as did South Carolina on May 23 (149–73).

The Federalists knew they could not count on Rhode Island, a staunchly independent state which had refused even to send delegates to the Constitutional Convention. In fact, Rhode Island's boycott contributed to the decision to require ratification by only 9 of the 13 states. Had unanimity been required, Rhode Island could have single-handedly vetoed the entire Constitution. Rhode Island refused to call a ratifying convention and instead submitted the new Constitution to numerous town meetings. In late May 1788, with most Federalists refusing to participate, the state *rejected* the Constitution by a vote of 2,708 to 237.

Most of the attention in the ratification debate was focused on Virginia. Eight states had thus far ratified the new Constitution. Would Virginia, the home of George Washington (who supported ratification but remained aloof from the campaign) and James Madison become the ninth state necessary to put the Constitution over the top? Not if Mason and Henry had anything to do with it.

As the Virginia ratifying convention began in Richmond, the Anti-Federalists were in the majority, but not all their supporters were die-hard opponents of the Constitution. A Federalist, Edmond Pendleton, a venerable figure in Virginia politics, was elected president of the ratifying convention and another Federalist, George Wythe, was chosen as president of the important Committee of the Whole.

Pendleton promptly handed the Federalists a critical victory by ruling out of order Henry's request to take up the question whether the Constitutional Convention had acted illegally in defiance of existing law under the Articles of Confederation. Pendleton ruled that, based on the actions of the Congress, the state legislature, and the voters, the Constitution was properly before them for debate.

Next, the Virginia convention adopted a rule requiring clause-by-clause debate on the proposed Constitution. Federalists may have believed this would help them expose errors and inconsistencies in the Anti-Federalist arguments, while Anti-Federalists may well have hoped this approach would highlight specific defects in the documents that Federalists preferred to gloss over.

What emerged as a result of the clause-by-clause debate was an advantage for Madison's patient, careful analysis of each provision of the document as against the legendary oratory of Henry, who was more comfortable holding forth with broad denunciations of his opponents but was no match when it came to Madison's intimate personal knowledge of the debates at the Constitutional Convention.

The Federalists also had the help of *The Federalist*. When Madison left New York in March, 1788 to return to his home state to join the ratification debate, he brought several copies of the first volume of *The Federalist*. When the second volume was published in May 1788, Hamilton saw to it that every prominent Federalist at the Virginia ratifying convention had his own personal two-volume set.

As the Virginia ratifying convention approached its historical vote on June 25, 1788, no one there knew that four days earlier on June 21, far to the north, the state of New Hampshire had quietly ratified the Constitution (57–46), becoming the ninth state to do so, and thereby bringing the Constitution into effect. Unaware that the Constitution had been safely ratified, the Virginia convention voted its approval (89–79) on June 25, 1788. A month later, on July 26, New York, an Anti-Federalist stronghold, surprised everyone by also voting for ratification (30–27).

It took another sixteen months, until November 21, 1789, for North Carolina to ratify the Constitution (197–99), under which the new government was already operating.

And then there was feisty Rhode Island. Just shy of two years after the Constitution had been ratified, on May 29, 1790, Rhode Island took a second look, narrowly ratified (34–32), and became a full participant in the United States of America.

The new nation had its new Constitution. The product of private drafting and public debate, the Constitution charted a course for an energetic national government to lead America into the next century and beyond.

Notes

The U.S. Constitution

The U.S. Constitution serves as a blueprint for the federal government, outlining the powers and responsibilities of the legislative, executive, and judicial branches, together with other important provisions, including the process of amendment.

THE CONSTITUTION OF THE UNITED STATES OF AMERICA, 1787

WE the people of the United States, in Order to form a more perfect Union, establish Justice, insure domestic **Tranquility**, provide for the common defense, promote the general Welfare, and secure the Blessings of Liberty to ourselves and our **Posterity**, do **ordain** and establish this Constitution for the United States of America.

NOTES

Tranquility: freedom from agitation of mind or spirit.

Posterity: future generations.

ordain: officially establish with authority.

COMMENTARY

The U.S. Constitution begins with a brief, but meaningful Preamble written at the end of the long and momentous Constitutional Convention in the summer of 1787. As with the rest of the Constitution, the Preamble was the product of political compromise.

Most of the Convention's work was finished by July 26, 1787, at which point the task of organizing and drafting the final text was delegated first to the Committee of Detail and then to the Committee of Style. In the end, most of the actual drafting was done by Gouverneur Morris of New York, who was actually serving as a delegate from Pennsylvania. Morris had distinguished himself as the most talkative delegate, exhibiting a keen wit and great eloquence. Fortunately, his skill as a writer equaled or surpassed his skill as a public speaker. James Madison paid Morris a high compliment remarking that as far as the selection of Morris to write the final draft of the Constitution was concerned, a "better choice could not have been made."

The draft of the Preamble that Morris received from the Committee of Detail did not begin with the now famous words, "We the people of the United States . . ." Instead, it read "We the People of the States of . . ." followed by the names of the thirteen states. But this formulation presented several problems for Morris. To begin with, the state of Rhode Island had sent no delegates to the Convention and no one would be present to sign on its behalf. Furthermore, assuming the other twelve state delegations all voted to approve the Constitution, there was no guarantee that all twelve states would ratify the document. Although the Constitution would become effective upon ratification by nine of the states, if some or all of the rest balked, it would be awkward for the Preamble to presume to speak in their name.

Morris solved the problem by eliminating the list of states and trimming the opening phrase to simply "We the people of the United States. . ."

Patrick Henry of Virginia, a fierce opponent of the Constitution, would later seize on these words as incriminating evidence that the Convention was traducing the sovereignty of the states. The Constitution should begin "We the States" he argued, because the states, and only the states, were the existing political units that could establish a federal union.

Henry's criticism seems unfounded. By the time the Preamble was written, the Constitution was already drafted. It proposed a new central government, not a continuation of the existing Confederation. There's no reason to believe Morris had any nefarious ulterior motive.

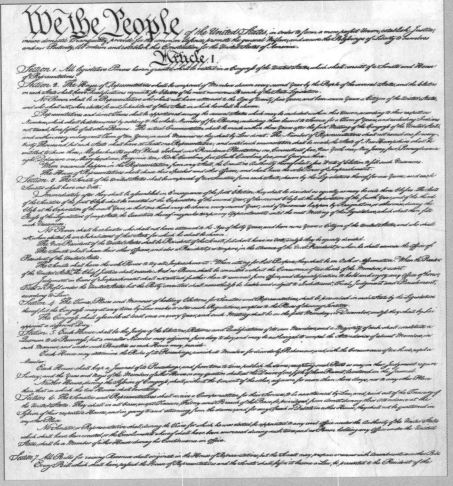

Preamble to the Constitution.
© Bettmann/CORBIS

lofty and the practical purposes for which the Constitution was written. By "a more perfect Union," the Preamble acknowledges that America is a work-in-progress aspiring to perfection, but as a human institution, not yet (or perhaps ever) attaining that ideal.

Surely establishing justice was a primary reason for the very existence of the United States. If injustice had marked the government under King George and Parliament, then justice should symbolize the essence of the new government.

Likewise "domestic tranquility"—peace at home—was something everyone yearned for. The problems with the Articles of Confederation and the lack of cooperation among the states had prompted the Constitutional Convention in the first place. Solving these problems, thereby allowing Americans to live in peace and to prosper, was an important goal of the new Constitution.

More than that, Henry's view of the existing union was outdated. The Declaration of Independence had declared Americans to be "one people" and had called the new union the "United States of America." Indeed, although the Declaration was focusing on breaking ties with Great Britain, its articulation of the right of one people to alter or abolish their former government and to establish a new government more conducive to their future safety and happiness equally applied to replacing the Articles of Confederation with the Constitution, all rightfully in the name of the American people.

For the balance of the Preamble, Morris drew on various sources to compose an eloquent list of purposes for the new government. The Preamble captures both the

Providing for the "common defence" was not so much an idealistic goal as a practical necessity. Foreign attack from England, France, or elsewhere was a serious threat. One of the most glaring defects in the Articles of Confederation and the loose alliance of American states was the absence of any national defense. If the new government was to live up to its central role, it must organize, finance, train, and maintain a "common defence."

Promoting the "general Welfare" covered a host of domestic and international responsibilities that the new national government was expected to address. Everything that would serve the national interest and make life better for its citizens was encompassed in the broad phrase "general Welfare."

Finally, the Constitution pledged that the new government would have as a primary purpose securing "the Blessings of Liberty." This provision delivered on the promise of the Declaration of Independence—that securing "Life, Liberty, and the pursuit of Happiness" was among the reasons "Governments are instituted among Men," and linked this portion of the Preamble to the Constitution to that seminal document signed on July 4, 1776. Securing liberty put the new government on the side of the people. It meant that the Constitution and the new government it created were intended to advance and protect liberty among the people. Unlike governments elsewhere in the world and throughout history that had been the enemies of liberty, this government would be the friend of liberty.

The worthy purposes expressed in the Preamble were promised "to ourselves and our Posterity," ensuring the permanence and continuity of the Constitution for future generations.

The Preamble concludes—in the active voice and the present tense—by declaring that the people "do ordain and establish this Constitution for the United States of America." The establishment of the Constitution occurs at a specific time and place, but it is not over and done with: It happens in the continuing present, and only with the continuing consent of the governed.

The legal status of the Preamble has been debated over the years. Is it an independent source of any inherent powers conferred on the national government? May Congress, the president, or the federal courts take any action based solely on the words of the Preamble? Some commentators support this view, but in *Jacobson v. Massachusetts* (1905), the Supreme Court specifically rejected that interpretation.

Whether or not the Preamble has the force of law, it has the force of inspiration. Quoted from grade schools to the halls of Congress, it expresses the spirit of the Constitution.

Article I

Article I establishes the legislative branch and specifies the powers of Congress.

ARTICLE I

SECTION 1. All legislative Powers herein granted shall be vested in a Congress of the United States, which shall consist of a Senate and House of Representatives.

Section 2. The House of Representatives shall be composed of Members chosen every second Year by the People of the several States, and the electors in each State shall have the qualifications requisite for electors of the most numerous branch of the State legislature.

No Person shall be a Representative who shall not have attained to the Age of twenty five Years, and been seven Years a citizen of the United States, and who shall not, when elected, be an Inhabitant of that State in which he shall be chosen.

Representatives and direct Taxes shall be **apportioned** among the several States which may be included within this Union, according to their respective Numbers, which shall be determined by adding to the whole number of free Persons, including those bound to Service for a Term of Years, and excluding Indians not taxed, three fifths of **all other Persons**. The actual **Enumeration** shall be made within three Years after the first Meeting of the Congress of the United States, and within every subsequent Term of ten Years, in such Manner as they shall by law Direct. The number of Representatives shall not exceed one for every thirty Thousand, but each State shall have at least one Representative; and until such enumeration shall be made, the State of New Hampshire shall be entitled to choose three, Massachusetts eight, Rhode Island and Providence Plantations one, Connecticut five, New York six, New Jersey four, Pennsylvania eight, Delaware one, Maryland six, Virginia ten, North Carolina five, South Carolina five, and Georgia three.

When vacancies happen in the Representation from any State, the Executive Authority thereof shall issue **Writs of Election** to fill such Vacancies.

The House of Representatives shall choose their Speaker and other Officers; and shall have the sole Power of **Impeachment**.

Section 3. The Senate of the United States shall be composed of two Senators from each State, chosen by the legislature thereof, for six Years; and each Senator shall have one Vote.

Immediately after they shall be assembled in Consequence of the first Election, they shall be divided as equally as may be into three Classes. The Seats of the Senators of the first Class shall be vacated at the expiration of the second Year, of the second Class at the expiration of the

NOTES

apportioned: divided up.

all other Persons: slaves.

Enumeration: census; counting of all persons.

Writs of Election: official notifications.

Impeachment: bringing charges to remove an official from office.

fourth Year, and of the third Class at the expiration of the sixth Year, so that one third may be chosen every second Year; and if vacancies happen by Resignation, or otherwise, during the recess of the Legislature of any State, the Executive thereof may make temporary Appointments until the next meeting of the Legislature, which shall then fill such Vacancies.

No person shall be a Senator who shall not have attained to the Age of thirty Years, and been nine Years a Citizen of the United States, and who shall not, when elected, be an Inhabitant of that State for which he shall be chosen.

The Vice-President of the United States shall be President of the Senate, but shall have no Vote, unless they be equally divided.

The Senate shall choose their other Officers, and also a **President pro tempore,** in the Absence of the Vice-President, or when he shall **exercise** the Office of President of the United States.

President pro tempore: temporary president.

The Senate shall have the sole Power to try all Impeachments. When sitting for that Purpose, they shall be on **Oath or Affirmation.** When the President of the United States is tried, the Chief Justice shall preside: And no Person shall be convicted without the Concurrence of two thirds of the Members present.

Oath or Affirmation: a declaration before God or upon penalty of perjury.

Judgment in cases of Impeachment shall not extend further than to removal from Office, and disqualification to hold and enjoy any **Office of honor, Trust or Profit** under the United States: but the Party convicted shall nevertheless be liable and subject to Indictment, Trial, Judgment and Punishment, according to Law.

Office of honor, Trust or Profit: any official position, whether compensated or not.

Section 4. The Times, Places and Manner of holding Elections for Senators and Representatives, shall be prescribed in each State by the Legislature thereof; but the Congress may at any time by Law make or alter such Regulations, except as to the Places of choosing Senators.

The Congress shall assemble at least once in every Year, and such Meeting shall be on the first Monday in December, unless they shall by law appoint a different Day.

Section 5. Each House shall be the Judge of the Elections, Returns and Qualifications of its own Members, and a Majority of each shall constitute a **Quorum** to do Business; but a smaller Number may adjourn from day to day, and may be authorized to compel the Attendance of absent Members, in such Manner, and under such Penalties as each House may provide.

Quorum: the minimum number of members of a group necessary to be present in order to conduct business.

Each house may determine the Rules of its Proceedings, punish its Members for disorderly Behavior, and, with the Concurrence of two-thirds, expel a Member.

Each house shall keep a Journal of its Proceedings, and from time to time publish the same, excepting such Parts as may in their Judgment require Secrecy; and the **Yeas and Nays** of the Members of either House on any question shall, at the Desire of one fifth of those Present, be entered on the Journal.

Yeas and Nays: votes for and against.

Neither House, during the Session of Congress, shall, without the Consent of the other, adjourn for more than three days, nor to any other Place than that in which the two Houses shall be sitting.

Section 6. The Senators and Representatives shall receive a Compensation for their Services, to be ascertained by Law, and paid out of the Treasury of the United States. They shall in all Cases, except Treason, Felony and Breach of the Peace, be privileged from Arrest during their Attendance at the Session of their respective Houses, and in going to and returning from the same; and for any Speech or Debate in either House, they shall not be questioned in any other Place.

No Senator or Representative shall, during the Time for which he was elected, be appointed to any civil Office under the authority of the United States, which shall have been created, or the **Emoluments** whereof shall have been increased during such time; and no Person holding any Office under the United States, shall be a Member of either House during his Continuance in Office.

Emoluments: financial compensation or other things of value.

Section 7. All Bills for raising Revenue shall originate in the House of Representatives; but the Senate may propose or concur with Amendments as on other Bills.

Every Bill which shall have passed the House of Representatives and the Senate, shall, before it become a Law, be presented to the President of the United States; If he approve he shall sign it, but if not he shall return it, with his Objections to that House in which it shall have originated, who shall enter the Objections at large on their Journal, and proceed to reconsider it. If after such Reconsideration two thirds of that house shall agree to pass the Bill, it shall be sent, together with the Objections, to the other House, by which it shall likewise be reconsidered, and if approved by two thirds of that House, it shall become a law. But in all such Cases the Votes of both Houses shall be determined by Yeas and Nays, and the Names of the Persons voting for and against the Bill shall be entered on the Journal of each House respectively. If any Bill shall not be returned by the President within ten Days (Sundays excepted) after it shall have been presented to him, the Same shall be a Law, in like Manner as if he had signed it, unless the Congress by their Adjournment prevent its Return, in which case it shall not be a Law.

Every Order, Resolution, or Vote to which the Concurrence of the Senate and House of Representatives may be necessary (except on a question of Adjournment) shall be presented to the President of the United States; and before the Same shall take Effect, shall be approved by him, or being disapproved by him, shall be repassed by two thirds of the Senate and House of Representatives, according to the Rules and Limitations prescribed in the Case of a Bill.

Section 8. The Congress shall have Power to **lay** and collect Taxes, **Duties, Imposts** and **Excises,** to pay the Debts and provide for the common Defense and general Welfare of the United States; but all Duties, Imposts and Excises shall be uniform throughout the United States;

To borrow Money on the credit of the United States;

lay: impose.

Duties: taxes on imports.

Imposts: taxes.

Excises: taxes on goods.

To regulate Commerce with foreign Nations, and among the several States, and with the Indian Tribes;

To establish an uniform Rule of **Naturalization,** and uniform Laws on the subject of Bankruptcies throughout the United States;

Naturalization: process for a foreigner to became a citizen.

To coin Money, regulate the Value thereof, and of foreign Coin, and fix the Standard of Weights and Measures;

To provide for the Punishment of counterfeiting the Securities and current Coin of the United States;

To establish Post Offices and Post Roads;

To promote the Progress of Science and useful Arts, by securing for limited Times to Authors and Inventors the exclusive Right to their respective Writings and Discoveries;

To constitute Tribunals inferior to the supreme Court;

To define and punish Piracies and Felonies committed on the high Seas, and Offenses against the Law of Nations;

To declare War, grant **Letters of Marque and Reprisal,** and make Rules concerning Captures on Land and Water;

Letters of Marque and Reprisal: official permission to seize enemy property.

To raise and support Armies, but no Appropriation of Money to that Use shall be for a longer term than two Years;

To provide and maintain a Navy;

To make Rules for the Government and Regulation of the land and naval Forces;

To provide for calling forth the **Militia** to execute the Laws of the Union, suppress Insurrections and repel Invasions;

Militia: an organized armed force composed of able-bodied private citizens.

To provide for organizing, arming, and disciplining, the Militia, and for governing such Part of them as may be employed in the Service of the United States, reserving to the States respectively, the Appointment of the Officers, and the Authority of training the militia according to the discipline prescribed by Congress;

To exercise exclusive Legislation in all Cases whatsoever, over such District (not exceeding ten Miles square) as may, by **Cession** of particular States, and the Acceptance of Congress, become the Seat of the Government of the United States, and to exercise like Authority over all Places purchased by the Consent of the Legislature of the State in which the Same shall be, for the Erection of Forts, **Magazines,** Arsenals, Dockyards, and other needful Buildings;—And

Cession: yielding.

Magazines: warehouses where powder and other explosives are stored.

To make all Laws which shall be necessary and proper for carrying into Execution the foregoing Powers, and all other Powers vested by this Constitution in the Government of the United States, or in any Department or Officer thereof.

Section 9. The Migration or Importation of such Persons as any of the States now existing shall think proper to admit, shall not be prohibited by the Congress prior to the Year one thousand eight hundred and eight, but a Tax or Duty may be imposed on such Importation, not exceeding ten dollars for each Person.

The Privilege of the **Writ of Habeas Corpus** shall not be suspended, unless when in Cases of Rebellion or Invasion the public Safety may require it.

No **Bill of Attainder** or **ex post facto Law** shall be passed.

No **Capitation**, or other direct, Tax shall be laid, unless in Proportion to the Census or Enumeration herein before directed to be taken.

No Tax or Duty shall be laid on Articles exported from any State.

No Preference shall be given by any Regulation of Commerce or Revenue to the Ports of one State over those of another: nor shall **Vessels** bound to, or from, one State, be obliged to enter, clear, or pay Duties in another.

No Money shall be drawn from the Treasury, but in Consequence of Appropriations made by Law; and a regular Statement and Account of the Receipts and Expenditures of all public Money shall be published from time to time.

No **Title of Nobility** shall be granted by the United States; and no Person holding any Office of Profit or Trust under them, shall, without the Consent of the Congress, accept of any present, Emolument, Office, or Title, of any kind whatever, from any King, Prince, or foreign State.

Section 10. No State shall enter into any Treaty, Alliance, or Confederation; grant Letters of Marque and Reprisal; coin Money; emit Bills of Credit; make any Thing but gold and silver Coin a **Tender** in Payment of Debts; pass any Bill of Attainder, ex post facto Law, or Law impairing the Obligation of Contracts, or grant any Title of Nobility.

No State shall, without the Consent of the Congress, lay any Imposts or Duties on Imports or Exports, except what may be absolutely necessary for executing it's inspection Laws: and the net Produce of all Duties and Imposts, laid by any State on Imports or Exports, shall be for the Use of the Treasury of the United States; and all such Laws shall be subject to the Revision and Control of the Congress.

No State shall, without the Consent of Congress, lay any **Duty of Tonnage**, keep Troops, or Ships of War in time of Peace, enter into any Agreement or Compact with another State, or with a foreign Power, or engage in War, unless actually invaded, or in such imminent Danger as will not admit of delay.

Writ of Habeas Corpus: official order requiring that a person in custody be brought to court to determine the legality of his or her detention or imprisonment.

Bill of Attainder: a law directed at a specific person.

Ex post facto Law: a law which retroactively increases the punishment for a crime committed before the law was enacted.

Capitation: a direct uniform tax imposed upon each head or person.

Vessel: a boat or ship.

Title of Nobility: hierarchieal social and/or political designation.

Tender: form of currency or legal payment.

Duty of Tonnage: tax imposed according to the weight of cargo.

COMMENTARY

It should not come as a surprise that the first and longest Article of the Constitution establishes the legislative branch of the federal government. While the framers formally treated all three branches of government as co-equal, in their hearts the legislative branch was more equal than the rest.

Congress, with its two-chamber structure, is the most democratic branch of government since members of the House of Representatives are elected directly by the people. The president is elected only indirectly by the people through the Electoral College, and the members of the judiciary, specifically the Supreme Court, are not elected at all but are appointed by the president and confirmed by the Senate. Consequently, Congress, the most democratic body created by the Constitution, takes a prominent place in Article I.

The term "Congress" refers to both the House of Representatives and the Senate, although sometimes people use the term "Congress" to mean only the House of Representatives.

The Founding of the House of Representatives

Believing that frequent elections would ensure a more representative government, Section 2 of Article I provides that members of the House of Representatives be elected every two years by direct election. The framers believed that representatives would stay in closer touch with their constituents, listen to their concerns and represent their interests in the halls of Congress, if for no other reason than that each representative had to stand for election every two years.

Article I provides that in order to qualify to be a representative, an individual must be at least 25 years old, a citizen of the United States for at least seven years, and a resident of the state he or she represents.

The original Constitution (until it was changed by the Fourteenth Amendment in 1868) provides that representatives be apportioned among the states according to their respective populations (referred to as *Numbers*). The population included every man, woman, and child who wasn't a Native American (who were not counted) or a slave (slaves counted as three-fifths of a person). This bizarre and shameful method of counting the population of the states was the product of a political compromise at the Constitutional Convention in 1787.

The first census (or what the Constitution calls *enumeration*) was set for three years after the first meeting of Congress and every ten years thereafter. The total number of representatives would not exceed one for every thirty thousand and each state was guaranteed at least one representative, regardless of its population.

In order to get the new national government started, since there would not be an enumeration for three years, the Constitution specified the number of representatives for each state in the interim. Virginia had ten; Massachusetts and Pennsylvania each eight; New York and Maryland each six; Connecticut, North Carolina, and South Carolina each five; New Jersey four; New Hampshire and Georgia each three; and Rhode Island and Delaware each one.

While today these figures are of only historical importance, they reveal how evenly divided the country was at its birth, in terms of the geographical distribution of representatives. Counting Maryland and Delaware with the South, of the 65 representatives in the First Congress, 34 were from northern states and 31 were from southern states. This balance of power explains many of the sectional compromises that went into creating the Constitution.

Section 2 of Article I concludes by providing that a vacancy in the House of Representatives be filled by the "Executive Authority" (generally the governor) of that state. Finally, the House is authorized to choose its presiding officer and other officers and is given "the sole Power of Impeachment."

The Founding of the Senate

Section 3 of Article I describes the formalities of the Senate. Two senators are assigned to each state, regardless of population. Thus, Delaware with only one representative in the First Congress and Virginia with ten, were each entitled to two senators. Like so much else in the Constitution, this was the result of political compromise. The small states (rightfully) feared that if representation in the entire Congress (House and Senate) was based solely on population, the larger states would perpetually dominate the national legislature, pursuing their own interests and ignoring those of the smaller states. Consequently, in the First Congress, with a Senate of 26 members, each state had equal representation of two senators. Each senator had a term of six years and the Constitution curiously confirmed that "each Senator shall have one Vote."

In the original Constitution, Section 3 of Article I provided that senators would be chosen by the state legislatures, not directly by the people as representatives were chosen. This is cited as one of the "undemocratic" features of the original Constitution. The framers denied that accusation and claimed it was only democracy once-removed, in that the people elected the state legislatures, which in turn chose the Senators. The framers justified the idea (as they did the Electoral College) on the grounds that the state legislatures were best equipped to pick senators of virtue and talent, who would serve at least three times as long as representatives. (In 1913, this portion of the Constitution was changed by the Sixteenth Amendment, which provided that Senators would henceforth be "elected by the people.")

Unlike the House of Representatives where all seats are up for election every two years, only one-third of the seats in the Senate are up for election every two years. Again to get started, the senators in the First Congress were divided into three classes, with the term of the first class expiring in two years; the second class in four years; and the third class in six years.

Vacancies in the Senate are to be filled by the state legislature, unless it is in recess, in which case the Executive (again, the governor) makes a temporary appointment until the next meeting of the state legislature.

A senator must be at least 30 years old, a citizen of the United States for at least nine years, and a resident of the state he or she represents.

The vice president of the United States serves as the president of the Senate but has no vote, except in the case of a tie. The Senate chooses its other officers, including a *president pro tempore*, who serves in the absence of the vice president or when the vice president is serving as president of the United States. The Senate has the sole power to try all impeachments (discussed in more detail later).

Rules of Congress

Section 4 of Article I sets forth various details regarding the meetings of Congress. Each state legislature is authorized to set the times, places, and manner for holding elections of senators and representatives. Congress can alter such matters, other than the places where senators are chosen. The Constitution requires Congress to meet at least once each year on the first Monday in December, unless Congress appoints a different day.

Section 5 of Article I provides that each chamber of Congress shall be the judge of the elections, returns, and qualifications of its members. Thus, the Senate has no say in such matters in the House of Representatives and vice versa. To conduct any official business, a *quorum* must be present, which the Constitution specifies as a majority. However, if less than a majority is present, each House may compel the attendance of absent members, with such penalties as each House may specify. Each House sets its own rules, can punish members for "disorderly behavior," and can expel a member on a two-thirds vote. Each House is required to keep a Journal of its proceedings, which is published from time to time (today known as the "Congressional Record"). The members of Congress may decide that parts of the record be kept secret. At the request of one-fifth of those present, the "Yeas and Nays" of the members are entered in the Journal. While Congress is in session, neither House may adjourn for more than three days without the consent of the other House and may not convene in any place except where both Houses sit.

Section 6 of Article I deals with compensation and other matters. Senators and representatives are entitled to the compensation set by Congress, to be paid by the Treasury of the United States. No member may be arrested while in the Senate or House, or while going to or from, except for treason, felony, or breach of the peace. The framers created this special sanctuary out of a concern that their work in the Congress could be disrupted by an overzealous (or corrupt) president, who could have opposition leaders arrested in order to silence them. Likewise, the Constitution provides that no member may "be questioned in any other Place" for any speech or debate made in the Senate or House. Again, the framers feared that opponents could try to silence or punish senators or representatives, through libel suits or criminal prosecutions, for what they said in their speeches in Congress. Instead, the Constitution establishes an absolute privilege for such speeches, regardless of whether they were false or defamatory. The framers did so because they placed such importance on candor and freedom of speech during the deliberations in the halls of Congress.

Section 6 also provides that for so long as members of the Senate or House serve in Congress, they may not also be appointed to any civil position created during their term, or for which the compensation or benefits (referred to as *Emoluments*) have been increased during their term. Essentially, the framers wanted to avoid the situation where a senator or representative plays a role in creating a government job (or increasing the compensation for that job) and then is rewarded with that very job. The restriction also works the other way around: No person who holds an office in the federal government can simultaneously be a senator or representative.

Section 7 of Article I is a very important part of the Constitution since it relates to money. All bills to raise revenue for the operation of the national government must originate in the House of Representatives, although the Senate may propose or concur in amendments to such bills as it does on other legislation. The framers felt very strongly that the power to tax the people must only begin in the body elected directly by the people. The revolutionary refrain "no taxation without representation" was still remembered in America.

Section 7 goes on to describe in detail the process by which legislation is enacted by Congress: Each bill must first be approved by both the House of Representatives and the Senate and then sent to the president for signature. If the president signs the bill, it becomes law. If the president returns the bill with objections (*vetoes* the bill), and both the House and Senate override the presidential veto by two-thirds votes, the bill becomes law. If the president does not sign or return a bill within ten days, excluding Sundays, it automatically becomes law, unless Congress is not in session, in which case it does not become law. This is known as a *pocket veto,* meaning that while Congress is in recess, the president can silently veto a bill by leaving it in his or her pocket. Under Section 7, a comparable process applies to orders, resolutions, and votes of Congress other than bills.

The procedures just described are some of the most important checks and balances devised by the framers. Here the legislature proposes laws which the president must first approve. But to limit the president's power to block laws with which he or she disagrees, the Constitution provides a safety valve through the override vote. But the override vote is pegged at two-thirds to ensure that a simple majority in Congress cannot ram through any and all laws it wants regardless of the president's wishes.

This carefully balanced scheme, reminiscent of the moves on a chessboard, tests the resolve of the legislative and executive branches. Is the president so vehemently opposed to a bill that he or she will go so far as to veto it? Is Congress so eager to pass a vetoed bill that it can muster a super majority to override a presidential veto? And throughout the process, what do the people think? A president may believe that he or she is more attuned to public opinion and that regardless of what a majority in Congress may want, a veto is in the country's best interest and that Congress will be unable to gather a two-thirds vote to pass the bill. Likewise, if public opinion overwhelmingly supports a bill and Congress votes in favor by two-thirds or more, the bill becomes veto-proof and there's nothing the president can do except publicly object and later seek new legislation to limit or repeal such a law.

The Powers of Congress

Section 8 is the centerpiece of Article I, setting forth all the specific powers granted to Congress by the Constitution. These are sometimes referred to as Congress' *enumerated powers,* in other words, the powers expressly spelled out in the Constitution, in contrast to its *implied powers,* discussed later.

In total, Section 8 sets forth 27 specific powers granted to Congress. Consequently, the first question Congress, the president, the courts, or the public must always ask in determining whether a law passed by Congress is constitutional is whether the Constitution granted Congress the power (express or implied) to enact such a law. (The second question is whether the law violates any of the amendments to the Constitution, including the Bill of Rights.)

Again, the first powers listed have to do with money. Congress is authorized to:

(a) impose and collect taxes, *duties* (taxes on imported goods) and *excises* (taxes on manufactured goods) so long as these taxes are "uniform" throughout the country

(b) pay debts and provide for the "common Defense and general Welfare of the United States."

Right off the bat, it's evident that one of Congress' "enumerated" primary powers is actually quite broad and undefined. While "common Defense" presumably refers to maintaining an army and navy (although the Article also contains specific provisions for armed forces), what exactly does "provide for the general Welfare of the United States" mean? Surely, an imaginative senator could justify virtually any bill as helping to provide for the "general Welfare." The very term "general" renders the term a generality, leaving it open to a wide range of interpretations. Of course, this is precisely what the framers intended: They realized that they could not imagine or anticipate every need that would call for congressional action. Yet the unlimited breadth of this term underscores why Anti-Federalists were so concerned that the Constitution created what they saw as such a powerful and limitless federal government.

Section 8 also grants Congress several more precise and limited powers such as the ability to borrow money; to establish rules for *naturalization* (the process for foreigners to become U.S. citizens) and bankruptcy; to coin money (and regulate its value, as well as the value in the United States of foreign money); to fix standard weights and measures; to provide punishments for counterfeiting securities and U.S. currency; to establish post offices and post roads; and to define and punish piracies and felonies committed on the high seas and offenses against the law of nations.

The Commerce Clause

One power granted to Congress which has proven to be an inexhaustible source of federal legislation may not at first have seemed so broad: the power to "regulate Commerce." Little controversy has arisen over regulating commerce with foreign nations and Native American tribes, but the simple phrase, to "regulate Commerce . . .

among the several States," (known as *the Commerce Clause*) has become one of the most significant in all of the Constitution.

For all that the Constitution means to us today, it may easily be overlooked that problems over trade and commerce were the driving force behind its creation. The Constitutional Convention of 1787 grew out of concerns over "the trade of the United States" and "how far a uniform system in their commercial regulation may be necessary to their common interest and their permanent harmony." Despite the fact that the needs of commerce prompted the calling of the Convention in the first place, the Commerce Clause was written, adopted, and ratified with hardly any debate or opposition. To regulate commerce *between* the states, known as *interstate commerce,* seemed a perfectly appropriate role for Congress to play, so long as commerce *within* each state, called *intrastate commerce,* was off-limits to national control. Indeed, this is the interpretation of the Commerce Clause unanimously upheld by the U.S. Supreme Court in *Gibbons v. Ogden* (1824).

For the first century under the Constitution, the Commerce Clause prompted little controversy. Legislation was limited to navigation on the oceans, lakes, and rivers which cut across state boundaries and therefore clearly affected interstate commerce. Beginning in 1887, Congress began to address the need for uniform rates for railroads carrying goods across the country by enacting the Interstate Commerce Act, the first federal regulation of land transportation. Three years later Congress passed the Sherman Anti-Trust Act, which prohibited combinations of large companies from restraining or monopolizing interstate commerce and foreign trade.

Effects of the New Deal

As the economy became more dependent on the nationwide distribution of goods and services, Congress acted more frequently to regulate interstate commerce. But the federal government's role in the economy was jolted into high gear by the Great Depression, which lasted from 1929 through the 1930s. With 13 million people unemployed, prices and wages dropping, and businesses failing, the people elected Franklin D. Roosevelt as president to get the country back on track. He announced the New Deal, and Congress began using the Commerce Clause to enact a wide range of legislation designed to increase national employment, boost national purchasing power, and improve the national economy,

including maximum hours, minimum wages, and production quotas for oil producers and farmers.

While Congress and Roosevelt generally saw eye to eye on the need for measures to combat the devastating consequences of the Depression, a majority in the Supreme Court certainly did not. In case after case, the Court struck down "New Deal" legislation on the grounds that the Constitution prohibited Congress from solving the economy's problems by controlling intrastate transactions at the manufacturing or production level.

On the eve of Supreme Court arguments in yet another challenge to the "New Deal," President Roosevelt, who had recently been re-elected by a huge majority, announced that he would ask Congress to expand the number of justices on the Court. Ostensibly to bring on more and younger judges to help keep up with the Court's workload, most observers saw Roosevelt's plan as a scheme to dilute the impact of the Court's current conservative majority. Two months later, however, the Court upheld the National Labor Relations Act and then two of the more conservative justices retired, giving Roosevelt the opportunity to appoint justices who took a broader view of the Commerce Clause without pursuing his court-packing plan.

In rapid succession, the Court began upholding the "New Deal," finding that the Commerce Clause extended not merely to the regulation of interstate commerce, but to those intrastate activities that exerted "a substantial economic effect" on interstate commerce. The Court held that this interpretation was "essential to weld a loose confederacy into a single, indivisible Nation."

Broadening the Scope in the 1960s

By the 1960s, Congress' authority to regulate all aspects of the interdependent national economy was used to uphold federal legislation prohibiting racial discrimination in restaurants, hotels, and resorts. Although at first glance such businesses seem uniquely local in their operations, Congress found that the movement of food and travelers across state lines implicated interstate commerce and the Court agreed in a series of decisions beginning with *Heart of Atlanta Motel v. United States* (1964).

The history of the Commerce Clause is a classic example of the development of constitutional interpretation to meet the needs of economic and technological change, as the country grew from an agrarian economy dominated by farms, small towns, and family businesses to a complex, mobile, national economy characterized by large, multifaceted corporations that manufacture, advertise, distribute, and market goods and services nationwide, without regard to state borders.

Other Powers of Congress

Section 8 of Article I contains other important powers granted to Congress. It authorizes Congress to issue copyrights, patents, and trademarks. The framers were acutely aware of the role copyright, patent, and trademark protection would play in the development of the new economy and in fostering the intellectual life of America.

Although Article III is devoted entirely to the judiciary, Section 8 of Article I authorizes Congress to establish lower federal courts, which it did by passing the Judiciary Act of 1789 during the First Congress.

Congress and the Armed Forces

Six separate provisions of Section 8 are devoted to Congress' authority over the military. To begin with, Congress is empowered to declare war. This awesome power is placed in the hands of the national legislature, *not* the president, which speaks volumes to the framers' conviction that a president should not have the powers of a king. Only the people's representatives in Congress should have the authority to make war.

Congress also was authorized to "raise and support Armies," "provide and maintain a Navy," and make rules and regulations for all land and naval forces. Wary of the power of a permanent army, which could potentially become a threat to democracy, the Constitution provides that funds to support the armed forces be allotted for only two years. In this way, the Constitution expected Congress to revisit the funding of the army every two years—not coincidentally the same schedule as the election of representatives. Today, the two-year restriction is a mere formality and there is not only a standing army, but marines and air force as well. Interestingly, the navy was not subject to the same two-year limitation on its funding, presumably because the framers saw a greater need to maintain a permanent defense at sea from foreign attack and because the navy posed less of a threat of military tyranny than a standing army.

Section 8 also provides for Congress to call forth, organize, arm, and discipline a militia. The militia had a long history in defending Americans before there was an army or navy. Today, the federal militia is known as the National Guard and continues to act in times of civil unrest and national emergencies.

Section 8 also authorized Congress to establish and administer a seat of government (which eventually became the District of Columbia, also known as Washington, D.C.) and to purchase land in the various states and erect forts, supply depots, arsenals, dockyards, and "other needful Buildings."

The Necessary and Proper Clause

Finally, Section 8 concludes with a few words which, like the Commerce Clause, have prompted great debate and controversy over the true nature of congressional power. The Constitution empowers Congress to "make all Laws which shall be necessary and proper for carrying into Execution the foregoing Powers and all other Powers rested by this Constitution in the Government of the United States, or in any Department or Officer thereof." Anti-Federalists, fearing that the Necessary and Proper Clause was a huge loophole through which Congress could exercise sweeping powers beyond those enumerated in Section 8, called it the "elastic clause." Thomas Jefferson agreed, claiming it would allow Congress to encroach on powers reserved to the states. In fact, Jefferson argued that the clause should actually be seen as a *limitation* on congressional power, allowing Congress to pass only laws indispensable to carrying out the powers granted by the Constitution. But James Madison and Alexander Hamilton disagreed, and eventually their broader view of the Necessary and Proper Clause prevailed in the Supreme Court in the historic decision in *McCulloch v. Maryland* (1819), which upheld the constitutionality of a second national bank.

Over the years, the Necessary and Proper Clause has been invoked by Congress and the Court to justify an ever-widening scope of the federal legislation in areas previously considered to be within the province of the states. Only recently, beginning in the 1990s, has a conservative majority on the Supreme Court begun to tighten the reins around the Necessary and Proper Clause, striking down federal legislation that the justices see as exceeding Congress' enumerated powers and invading the sovereignty of the states.

The Question of Rights

Section 9 of Article I places specific limitations on the powers of Congress. Thus, some of what the Constitution giveth in Section 8, the Constitution taketh away in Section 9.

Section 9 begins with another indirect reference to—indeed, endorsement of—slavery. Cleverly worded to avoid the term "slavery" but surely understood that way to the framers, Section 9 says that the "Migration or Importation of such Persons as any of the States now existing shall think proper to admit, shall not be prohibited by the Congress prior to the Year one thousand eight hundred and eight, but a Tax or Duty may be imposed on such Importation, not exceeding ten dollars for each Person." Any suggestion that this provision merely dealt with immigration is belied by the term "Importation." Human beings migrate; goods are imported. The clause unmistakably treats "such Persons" as goods.

Under this provision, Congress could not prohibit the slave trade until 1808. This ignominious clause was part of the price non-slave states paid to gain approval from the slave states for the rest of the Constitution. Calling the African slave trade a violation of "human rights," President Thomas Jefferson signed legislation ending the importation of slaves effective January 1, 1808, yet the owning and selling of slaves within the United States continued for more than half a century.

The Writ of Habeas Corpus

The next clause of Section 9 is the first of a handful of provisions in the Constitution that protect personal freedoms, even before there was a Bill of Rights. The Writ of Habeas Corpus, known as the Great Writ because it is a hallmark of any system which values personal liberty over the authority of the state, originated in English common law. The term *habeas corpus* means "you shall have the body" and refers to the opening words of a writ, or court order, commanding any person who holds another in custody, such as a sheriff, jailer, warden, or military officer, to bring the person to court and once there, justify the lawfulness of that person's detention, conviction, or sentence. In 1868, Chief Justice Salmon P. Chase recognized the Great Writ as the basic safeguard of liberty when he wrote that it has been "for centuries esteemed the best and only sufficient defense of personal freedom."

In *habeas corpus* proceedings, which can be filed in state or federal court, an individual can attack the constitutionality or legality of his or her conviction or sentence, even after all other appeals have been exhausted. Under Chief Justice Earl Warren, who served from 1953 to 1969, the Court took an expansive view of *habeas corpus*. For example, in *Fay v. Noia* (1953), in an opinion by Justice William J. Brennan, Jr., the Court overturned a criminal conviction based on a coerced confession in violation of the Fifth Amendment, calling *habeas corpus* the "ultimate remedy" in the struggle for personal liberty.

The Constitution does allow for the suspension of *habeas corpus* in the event of rebellion or invasion. This has occurred only rarely: during the Civil War; in 1871 to combat the Ku Klux Klan in North Carolina; in 1905 when the United States occupied the Philippines; and in Hawaii during World War II.

Of more serious concern to civil libertarians is the extent to which the Supreme Court and Congress have restricted *habeas corpus* in the past 25 years. In *Stone v. Powell* (1976), the Court held that a conviction based on evidence obtained by police in an illegal search and seizure could not be overturned in a *habeas corpus* proceeding so long as there was a fair chance to litigate that issue in the state courts. And in *Herrera v. Collins* (1993), the Court allowed the petitioner to be executed despite his claim that newly discovered evidence would prove his actual innocence of the crime, because he had not also shown procedural errors at his original trial. In 1996, Congress passed and President Bill Clinton signed the Anti-Terrorism and Effective Death Penalty Act, which severely restricted *habeas corpus* by setting a one-year filing deadline among other things. Whether the Great Writ will be restored to its historic role in protecting legal and constitutional rights will depend on the views of the members of Congress, the Supreme Court, and ultimately, the general public.

Laws, Crimes, and Taxes

Section 9 of Article I next prohibits *bills of attainder* (laws targeting specific individuals) and *ex post facto laws* (laws applied retroactively to make something a crime that wasn't a crime when it took place). In addition, a tax must be imposed in proportion to the latest census. (This provision was modified by the Sixteenth Amendment.) Furthermore, articles exported from states aren't subject to duty, and Congress can't give preference to one state over others as it regulates commerce or collects trade revenues. The government is required to publish its receipts and expenditures of all public money from time to time, and in order to withdraw funds from the U.S. Treasury, Congress must pass a law.

Section 9 concludes by prohibiting the United States from granting titles and prohibiting any federal official from accepting any gifts, office, or title from any foreign state, without the consent of Congress. Here again, the framers were deeply concerned that neither the president nor any other United States official assume any of the trappings of royalty. Indeed, a proposal at the Constitutional Convention to refer to the president as "his Excellency" was soundly rejected.

Limitations on the States

Article I concludes with Section 10, which deals with limitations on the states and international relations. It prohibits states from entering into a treaty, alliance, or confederation; coining money; issuing bills of credit; making anything but gold and silver coin a form of payment of debts; passing any bill of attainder, *ex post facto* law, or law impairing the obligation of contracts; or granting any title of nobility.

Furthermore, no state may, without the consent of Congress, impose any duties on imports or exports, with minor exceptions; and the net revenues from such duties belong to the federal government.

Finally, Section 10 prohibits states from imposing any duty on the tonnage of ships, or from keeping troops on ships of war in time of peace; or entering into any agreement or compact with another state or foreign power or engage in war, "unless actually invaded, or in such imminent Danger as will not admit of delay."

Article II

Article II establishes the executive branch and specifies the powers and responsibilities of the president.

ARTICLE II

SECTION 1. The executive Power shall be vested in a President of the United States of America. He shall hold his Office during the Term of four Years, and, together with the Vice President chosen for the same Term, be elected, as follows:

Each State shall appoint, in such Manner as the Legislature thereof may direct, a Number of **Electors**, equal to the whole Number of Senators and Representatives to which the State may be entitled in the Congress: but no Senator or Representative, or Person holding an Office of Trust or Profit under the United States, shall be appointed an Elector.

The Electors shall meet in their respective States, and vote by Ballot for two Persons, of whom one at least shall not lie an Inhabitant of the same State with themselves. And they shall make a List of all the Persons voted for, and of the Number of Votes for each; which List they shall sign and certify, and transmit sealed to the **Seat of the Government** of the United States, directed to the President of the Senate. The President of the Senate shall, in the Presence of the Senate and House of Representatives, open all the Certificates, and the Votes shall then be counted. The Person having the greatest Number of Votes shall be the President, if such Number be a Majority of the whole Number of Electors appointed; and if there be more than one who have such Majority, and have an equal Number of votes, then the House of Representatives shall immediately choose by Ballot one of them for President; and if no Person have a Majority, then from the five highest on the List the said House shall in like Manner choose the President. But in choosing the President, the Votes shall be taken by States, the Representation from each State having one Vote; a Quorum for this Purpose shall consist of a Member or Members from two thirds of the States, and a Majority of all the States shall be necessary to a Choice. In every Case, after the Choice of the President, the Person having the greatest Number of Votes of the Electors shall be the Vice President. But if there should remain two or more who have equal Votes, the Senate shall choose from them by Ballot the Vice President.

The Congress may determine the Time of choosing the Electors, and the Day on which they shall give their Votes; which Day shall be the same throughout the United States.

No Person except a natural born Citizen, or a Citizen of the United States, at the time of the Adoption of this Constitution, shall be eligible to the Office of President; neither shall any Person be eligible to that

NOTES

Electors: persons chosen to vote for an elected official.

Seat of the Government: the location of the capital of a country or state.

Office who shall not have attained to the Age of thirty five Years, and been fourteen Years a Resident within the United States.

In Case of the Removal of the President from Office, or of his Death, Resignation, or Inability to discharge the Powers and Duties of the said Office, the Same shall **devolve** on the Vice President, and the Congress may by Law provide for the Case of Removal, Death, Resignation or Inability, both of the President and Vice President, declaring what Officer shall then act as President, and such Officer shall act accordingly, until the Disability be removed, or a President shall be elected.

devolve: transfer from one person to another.

The President shall, at stated Times, receive for his Services, a Compensation, which shall neither be increased nor diminished during the Period for which he shall have been elected, and he shall not receive within that Period any other Emolument from the United States, or any of them.

Before he enter on the Execution of his Office, he shall take the following Oath or Affirmation:—"I do solemnly swear (or affirm) that I will faithfully execute the Office of President of the United States, and will to the best of my Ability, preserve, protect and defend the Constitution of the United States."

Section 2. The President shall be Commander in Chief of the Army and Navy of the United States, and of the Militia of the several States, when called into the actual Service of the United States; he may require the Opinion, in writing, of the principal Officer in each of the executive Departments, upon any Subject relating to the Duties of their respective Offices, and he shall have Power to grant **Reprieves** and **Pardons** for Offenses against the United States, except in Cases of impeachment.

Reprieves: temporary delays of punishment.

He shall have Power, by and with the Advice and Consent of the Senate, to make Treaties, provided two thirds of the Senators present concur; and he shall nominate, and by and with the Advice and Consent of the Senate, shall appoint Ambassadors, other public Ministers and Consuls, Judges of the supreme Court, and all other Officers of the United States, whose Appointments are not herein otherwise provided for, and which shall be established by Law: but the Congress may by Law vest the Appointment of such inferior Officers, as they think proper, in the President alone, in the Courts of Law, or in the Heads of Departments.

Pardons: official releases from legal penalties.

The President shall have Power to fill up all Vacancies that may happen during the **Recess** of the Senate, by granting Commissions which shall expire at the End of their next session.

Recess: a suspension of business.

Section 3. He shall from time to time give to the Congress Information of the State of the Union, and recommend to their Consideration such Measures as he shall judge necessary and expedient; he may, on extraordinary Occasions, convene both Houses, or either of them, and in Case of Disagreement between them, with Respect to the Time of Adjournment, he may adjourn them to such Time as he shall think proper; he shall receive Ambassadors and other public Ministers; he shall take Care that the Laws be faithfully executed, and shall Commission all the Officers of the United States.

Section 4. The President, Vice President and all civil Officers of the United States, shall be removed from Office on Impeachment for, and Conviction of, Treason, Bribery, or other high Crimes and Misdemeanors.

COMMENTARY

Article II of the U.S. Constitution, which deals with the executive branch, spells out very little in terms of the powers granted to the president in contrast to the detailed rundown of the legislative branch's powers found in Article I.

Section 1 of Article II begins by declaring that the "executive Power shall be vested in a President of the United States of America," who holds office for a four-year term, as does the vice president.

Electing the President

Section 1 sets forth in detail the manner by which the president and vice president are chosen. (Some of the original procedures, as noted later on, were modified in 1804 by the Twelfth Amendment.) The framers of the Constitution decided against the direct election of the president and vice president and opted instead for the use of Electors in what has come to be known as the *Electoral College*. The Constitution provides that each state appoint a number of Electors equal to the total number of senators and representatives from that state. Current federal officeholders cannot be electors.

As originally written, the Constitution specified that the Electors vote for two persons, at least one of them from another state. The senate received and counted the votes. The person with the greatest number of votes was elected president, provided he or she received a majority of the votes from all the Electors appointed. If there was a tie, the House of Representatives chose the winner. If no candidate got a majority of the votes, the five highest vote-getters were voted on by the House, with each state delegation having one vote.

The person having the second greatest number of votes was elected vice president (except that in the case of a tie for second, the Senate would vote to break the tie). Section I goes on to provide that Congress shall determine the time for choosing Electors and the day they vote. Since political parties had not emerged in America by the time the Constitution was written, it seemed quite appropriate for the president to be the highest vote getter, the vice president the next. This would soon change.

The Electoral College was devised by the framers as a means to satisfy both the large and small states, which disagreed over how to select the president. The framers anticipated that the Electoral College would choose the most highly qualified individual—someone with a continental or national outlook who would serve the best interests of all the people, not only certain sectional interests.

According to some historians, the electoral system may have been put into place to ensure the election of George Washington as the first president of the United States. A wide-open direct election could have resulted in the election of a popular figure such as Patrick Henry, who fiercely opposed the new national government.

When the Electoral College Fails

By 1800, the Federalist and Democratic-Republican parties had emerged. Thomas Jefferson tied with his own running mate Aaron Burr, both of whom were members of the Democratic-Republican party. Consequently, under the procedures set forth in Article II, Section 1 of the Constitution, the House of Representatives chose Jefferson, and Burr became the vice president. In 1824, the House chose John Quincy Adams over Andrew Jackson, despite the fact that Jackson won both the popular and electoral votes. In 1876, with disputed returns in four states, the House appointed a special commission (nowhere provided for in the Constitution) which put Rutherford B. Hayes in office, even though his opponent, Samuel J. Tilden, had 264,000 more popular votes. And in 1888, Grover Cleveland, the incumbent president, won the popular vote but lost the Electoral College to Benjamin Harrison.

Most recently, Al Gore, the Democratic candidate for president, lost to George W. Bush, the Republican candidate, even though Gore won the popular vote by more than 550,000 votes. The electoral votes were undecided for 35 days, due to discrepancies in the vote tallies in Florida. Although the Florida Supreme Court ordered a recount of certain manual ballots, the U.S. Supreme Court, in two 5-4 decisions, first stayed the Florida recount and then ruled that the recount violated the equal protection guarantee of the Constitution. As a result of the Court's controversial ruling, Bush was certified as the 43rd president, amidst complaints that all the votes had never been properly counted and that five conservative Justices, including one appointed by Bush's father, who was president from 1989 to 1993, had installed Bush as president.

The 2000 election renewed calls to eliminate the Electoral College. Defenders of the system claim it encourages presidential candidates to campaign in every state, while opponents complain that campaigns are fought mostly over television, which reaches everyone, and that in any case, it is undemocratic for someone to become president when his or her opponent received more popular votes. It would take a constitutional amendment to repeal the Electoral College, which requires ratification by three-fourths of the states. Because more than one-fourth of the states are smaller states which generally benefit from the Electoral College, the passage of such an amendment seems unlikely.

Becoming President

Section 1 of Article II provides that the president must be at least 35 years old, a resident of the United States for at least 14 years and either a natural born citizen or a citizen of the United States at the time of the adoption of the Constitution.

Presidential succession—who serves in the president's absence—has proved to be a delicate and difficult matter. As originally written (and until the adoption of the Twenty-Fifth Amendment in 1967), the Constitution provided that in the event the president died or was removed from office, the vice president would take over and serve until the disability was removed or a new president was elected. Congress is authorized to enact the details of succession.

The president is entitled to compensation, which may not be increased or decreased during his or her term, and is not entitled to any other payments, wages, fees, and so on from the United States or any state.

Inauguration

Section 1 concludes by quoting the oath or affirmation the president takes. At the first inauguration of George Washington on April 30, 1789, he added the words "So help me God" to the oath of office, despite the fact that those words are not in Section 1. Each president since has followed suit. Washington's second inaugural address on March 4, 1793 was the shortest (135 words)

and William Henry Harrison's on March 4, 1841 was the longest (10,000 words).

With the development of technology, inaugural speeches have gone beyond those present to reach people all over the world. James Polk's inaugural address (March 4, 1845) was the first covered by the telegraph, William McKinley's (March 4, 1897) the first recorded by a motion picture camera, Harry S. Truman's (January 20, 1949) the first broadcast by television, and Bill Clinton's second inaugural address (January 20, 1997) the first carried live on the Internet.

Perhaps the most memorable words spoken by any president at his swearing in were those of Abraham Lincoln at his second inaugural, at the height of the Civil War, when he sought to bring the nation together. " . . . With malice toward none, with charity for all, with firmness in the right as God gives us to see the right, let us strive on to finish the work we are in, to bind up the nation's wounds, to care for him who shall have borne the battle and for his widow and his orphan, to do all which may achieve and cherish a just and lasting peace among ourselves and with all nations." (*CliffsComplete U.S. Presidential Addresses* [Hungry Minds, Inc.] contains the complete text and commentary on this and other presidential speeches.)

Powers of the President

Section 2 of Article II states six of the powers granted to the president by the Constitution. First, the president is Commander-in-Chief of the army and navy of the United States, and of state militias when they're called into the service. The framers believed strongly in civilian control of the military, as a counterweight to the risk of military domination of the country.

Second, the president may instruct executive departments to provide reports.

Third, the president may grant reprieves and pardons for persons convicted of violating federal law, except that the president cannot pardon any office holder who has been impeached. (See the "Impeachment" section later in this commentary for a discussion of this term.)

Fourth, the president has the power to make treaties with the advice and consent of the Senate and the concurrence of two-thirds of the senators present.

Fifth, the president has the power to appoint ambassadors, other public ministers and consuls, judges of the Supreme Court, and all other officers of the United States, subject to Senate approval.

Sixth, and finally, the president has the power to fill vacancies in any offices that require Senate approval during any Senate recess by granting commissions which shall expire at the end of the next session of the Senate.

These powers contain certain checks and balances that the framers felt were appropriate to limit presidential power. Thus, the president can make treaties and appoint individuals to the Supreme Court and other positions in government, but always with the "advice and consent" of the Senate. While presidents make thousands of appointments, only rarely does the Senate reject them under its advice and consent power. In modern times, the Senate has particularly scrutinized presidential nominees to the Supreme Court since the Court plays such a pervasive role on a wide range of important issues. There is an ongoing debate over whether the Senate may reject Supreme Court nominees on the basis of their views on the important legal and constitutional issues likely to come before them or only on the basis of their general qualifications and fitness to serve.

Clashes with the Senate

In 1795, the Senate rejected John Rutledge, nominated by George Washington to serve as Chief Justice, largely because Rutledge had criticized the Jay Treaty of 1794, which the Senate supported.

In 1987, President Ronald Reagan nominated Robert Bork to the Supreme Court. A bitter confirmation battle ensued, in which Bork's conservative views on the interpretation of the Constitution, civil rights, privacy, and free speech were scrutinized in detail. The Senate Judiciary Committee voted, 9-5, not to recommend his confirmation and he was rejected by the full Senate on a vote of 58-42.

In rejecting Bork, the Senate Judiciary Committee concluded that his "narrow definition of liberty" set him apart "from every Justice who ever sat on the Supreme Court" and that his "rejection of the concept of unenumerated rights and liberties" and his theory that "the Constitution should not be read as recognizing an individual right unless that right can be specifically found in a particular provision of the document" were "fundamentally at odds with the express understanding of the Framers and with the history of the Supreme Court in building our tradition of constitutionalism."

In 1991, President George Bush nominated Clarence Thomas, a conservative African-American, to the Supreme Court to fill the seat vacated by Thurgood Marshall, the first African-American Justice. Although Thomas was criticized for such things as his reluctance to pursue civil rights complaints while he served as chair of the Equal Employment Opportunity Commission (EEOC) and his conservative views on affirmative action and other civil rights issues, his confirmation hearings are best remembered because he was accused of having sexually harassed Anita Hill, one of his employees at the EEOC. Thomas condemned the hearings as a "high-tech lynching" and several Republican senators responded by attacking Hill's credibility. In the end, the Senate confirmed Thomas by a 52-48 margin.

Most recently, in 2001, President George W. Bush's nomination of former Senator John Ashcroft as Attorney General triggered widespread opposition from civil rights and women's groups, who criticized Ashcroft's highly conservative record of opposing desegregation, affirmative action, gun control, abortion rights, and other civil rights positions. In addition, Ashcroft was accused of characterizing as pro-criminal the record of Justice Ronnie White, an African-American member of the Missouri Supreme Court, who had been nominated to the U.S. District Court. Following Justice White's appearance at Ashcroft's confirmation hearings, opposition mounted. In the end, however, Ashcroft was approved by the Senate 58 to 42.

Additional Powers of the President

Section 3 of Article II contains additional powers and responsibilities granted to the president. The president is required to give Congress information on the State of the Union from time to time. Until 1913 and the administration of President Woodrow Wilson, the State of the Union address was always delivered in writing. Since then it has been given by the president in person before a joint session of the Senate and House.

The president may also recommend proposed legislation to Congress and may, on extraordinary occasions, convene both chambers of Congress, or either of them, and if the two chambers disagree on the time of adjournment, the president may adjourn them. The president also receives ambassadors and other public ministers and commissions all officers of the United States.

Perhaps the president's most important power and responsibility is to "take care that the Laws be faithfully executed." It is from these few words that the president and the entire executive branch derive their authority to enforce all federal laws. The provision also means that a president only *executes* the laws; he or she does not *make* the laws. When President Harry S Truman attempted by executive order to take control of steel mills, the Supreme Court in *Youngstown Sheet and Tube Company v. Sawyer* (1951) found his actions unconstitutional saying that "the president's power to see that the laws are faithfully executed refutes the idea that he is to be a lawmaker."

The Cabinet

In order to execute the laws faithfully, presidents have established various cabinet departments, such as the Departments of State, Defense, Justice, Interior, and Education, some of which have varied from president to president. Today considered indispensable to the operation of the federal government, they are not delineated in the Constitution. Since the founding of the nation, this "headless fourth branch" of government has emerged. Administrative agencies have proliferated, including the Federal Trade Commission, Federal Communications Commission, Federal Aviation Administration, Securities and Exchange Commission, Food and Drug Administration, and scores of others. These agencies routinely promulgate rules and regulations which affect virtually every aspect of business, commerce, transportation, communications, the environment, and other aspects of American life.

These agencies function as part of the executive branch with powers delegated to them by the Congress. As such they are a hybrid, spanning two different branches of government. They have been called "quasi-legislative, quasi-executive, or quasi-judicial" by Justice Robert H. Jackson in *Federal Trade Commission v. Ruberoid Company* (1952).

Impeachment

The final section of Article II provides that the president, vice president, and all civil officers of the United States are subject to impeachment for treason, bribery, or other "high Crimes and Misdemeanors."

Contrary to popular belief, impeachment does not mean removal from office. *Impeachment* is the equivalent of an accusation or indictment. Once impeached by the House of Representatives, an official must then be convicted by the Senate to be removed from office. Since the Constitution was adopted, three presidents, one Supreme Court Justice, and several U. S. District judges have faced impeachment.

Although treason and bribery have well-established meanings, there is continuing debate over what the framers meant by "other high Crimes and Misdemeanors." Some believe that phrase covers only indictable crimes. But when then-Congressman Gerald Ford sought the impeachment of Justice William O. Douglas in 1970 over allegations that he accepted money from someone involved in a case that could have gone to the Supreme Court, Ford held that an indictable offense is whatever the House and Senate "consider [it] to be." Generally, commentators agree that an impeachable offense is one that subverts the Constitution or constitutes an abuse of power with respect to the duties of one's office, as opposed to purely private matters outside one's constitutional responsibilities.

On March 12, 1804, the House voted to impeach Supreme Court Justice Samuel P. Chase for his conduct in presiding over the trials of several editors charged with seditious libel for criticizing President John Adams. In one trial, Chase so hampered the defense attorneys that they withdrew from the case. After a two-month trial in the Senate, Chase was acquitted.

On March 3, 1868, President Andrew Johnson, who had assumed the office after Abraham Lincoln's assassination, was impeached by the House on 11 articles stemming from his firing of a cabinet minister of the opposing party. In the Senate, only 2 of the 11 articles came to a vote, and on each Johnson was acquitted by a single vote.

On July 27, 1974, President Richard M. Nixon was impeached on charges that he subverted the Constitution and abused his power as president by participating in the cover-up of the notorious Watergate scandal. Facing certain conviction in the Senate, Nixon resigned on August 9, 1974. His vice president, Gerald Ford, upon becoming president, pardoned Nixon for any and all offenses.

On December 19, 1998, President Bill Clinton was impeached on two counts of perjury and obstruction of justice, growing out of his testimony regarding accusations that he had a sexual affair with a White House intern, Monica Lewinsky. In the Senate, with Chief Justice William Rehnquist presiding, Clinton's opponents claimed he had demeaned the presidency, while his defenders argued that regardless of his bad judgment or marital infidelity, nothing Clinton did rose to the level of an impeachable offense. On February 14, 1999, the Senate found him not guilty on both charges.

Article III

Article III establishes the judicial branch and the powers and jurisdiction of the federal courts.

ARTICLE III

SECTION 1. The judicial Power of the United States, shall be vested in one supreme Court, and in such **inferior Courts** as the Congress may from time to time ordain and establish. The Judges, both of the supreme and inferior Courts, shall hold their Offices during **good behavior**, and shall, at stated Times, receive for their Services, a Compensation, which shall not be diminished during their Continuance in Office.

Section 2. The judicial Power shall extend to all Cases, in **Law and Equity**, arising under this Constitution, the Laws of the United States, and Treaties made, or which shall be made, under their Authority;—to all Cases affecting Ambassadors, other public Ministers and Consuls;—to all Cases of admiralty and maritime Jurisdiction;—to Controversies to which the United States shall be a Party;—to Controversies between two or more States;—between a State and Citizens of another State;—between Citizens of different States; —between Citizens of the same State claiming Lands under Grants of different States, and between a State, or the Citizens thereof, and foreign States, Citizens or Subjects.

In all cases affecting Ambassadors, other public Ministers and Consuls, and those in which a State shall be Party, the supreme Court shall have original Jurisdiction. In all the other Cases before mentioned, the supreme Court shall have appellate Jurisdiction, both as to Law and Fact, with such Exceptions, and under such Regulations as the Congress shall make.

The Trial of all Crimes, except in Cases of Impeachment, shall be by Jury; and such Trial shall be held in the State where the said Crimes shall have been committed; but when not committed within any State, the Trial shall be at such Place or Places as the Congress may by Law have directed.

Section 3. Treason against the United States, shall consist only in **levying War** against them, or in adhering to their Enemies, giving them Aid and Comfort. No Person shall be convicted of Treason unless on the Testimony of two Witnesses to the same overt Act, or on Confession in open Court.

The Congress shall have power to declare the punishment of Treason, but no Attainder of Treason shall work **Corruption of Blood**, or **Forfeiture** except during the Life of the Person attainted.

NOTES

inferior Courts: Federal courts below the U.S. Supreme Court, including U.S. Circuit Courts of Appeals and U.S. District Courts.

good behavior: proper conduct above reproach or ethical lapses.

Law and Equity: legal remedies of monetary damages and injunctive or declaratory relief, respectively.

levying War: waging war.

Corruption of Blood: a ban preventing a person from inheriting, retaining, or transmitting any estate, rank, or title.

Forfeiture: the loss of property or money because of a breach of a legal obligation.

COMMENTARY

Article III of the Constitution deals with the judicial branch of the federal government. Under Section 1, the only court established by the Constitution—one Supreme Court—is specifically identified. Congress is authorized to establish other inferior courts. The judges of the Supreme Court and the inferior courts hold office during good behavior, which means for life, although that is not spelled out in the Constitution. The framers believed (quite rightly) that lifetime appointments of federal judges would assure them the greatest independence from the political branches of government, thereby serving as another check and balance. Judges are to be compensated for their services, but the compensation cannot be reduced so long as they continue in office. This too was meant to insulate federal judges from outside influence or threats tied to their pay.

The Powers of the Supreme Court

Section 2 of Article III defines the scope of federal judicial power. It extends to

(a) all cases involving damages, injunctions (court orders to prevent an act), and declarations of law arising under the Constitution and the laws of the United States
(b) all cases affecting ambassadors, other public ministers, and consuls
(c) all cases related to the laws of the sea
(d) controversies in which the United States is a party
(e) controversies involving a state's conflicts with another state, with its own citizens or citizens of another state, or foreign powers or citizens

These provisions are clarified by the Eleventh Amendment, which was ratified in 1798.

The Supreme Court has *original jurisdiction* over cases covered under (b) above and in cases where a state is a party. In other words, those matters are filed *directly* in the Supreme Court. In other cases, the Supreme Court has *appellate jurisdiction,* which means it reviews cases which originate in lower federal or state courts.

The U.S. Court System

America has a dual system of courts, each culminating in the U.S. Supreme Court. The two sets are *federal* and *state.* In the federal system, cases are filed in the U.S. District Courts, which hear trials. Decisions in the District Courts are then appealed to the U.S. Circuit Courts of Appeals, which serve as intermediate appellate courts.

In the state courts, the system may vary, but generally cases are filed in a *trial court* (sometimes known as Justice, Municipal, or Superior courts). Decisions in the trial courts are generally appealed to an intermediate court of appeal and then to a state supreme court. At that point, some cases may be appealed to the U.S. Supreme Court.

Trial by Jury

Section 2 of Article III also provides that the trial of all crimes, except in cases of impeachment, shall be heard by a jury and shall be held in the state where the crime was committed. This provision is another example of an important right included in the text of the Constitution even before the Bill of Rights was adopted. The right to a trial by jury is considered a hallmark of any constitutional democracy. Often referred to as a "jury of one's peers," it means that people are judged by jurors of their own background and status. Indeed, originally jurors were chosen from the community where the crime was committed and often knew the victim, the suspect, or both. Today, by contrast, the judicial system goes to great lengths to exclude jurors who are personally acquainted with anyone involved in a case.

A jury serves as the "conscience of the community" and decides all questions of fact, while the judge instructs the jury on all questions of law. Jurors are expected to follow the law as explained by the judge, regardless of their own views of what the law is or should be. Some legal theorists believe that inherent in our system is the concept of *jury nullification,* by which juries can ignore the law in order to serve a higher moral purpose, but the courts have generally rejected this concept.

Treason and the Court

Section 3 of Article III defines *treason* as conducting war against the United States or providing aid and support to its enemies. Given the seriousness of a charge of treason, the Constitution also provides that a defendant may not be convicted unless two witnesses testify to the same overt act, or the defendant confesses in open court. The framers knew only too well how kings and unscrupulous political opponents used treason to silence criticism. They believed that wrongful convictions for treason could be prevented by requiring two witnesses or a confession in open court, not in a jail somewhere under questionable circumstances. As much as the Constitution establishes the crime of treason, it limits it in order to avoid the experience in England where even imagining the death of the King was treasonous, thereby jeopardizing freedom of conscience, freedom of speech, and freedom of the press. The Supreme Court held in *Cramer v. United States* (1945) that it is "consonant to the principles of our constitution, that the crime of treason should not be extended by construction to doubtful cases."

Deciding Constitutionality

The Constitution left open a fundamental question regarding the balance of authority between Congress and the Supreme Court when it came to deciding the constitutionality of laws passed by Congress. Today we take it for granted that the Supreme Court is the last word in deciding whether an act of Congress (or a state law) violates the Constitution, but searching the Constitution for language to that effect is fruitless.

While the Constitution and the Laws of the United States are the "supreme Law of the Land" and every judge is obligated to uphold them, the Constitution does not specify which branch of government has the power and authority to decide the constitutionality of federal or state laws.

Yet every year lower courts, and ultimately the U.S. Supreme Court, strike down laws on the grounds that they violate certain provisions of the Constitution, the Bill of Rights, or the other amendments. We recognize and accept the fact that nine individuals, who are not elected and who serve for life, can overturn a law passed by the duly elected members of Congress and signed by the duly elected president or passed by the duly elected members of a state legislature and signed by a duly elected governor.

Why does the Supreme Court have the power to strike down laws if no such power can be found in the Constitution? To put it bluntly: Because the Supreme Court said so. In 1803, barely 15 years after the Constitution was ratified, the Court decided in *Marbury v. Madison* that it had the duty and authority to exercise *judicial review*—to judge whether or not laws are constitutional.

In *Marbury*, Chief Justice John Marshall speaking for a unanimous Court ruled that Section 13 of the Judiciary Act of 1789 improperly extended the Court's original jurisdiction beyond the scope granted in Article III of the Constitution. This was the first time that the Court declared a law passed by Congress unconstitutional. It is indeed ironic that the first occasion on which the Court exercised the power to invalidate an act of Congress (a power nowhere found in the Constitution) it held that Congress had granted the Court powers beyond those specified in the Constitution.

Marshall offered several reasons why the Court had the duty and authority to declare laws unconstitutional. He began with the principle that the Constitution was designed to establish a limited government confined by the boundaries of that charter. By itself, this self-evident statement would prove little since it hardly follows that it is the job of the *courts* to police those boundaries. Why not Congress itself or the president? Likewise, the fact that judges take an oath to support the Constitution does not elevate judges above any other official who swears a similar oath.

Marshall found surer ground when he turned to the text of the Constitution itself. There he noted that Article III lists cases "arising under the Constitution" as one of the subjects included within the judicial power of the United States, suggesting that the federal courts, including the Supreme Court, had a judicial role to play in constitutional questions. Furthermore, Marshall noted that first among the sources of law specified in Article VI as being "the supreme Law of the Land" was the Constitution itself, implying that the Constitution stood at the apex of the legal hierarchy.

These textual references establish that the Constitution is a law, the highest law, the "supreme Law of the Land." The reason it was important to treat the Constitution as a law—and not merely as a set of general abstract principles—is that no one would question that judges, at every level, have a duty and authority to apply the law to the cases that come before them. Since this is the normal task of judges, Marshall could declare with great confidence that it was "emphatically the province and duty of the judicial department to say what the law is." It therefore followed, according to Marshall, that where a statute and the Constitution came into conflict, the Courts must enforce the higher of the two—the Constitution—and disregard the statute. For Marshall that was "of the very essence of judicial duty."

Marshall's views on judicial review were in keeping with other contemporary expressions on the subject. In *Federalist* No. 78, Alexander Hamilton wrote that the "interpretation of laws is the proper and peculiar province of the courts," and legal commentators often cited Edward Coke in the case of *Bonham's Case* (1610) in England for the proposition that "the common law will controul Acts of Parliament, [and] adjudge them to be utterly void" when they are "against common right and reason."

Advocates of judicial review are fond of citing one statement by delegate Luther Martin from Maryland who, in opposing a proposal that the Supreme Court and the president jointly exercise the power to veto Congressional acts, argued that "as to the Constitutionality of laws, that point will come before the Judges in their proper official character."

Judicial review has never been without its critics, especially among U.S. presidents. Thomas Jefferson insisted that "nothing in the Constitution has given [the judges] a right to decide for the Executive, more than to the Executive to decide for them." He vehemently argued that treating "the judges as the ultimate arbiters of all constitutional questions" was "a very dangerous doctrine indeed, and one which would place us under the despotism of an oligarchy." Similar concerns have been raised down through the years by Presidents Andrew Jackson, Abraham Lincoln, and Franklin D. Roosevelt.

Despite such criticism, obviously expressed by men who felt the brunt of the Court's rulings, the public has generally accepted the Court as the constitutional watchdog. The Court has in turn flexed its rhetorical muscle in declaring the scope of judicial review in stronger terms than any found in *Marbury v. Madison*. For example, in *Cooper v. Aaron* (1958), the Court, in a unanimous opinion, sternly admonished the Arkansas governor and legislature not to defy the historic integration ruling in *Brown v. Board of Education* (1954), warning them to "recall some basic constitutional propositions which are settled doctrine." Citing *Marbury*, the Court declared "the basic principle that the federal judiciary is supreme in the exposition of the law of the Constitution." A few years later in *Baker v. Carr* (1962), and *Purnell v. McCormack* (1969) the Court referred to the "responsibility of this Court as ultimate interpreter of the Constitution."

Since *Marbury*, the Justices and their critics have actively debated whether the Court is engaging in *judicial activism* or *judicial restraint*. The Court is applauded for exercising judicial restraint when the observer likes what the Court is doing and the Court is guilty of judicial activism when the observer disagrees with the result.

Supreme Court Guidelines

The Court tries to avoid having to decide whether a law or official action violates the Constitution, given the fact that all governmental officials, including the president, senators, representatives, and their counterparts in state government are bound by an oath to uphold the Constitution.

An institutional reluctance on the part of the Court to overturn laws and official actions as unconstitutional also reflects a sobering realization that the courts are the least democratic branch of government. The Supreme Court is purposely insulated from representative government, public opinion, and the hallowed, albeit elusive, "will of the people." Ideally, the actions of the Congress, the president, state legislatures, and other elected officials reflect the "will of the people," which in a democracy should not be easily or cavalierly overturned.

Tempering these concerns is the realization that the Constitution likewise reflects the "will of the people" and was equally the product of a democratic process, with duly elected representative bodies drafting and ratifying the seminal charter of our nation. Consequently, the Justices of the Supreme Court are carrying out important duties and responsibilities delegated to them by the people through the democratically enacted Constitution. When laws and official actions conflict with the Constitution, the Justices would fail to discharge their duties and responsibilities if they shirk from declaring an unconstitutional law or official action to be so by hiding behind the shield of judicial restraint.

Striking Down Federal and State Laws

When it comes to deciding whether Congress has acted within the bounds of its enumerated powers, the Court actually has shown considerable deference and exhibited great restraint. According to one survey, during its entire history, the Court has invalidated only about 125 of the tens of thousands of laws passed by Congress.

The Courts versus Discrimination

By far, the Court has exhibited the greatest degree of judicial activism in striking down federal and state laws and official actions found to violate the prohibitions on discrimination found in the Bill of Rights and the Fourteenth Amendment.

The Court cannot be expected to exercise restraint if a law violates an express clause of the Constitution. Critics of judicial activism urge that the democratic process, through free and fair elections, is the appropriate remedy, not the intervention of the courts. They argue that new legislators can be elected and that bad laws can be repealed and new ones enacted in their place, all through the democratic process expressing the "will of the majority."

Yet advocates of the Court playing a more active role in scrutinizing laws argue that when it comes to the constitutional rights of minorities, the "will of the majority" cannot control. The whole point of constitutional rights is that they exist beyond the reach of the majority. Under the Constitution, a majority cannot vote out of existence the rights of the minority. Otherwise, the Constitution and the Bill of Rights would be illusory; constitutional rights would exist only at the pleasure of the majority, which would remain free to deny those rights to any religious, ethnic, social, or political group.

The controversies over judicial restraint versus judicial activism and the proper scope of judicial review are sure to persist unabated. Public officials, whether elected to office or appointed to the courts, inevitably consider themselves ideally equipped to decide what is right and constitutional for the people they are sworn to serve. With the exception of individuals in all spheres of government who exercise their authority with selfish, corrupt, racist, sexist, or other improper motives, the vast number of legislators and judges take seriously their duty to protect and defend the Constitution. The hard part is living up to that ideal and having a process in place when they prove less than perfect. The founders knew all too well that governments are run by people and that people are hardly perfect. That is why they set the goal of a "more perfect Union."

Article IV

Article IV deals with the relationship between and among the states and between the national government and the states.

ARTICLE IV

SECTION 1. Full Faith and Credit shall be given in each State to the public Acts, Records, and judicial Proceedings of every other State. And the Congress may by general Laws prescribe the Manner in which such Acts, Records, and Proceedings shall be proved, and the Effect thereof.

Section 2. The Citizens of each State shall be entitled to all Privileges and Immunities of Citizens in the several States.

A Person charged in any State with Treason, Felony, or other Crime, who shall flee from Justice, and be found in another State, shall on Demand of the executive Authority of the State from which he fled, be delivered up, to be removed to the State having Jurisdiction of the Crime.

No person held to Service or Labor in one State, under the Laws thereof, escaping into another, shall, in Consequence of any Law or Regulation therein, be discharged from such Service or Labor, But shall be delivered up on Claim of the Party to whom such Service or Labor may be due.

Section 3. New States may be admitted by the Congress into this Union; but no new States shall be formed or erected within the Jurisdiction of any other State; nor any State be formed by the Junction of two or more States, or Parts of States, without the Consent of the Legislatures of the States concerned as well as of the Congress.

The Congress shall have Power to dispose of and make all needful Rules and Regulations respecting the Territory or other Property belonging to the United States; and nothing in this Constitution shall be so construed as to Prejudice any Claims of the United States, or of any particular State.

Section 4. The United States shall guarantee to every State in this Union a **Republican Form of Government**, and shall protect each of them against Invasion; and on Application of the Legislature, or of the Executive (when the Legislature cannot be convened) against domestic Violence.

NOTES

Republican Form of Government: a government in which supreme power resides in a body of citizens who elect representatives to govern according to law.

COMMENTARY

Section 1

Section 1 requires that the public acts, records, and judicial proceedings of one state be honored in every other state. In other words, all of the laws and orders, verdicts, sentences, and judgments rendered in the criminal and civil courts of one state must be recognized and accepted in all other states. This provision ensures a degree of uniformity and consistency throughout the United States.

Section 2

Section 2 provides another guarantee of uniformity and consistency between states by mandating that the rights granted the citizen of one state shall be granted to citizens of all states. In *Federalist* No. 80, Alexander Hamilton calls this provision nothing less than "the basis of the Union" because it ensures that the citizens of one state are not treated as "aliens" when they're in another state. In *Corfield v. Coryell* (1823), Justice Bushrod Washington held that this clause protects out-of-state citizens' fundamental rights—those that "belong, of right, to citizens of all free governments."

Until very recently, however, the Supreme Court has not used the clause to its fullest potential. In the *Slaughterhouse Cases* (1873), the Court ruled that the right to work was not covered by the Privileges and Immunities Clause, because it encompasses only privileges and immunities created by the national government. In dissent, Justice Stephen J. Field decried the majority's emasculation of the clause rendering it "a vain and idle enactment, which accomplished nothing."

In 1990, however, the Court breathed new life into the Privileges and Immunities Clause of the Fourteenth Amendment. In *Saenz v. Roe* (1999), the Court held, in a 7-2 decision, that a California law that limited welfare benefits payable to a pregnant mother and her husband to the amount they were receiving in Oklahoma ($307 per month) rather than the standard California benefit ($624 per month), violated the Privileges and Immunities Clause of the Fourteenth Amendment on the grounds that state citizenship rights cannot be conditioned on when a person arrived in the state or what they were receiving in a prior state.

The Privilege and Immunities Clause is another example of a protection for individual rights which was written into the original Constitution before the adoption of the Bill of Rights.

Section 2 also provides that if a person charged in any state with treason, a felony, or other crime flees to another state, he or she must be returned to the first state. More ominously, Section 2 states that no person "held to service or labor in one State,"—a slave or indentured servant—may obtain freedom by escaping to another state. Instead, he or she must be returned to the person to whom his or her service or labor was due. This is one of several provisions in the Constitution which perpetuate the practice of slavery. (It was nullified upon the adoption of the Thirteenth Amendment in 1865.)

Section 3

Section 3 of Article IV provides that Congress can admit new states into the Union. However, new states cannot be carved out of existing states or be created by joining two states together unless the affected state legislatures as well as Congress approves.

Section 4

Finally, Section 4 of Article IV guarantees each state a "Republican Form of Government" and protection against invasion and domestic violence. These provisions add significantly to the status of the national government as the superior level of government over the states.

A republican government has two complementary meanings well understood by the framers. For Alexander Hamilton, writing in *The Federalist*, it meant that instead of a monarchy there would be a central authority with sufficient power to suppress any attempt to impose a monarchy. For James Madison, a republican government meant a representative government rather than direct democracy—a government where the rule of the majority was expressed through elected officials.

Post Civil War Debates

As Congress began to rebuild the nation after the Civil War, many representatives reflected on the true nature of the American government. In 1868, Senator Jacob Howard of Michigan defined a republican form of government as one "in which the laws of the community are made by their representatives, freely chosen by the people. It is popular government; it is the voice of the people expressed through their representatives."

Article V — Article V sets forth the process by which the Constitution may be amended.

ARTICLE V

THE Congress, whenever two thirds of both Houses shall deem it necessary, shall propose Amendments to this Constitution, or, on the Application of the Legislatures of two thirds of the several States, shall call a Convention for proposing Amendments, which, in either Case, shall be valid to all Intents and Purposes, as Part of this Constitution, when ratified by the Legislatures of three fourths of the several States, or by Conventions in three fourths thereof, as the one or the other Mode of Ratification may be proposed by the Congress; Provided that no Amendment which may be made prior to the Year one thousand eight hundred and eight shall in any Manner affect the first and fourth Clauses in the ninth Section of the first Article; and that no State, without its Consent, shall be deprived of its equal Suffrage in the Senate.

COMMENTARY

Although the Declaration of Independence spoke boldly of the right of the people to alter or to abolish any government, once the founders established a new government themselves, they were eager to avoid revolution and to provide a stable and peaceful process for making changes. At the Constitutional Convention, George Mason of Virginia cautioned that since amendments may be necessary, it would be better to provide for them, in an easy, regular, and constitutional way than to trust the process to chance and violence.

Article V sets forth two separate methods to adopt amendments and two separate methods to ratify them.

An amendment to the Constitution may originate with Congress or with the people themselves. The framers wanted to ensure that when it came to the critical task of amending the Constitution, the people had a direct means to do so.

Thus, an amendment may be proposed by Congress upon a vote of two-thirds of both Houses. In the alternative, upon the request of the legislatures of two-thirds of the states, a constitutional convention may be called for the purpose of proposing amendments. In either case, an amendment must be ratified by the legislatures of three-fourths of the states or by conventions in three-fourths of the states. Congress has the authority to decide which method of ratification the states shall use.

Despite the possibility of four different ways to amend the Constitution, all 27 amendments have been proposed by Congress (none by the state legislatures) and, with the exception of the Twenty-First amendment (which Congress submitted to special state conventions), all amendments have been ratified by state legislatures.

Since 1789, 5,000 bills proposing constitutional amendments have been introduced in Congress, but only 33 have received the necessary two-thirds vote of both Houses of Congress to be sent to the states for ratification. Twenty-seven were ratified and six were not.

Amendment Arguments

The brief provisions of Article V left several unanswered questions about the amendment process. In the *National Prohibition Cases* (1920) and *Leser v. Garnett* (1922), the Supreme Court rejected the argument that certain amendments interfered with state sovereignty to such an extent that they required separate consent from the states. In *Hollingsworth v. Virginia* (1798), the Court confirmed that the president plays no role in the amendment process and his or her signature is not necessary for Congress to propose an amendment. In *Dillon v. Gloss* (1921), the Court ruled that Congress may set a reasonable time limit for ratification and that seven years is reasonable.

Some questions remain unresolved. May a state ratify an amendment but later rescind its ratification? More importantly, if a constitutional convention were called by the requisite number of states for a specific purpose, for example to require the federal government to balance its budget, could the convention, once convened, adopt unrelated amendments, such as one to repeal freedom of speech? After all, the only constitutional convention ever held in the United States was called for the express purpose of amending the Articles of Confederation; instead, the delegates wrote an entirely new Constitution.

Fortunately, the amendment process has served its intended purpose. It has allowed for flexibility in adapting the Constitution to new circumstances, thereby channeling resentments over perceived injustices into the political process and away from violent revolution. It has achieved what Madison in *Federalist* No. 43 called the proper balance between "that extreme facility, which would render the Constitution too mutable; and that extreme difficulty which might perpetuate its discovered faults."

Not to be Amended

Article V specifically provided that, until 1808, no amendment was permitted of:

- The clause that prevented Congress from prohibiting the importation of slaves until 1808
- The clause that prohibited Congress from imposing any tax unless in proportion to the census to be taken within three years of the First Congress

The first of these demonstrates just how important the framers considered the continuation of slavery. Of all the vital provisions in the new Constitution, the delegates resolved that the perpetuation of the slave trade until at least 1808 had to be insulated from amendment.

On a more favorable note, Article V provides that one provision in the Constitution may never be amended except with the consent of the state involved: The guarantee that each state have two senators.

Article VI

Article VI deals with several miscellaneous but important provisions having to do with debts, law enforcement, and the supremacy of the Constitution.

ARTICLE VI

ALL Debts contracted and **Engagements** entered into, before the Adoption of this Constitution, shall be as valid against the United States under this Constitution, as under the **Confederation**.

This Constitution, and the Laws of the United States which shall be made in Pursuance thereof; and all Treaties made, or which shall be made, under the Authority of the United States, shall be the supreme Law of the Land; and the Judges in every State shall be bound thereby, any Thing in the Constitution or Laws of any State to the Contrary notwithstanding.

The Senators and Representatives before mentioned, and the Members of the several State Legislatures, and all executive and judicial Officers, both of the United States and of the several States, shall be bound by Oath or Affirmation, to support this Constitution; but no religious Test shall ever be required as a Qualification to any Office or public Trust under the United States.

NOTES

Engagements: agreements or pledges.

Confederation: the American system of government from 1777 to 1788 under the Articles of Confederation.

COMMENTARY

Article VI covers three important subjects. First, it makes all debts and contracts entered into before the adoption of the Constitution valid against the new United States government. This provision assured creditors and others who had worked with the government under the Articles of Confederation that the new government would pay what was owed them.

The second portion of Article VI is one of the most important in the entire Constitution. It makes the Constitution, the laws of the United States, and all treaties made by the United States "the supreme Laws of the Land." So the federal constitution and laws supercede any state constitution or laws.

This clause leaves no doubt that the Constitution and the new national government are supreme over the individual states. To drive the point home, Article VI specifically requires state judges to adhere to the Constitution and the laws and treaties of the United States. Consequently, if state law conflicts with the Constitution or federal laws or treaties, national law prevails.

The last portion of Article VI mandates that all state and federal officials, including senators, representatives, state legislators, and executive and judicial officers, swear an oath or affirmation to support the Constitution.

In a final acknowledgment of the enlightened tolerance that animates much of the Constitution, Article VI also provides that candidates for any position shall not be subject to a religious test. Near the very end of the Constitution, this clause shows that the framers had firmly turned their backs on centuries of world history during which church and state had been inseparable. Henceforth, allegiance to any religion would no longer be a condition for service in the federal government.

Article VII

The very last provision of the Constitution provides that it be established upon the ratification of nine of the thirteen states.

ARTICLE VII

THE Ratification of the Conventions of nine States, shall be sufficient for the Establishment of this Constitution between the States so ratifying the Same.

Done in Convention by the Unanimous Consent of the States present the Seventeenth Day of September in the Year of our Lord one thousand seven hundred and eighty seven and of the Independence of the United States of America the Twelfth. In Witness whereof We have hereunto subscribed our Names,

Go. Washington—

Presid. and deputy from Virginia

New Hampshire	Delaware
John Langdon	Geo: Read
Nicholas Gilman	Gunning Bedford jun
Massachusetts	John Dickinson
Nathaniel Gorham	Richard Bassett
Rufus King	Jaco: Broom
Connecticut	Maryland
Wm. Saml. Johnson	James Mchenry
Roger Herman	Dan of St Thos. Jenifer
New York	Danl Carroll
Alexander Hamilton	Virginia
New Jersey	John Blair
Wil: Livingston	James Madison Jr.
David Brearley	North Carolina
Wm. Paterson	Wm. Blount
Jona: Dayton	Rich'd Dobbs Spaight
Pennsylvania	Hu Williamson
B Franklin	South Carolina
Thomas Mifflin	J. Rutledge
Robt Morris	Charles Cotesworth Pinckney
Geo. Clymer	Charles Pinckney
Thos FitzSimons	Pierce Butler
Jared Ingersoll	Georgia
James Wilson	William Few
Gouv Morris	Abr Baldwin

Attest:

William Jackson, Secretary

COMMENTARY

The concept of ratification by fewer that all the states was a departure from the Articles of Confederation, which required unanixmous ratification for any amendments. The framers were very eager to see their handiwork become the law of the land. None knew for sure whether it would. Some hoped it would not. All knew that if the Constitution were ratified it would have a profound and lasting impact on America and eventually the rest of the world.

Notes

Notes

Notes

AMERICAN WORDS OF FREEDOM

THE BILL OF RIGHTS

A Constitution without a Bill of Rights 71

Ratifying the Bill of Rights 75

First Amendment (1791) 77

Second Amendment (1791) 86

Third Amendment (1791) 88

Fourth Amendment (1791) 89

Fifth Amendment (1791) 92

Sixth Amendment (1791) 97

Seventh Amendment (1791) 100

Eighth Amendment (1791) 101

Ninth Amendment (1791) 103

Tenth Amendment (1791) 105

A Constitution without a Bill of Rights

The Bill of Rights—the first ten amendments to the U.S. Constitution, crowned by the First Amendment—was born out of dissent.

The Constitution written in Philadelphia in 1787 was not unanimously approved. While George Washington called it "little short of a miracle," many delegates to the Constitutional Convention had serious reservations, not the least of which that it lacked a bill of rights to protect individual freedoms. In the end, of the remaining 39 delegates (16 of the original delegates had gone home), 3 dissented and refused to sign the document. George Mason of Virginia said he would "sooner chop off this right hand" than put it to a Constitution without a Bill of Rights.

When Mason returned to Virginia and told the legendary Patrick Henry what had happened in Philadelphia, Henry was not surprised. A staunch defender of state sovereignty and an outspoken opponent of an all-powerful national government, Henry had refused to serve as a delegate to the Convention because he said he "smelt a rat."

Mason, Henry, and a few others came to be known as the Anti-Federalists. Those who unflinchingly promoted the Constitution adopted the more affirmative title of Federalists. The Anti-Federalists feared the powerful central government which the Federalists were actively sponsoring. Mason and Henry had fought valiantly in the Revolution. Other Anti-Federalists had signed the Declaration of Independence. But all Anti-Federalists dissented from the new Constitution because they refused to replace a foreign despot with a homegrown version. And they were deeply suspicious of a Constitution which granted government sweeping powers, but failed to guarantee individual freedoms in the form of a Bill of Rights.

Two Demand a Bill of Rights

Mason and Henry symbolized differing styles of American politics. Mason agonized over how to make the new nation work. He actively joined in the debates. He understood the tension between the need for a strong national government and the need to protect the people from that government. He worked within the system.

Henry stood aside from the deliberative process. For him, the issues were unambiguous. It was better to have no central government than one which would not secure individual liberty. Confident of his enormous popularity among the people, Henry challenged the political leadership to satisfy his demands or risk his wrath.

It is curious that George Mason is so little known to all but scholars of colonial history. At 62, he welcomed the opportunity to attend the Philadelphia Convention. In May of 1776, he had authored the seminal Virginia Declaration of Rights, which not only inspired the Declaration of Independence, several state constitutions, and the Bill of Rights, but gained widespread attention in Europe during the French Revolution. Thomas Jefferson considered Mason "the wisest man of his generation."

George Mason
© Bettmann/CORBIS

Mason believed deeply in the republican form of government. "We ought to attend to the rights of every class of the people . . . provide no less carefully for the . . . happiness of the lowest than of the highest orders of citizens." Mason was suspicious of an unrestrained central government far removed from the people. He believed that the American colonies had not succeeded in freeing themselves from the bonds of a tyrannical King only to be controlled by a more subtle form of domestic subjugation. "Is it to be thought that the people of America, so watchful over their interests, so jealous of their liberties, will give up their all, will surrender both the sword and the purse to the same body, and that, too, not chosen immediately by themselves?"

The serious doubts Mason harbored over endorsing a Constitution that created a powerful central government were fully confirmed when the delegates flatly refused to include a Declaration of Rights. Shortly before the Convention adjourned Mason called for a "bill of rights." The constitutions of eight states already included declarations of rights.

Mason was proud of his work in writing the Virginia Declaration of Rights. It declared that "all men are by nature equally free" and guaranteed the right to a speedy trial "by an impartial jury;" the right not to be compelled to give evidence against oneself; the right of freedom of the press as "one of the great bulwarks of liberty;" and the right to "the free exercise of religion, according to the dictates of conscience." On September 12, 1787, Mason rose and implored the delegates that a bill of rights would give "great quiet to the people."

Fearing that the growing consensus to approve the Constitution would unravel over this last-minute call for a bill of rights, Roger Sherman of Connecticut argued that "The State Declarations of Rights are not repealed by this Constitution, and being in force are sufficient." He assured his colleagues that when it came to the rights of the people, Congress could be trusted to preserve them. This was little solace to Mason, who pointed out that the new federal government, and its laws, would supersede state declarations of rights. But Mason had raised the issue too late and the weary delegates (voting by state) unanimously opposed even forming a Bill of Rights committee.

Elbridge Gerry of Massachusetts (a signer of the Declaration of Independence) tried a few days later to include a declaration "that the liberty of the press would be inviolably observed." But Sherman again objected that since the "power of Congress does not extend to the press," such a provision was "unnecessary." The majority again sided with Sherman.

The Arguments Begin

The Federalists committed a grave, if unforeseen, error in opposing a bill of rights. No Anti-Federalist argument would be more powerful during the contentious ratification debates than that the architects of this drastic new plan of government had deliberately refused to guarantee the very liberties and freedoms on which the nation had been founded.

When the secrecy that had shrouded the Convention was lifted, public opinion was far from unanimous in favor of the new plan. Most people were stunned. Had they sent their delegates to Philadelphia to "revise" the Articles of Confederation only to have them clandestinely fashion an entirely new government patterned after the English system?

Richard Henry Lee of Virginia saw a dangerous system of putting power in the hands of a few. "Either a monarchy or an aristocracy will be generated." Colonel William Grayson, an ardent revolutionary, belittled the Constitution "as a most ridiculous piece of business—something like the legs of Nebuchadnezzar's image . . . formed by jumbling a number of ideas together." (Grayson was alluding to the Babylonian king, prone to fits of madness.)

Of course, the ratification struggle was generally marked by more rational debate. The Anti-Federalists filled the daily newspapers with a stream of objections to the new constitution. Mason published his own list of objections, with the glaring absence of a bill of rights at the very top. James Madison, Alexander Hamilton, and John Jay countered with the now famous *Federalist Papers*. What the proponents had hoped would be a prompt and ceremonial ratification dragged on for months in a complex mixture of political, social, economic, religious, and personal debates. Again and again, the Anti-Federalists drew public attention to the twin dangers of a strong central government unrestrained by a Bill of Rights.

Hamilton challenged the Anti-Federalists: "Why declare that things shall not be done which there is no power [in Congress] to do?" James Wilson of Pennsylvania, one of the most learned and articulate Federalists, asked: "Enumerate all the rights of men? I am sure that no gentleman in the late Convention would have attempted such a thing."

The Anti-Federalists gained an unexpected ally when Thomas Jefferson sent his thoughts about the proposed Constitution from France, where he was serving as American ambassador. "I will now add what I do not like," Jefferson wrote, after generally approving the new plan. "First the omission of a bill of rights providing clearly & without the aid of sophisms for the whole catalog of civil rights commonly accepted as fundamental in America. A bill of rights," Jefferson insisted, "is what the people are entitled to against every government on earth, general or particular, & what no just government should refuse, or rest on inference." Jefferson proposed a strategy to get both a Constitution *and* a Bill of Rights. "I would advocate it [the Constitution] warmly till nine [states] should have adopted, & then as warmly take the other side to convince the remaining four that they ought not to come into it till the declaration of rights is annexed to it. By this means we should secure all the good of it, & procure so respectable an opposition as would induce the accepting states to offer a bill of rights. This would be the happiest turn the thing could take."

When the Virginia ratifying convention opened in June, 1788, Henry and Mason symbolized the range of Anti-Federalist thought. Henry was indomitable. "I declare," Henry intoned, "that if *twelve states and a half* had adopted it, I would with manly firmness, and in spite of an erring world, reject it." Henry was more popular than any Virginian save Washington, and Madison realized that Henry could single-handedly disrupt the Union if the Constitution was adopted over his strenuous objections.

Mason was less intransigent, but equally committed to a bill of rights. He insisted that "the great essential rights of the people are secured" *before* Virginia ratified the Constitution.

Henry persisted. One speech lasted seven hours. "Perhaps in these refined, enlightened days," Henry charged, "an invincible attachment to the dearest rights of man . . . may be deemed old-fashioned, if so, I am content . . . to become an old-fashioned fellow." A Bill of Rights, Henry insisted, "securing to the states and the people every right which was not conceded to the general government" was "indispensably necessary" before he could approve the Constitution.

Although Hamilton's defense of the Constitution is today considered the quintessential Federalist argument, during the ratification debates themselves, delegate James Wilson may have proved more persuasive and was certainly more influential. Less than a month after the Philadelphia Convention had adjourned, Wilson, considered by some as the most influential framer of the Constitution and as one of the great legal experts of his time, argued that it would have been "superfluous" and "absurd" to have agreed that the newly created government would not violate rights which the people had not given up in the first place.

Thus, far from endorsing the principle that by ratifying the Constitution Americans would be empowering the majority through their representatives to regulate their natural rights, the Federalists believed that nothing in the Constitution was intended to abridge those rights and therefore an enumerated list of specific rights was "superfluous" at best and "dangerous" at worst.

But the Anti-Federalists wanted to leave nothing to chance. Even if they accepted the good faith of the Federalists' intentions, they feared that other interpretations in other times would not be so benign. They wanted written and binding assurances that the Constitution meant what the Federalists said it meant—that the inalienable rights which they had fought for and other patriots had died for had not been bargained away as the price for a new and energetic national government.

Various Anti-Federalist writers searched the proposed Constitution for provisions which might, in the absence of a Bill of Rights, be construed by those in power as license to interfere with individual liberties in the name of the public interest. In the custom of the times, various pamphlets setting forth anonymous writers' political viewpoints were widely distributed and highly influential, particularly in New England and Virginia. Using the assumed name *A Democratic Federalist*, one opponent of the Constitution suggested that the broad judicial power of the United States under Article Three could be used by government officials to "claim a right to the cognizance of all offenses against the general government."

In a pamphlet by *A Federal Republican*, the anonymous writer posited that Congress could use its broad power to tax to impose stamp duties which would "as effectually abolish the freedom of the press as an express declaration."

Perhaps the most creative and prescient threat to freedom of the press was identified by Anti-Federalist Robert Whitehall. On December 1, 1787, at the Pennsylvania ratifying convention, he observed that under the Copyright Clause (Article I, Section 8), which gave Congress the power to grant copyrights, Congress could assume the power to "license the press . . . and under licensing the press, they may suppress it."

One of the most comprehensive Anti-Federalist polemics was contained in a series of letters signed by *The Federal Farmer*. He asserted that there "are certain unalienable and fundamental rights, which in forming a social compact, ought to be explicitly ascertained and fixed—a free and enlightened people, in forming this compact will not resign all their rights to those who govern, and they will fix limits to their legislators and rulers, which will soon be plainly seen by those who are governed, as well as by those who govern."

The Federal Farmer acknowledged the claim "that when the people make a Constitution, and delegate powers that all powers not delegated by them to those who govern is reserved in the people; and that the people, in the present case, have reserved in themselves, and in their state governments, every right and power not expressly given by the federal Constitution to those who shall administer the national government." But he warned that others would claim that "the people, when they make a constitution, yield all power not expressly reserved to themselves." *The Federal Farmer* concluded that in either case "it is mere matter of opinion and men usually take either side of the argument, as will best answer their purposes," since in doubtful cases the men who govern "constitute laws and constitutions most favorably for increasing their own powers." Only a bill of rights would settle the arguments in favor of the people.

Heeding the Call for a Bill of Rights

The incessant call for a bill of rights could not be ignored. Facile legal arguments would not silence the growing public opposition to the Constitution without a declaration of individual rights. If the Federalists were to win ratification and quell the recurring talk of a second Constitutional Convention, they had to commit to amending the Constitution to guarantee a bill of rights.

No one understood this better than Madison. "Let the enemies of the System wait until some experience shall have taken place, and the business will be conducted with more light as well as with less heat." Madison wrote. To quiet some of the fears being expressed, Madison urged that the states ratify the Constitution be ratified *first* and that they propose amendments *subsequently*.

In the midst of the Virginia Convention, New Hampshire quietly became the ninth state to ratify the Constitution (thereby constituting the necessary three-fourths). But communication methods being what they were, none of the delegates in Virginia knew of the New Hampshire vote when they met in Richmond to make their final decision.

Henry (with Mason's able guidance) had reworked the Virginia Declaration of Rights and proposed a federal Bill of Rights as a *condition* of ratification. The delegates voted. The tally sheets were counted. The motion was barely defeated 80 to 88. Madison promptly moved for ratification, arguing that *subsequent* amendments be recommended to Congress. The motion passed and two days later the Virginia convention unanimously adopted a proposed bill of rights containing 20 amendments.

Madison Embraces a Bill of Rights

After Virginia ratified the constitution, Madison moved swiftly to fulfill his promise to fight for a bill of rights. Running for Congress on a platform supporting a bill of rights, he defeated James Monroe to win a seat as a representative to the First Congress.

Ever the consummate scholar, Madison kept a scrapbook in which he mounted clippings from all over the country telling of proposed amendments to the new Constitution. Madison accumulated a list of the recommended amendments from the various ratifying conventions, including 9 from Massachusetts and 37 from New York.

As Madison trimmed the list and eliminated redundant rights, he faced a dilemma. Should these personal rights be woven into the text of the existing Constitution at appropriate points or should they stand apart, leaving the original document intact? Eventually he chose the latter, perhaps to show that the original was not defective, perhaps to emphasize that the amendments stood on their own.

On June 8, 1789, Madison took the floor of Congress (then meeting in New York City) and spoke for the better part of the day in favor of the amendments. He said their passage would prove Federalists were "friends of liberty." He reminded his colleagues that Rhode Island and North Carolina had yet to ratify the Constitution because of their suspicions that "it did not contain effectual provision against encroachment on particular rights." To those who doubted that a simple "parchment barrier" would prevent unscrupulous officials from trampling on personal rights, Madison acknowledged the vital role of the courts. "Independent tribunals of justice will consider themselves in a peculiar manner the guardians of those rights they will be an impenetrable barrier against every assumption of power in the legislative or executive [branch]. . . ."

Madison was keenly aware that his Bill of Rights had to overcome the criticism that if some rights are spelled out, others may be ignored. To answer this charge, he proposed an amendment (eventually the Ninth) which simply stated that the enumeration of rights in the Constitution did not limit or disparage others retained by the people.

Madison's proposals were taken up by a select committee that finally settled on 17 articles of amendment. The House sent them to the Senate for prompt consideration on August 24, 1789, but the Senate didn't take them up until September 2, 1789. Twelve amendments emerged, including all the fundamental principles Madison had offered in June. Congress passed the Bill of Rights on September 25, 1789.

Madison went on to serve in the new government he had helped establish and eventually became the fourth president of the United States. He is often referred to as the Father of the Constitution and the Father of the Bill of Rights.

Ratifying the Bill of Rights

The Bill of Rights, like the Constitution it was amending, had to be ratified before it became effective, and it met with opposition. The senators from Virginia, William Grayson and Richard Henry Lee, both Anti-Federalists, opposed the amendments because they left "the great points of the Judiciary, direct taxation, etc. to stand as they are . . ." Lee confided in Patrick Henry that it had been a mistake to ratify the Constitution with only a promise of subsequent amendments, and Grayson told Henry that the amendments are "good for nothing."

Within six months after the ratification process had begun, nine states approved the Bill of Rights, but Connecticut and Georgia refused on the grounds that it was unnecessary. (They belatedly ratified 140 years later in 1939, as did Massachusetts, which had ratified most of the amendments in 1790, but neglected to send official notice to Congress.)

While ratification was pending, Vermont was admitted as a state in 1791, which meant that 11 states needed to ratify the Bill of Rights. Vermont ratified it in November 1791, but with Georgia taking no action, the fate of the Bill of Rights fell to Virginia.

The Anti-Federalists in Madison's home state resisted ratifying the Bill of Rights written by their own favorite son. The lower house of the Virginia legislature finally adopted the amendments, but they remained stalled in the state senate controlled by Madison's political enemy, Patrick Henry. Frustrated that the Anti-Federalists had so vocally demanded a Bill of Rights during the debates over the ratification of the Constitution and were now stubbornly standing in its way, the Federalists decided to give their opponents a taste of their own obstructionist medicine. They simply suspended their drive for ratification and allowed popular support to grow, pointing out at every opportunity that all that stood in the way of a Bill of Rights were Virginia's Anti-Federalists.

Finally, Henry and his allies relented, brought the Bill of Rights to the floor, and voted for ratification on December 15, 1791. On March 1, 1792, Secretary of State Thomas Jefferson formally announced that the Bill of Rights had become part of the Constitution.

First Amendment (1791)

The First Amendment prohibits Congress from establishing religion; or prohibiting the free exercise of religion; or abridging freedom of speech; freedom of the press; the right of the people peaceably to assemble; and the right to petition the government for redress of grievances.

I

CONGRESS shall make no law respecting an establishment of religion, or prohibiting the free exercise thereof; or abridging the freedom of speech, or of the press, or the right of the people peaceably to assemble, and to petition the Government for a **redress** of grievances.

NOTES

redress: a means of seeking a remedy for a complaint.

COMMENTARY

When most people think of the Bill of Rights, they think of the First Amendment. Here, at the very threshold of the Bill of Rights, in a single amendment, the personal rights most cherished by Americans are guaranteed.

The First Amendment is a catalogue of the fundamental rights which every citizen in the United States enjoys: rights indispensable to a citizen's role in a democracy; rights essential to the twin goals of individual autonomy and collective self-government.

The structure of the First Amendment itself is very important. It is noteworthy that the First Amendment speaks in prohibitory terms, denying to Congress the power to infringe upon these critical rights. This formulation was in direct response to the Anti-Federalist attacks on the proposed Constitution during the ratification debates. In 1787 there was widespread fear that the new national government would exercise powers that would violate individual liberties. The First Amendment unequivocally prohibits Congress from making any law that would infringe on these fundamental rights. Regardless of whether the original Constitution granted any such power to Congress (and on this the Federalists and Anti-Federalists were sharply divided), the First Amendment operates to cut off Congress' authority in this area.

The next important point to recognize about the First Amendment is that since it originally was framed as a prohibition on *Congress*, it did not act as a prohibition on the *states*. It does *not* say: "Neither Congress nor any state shall make any law . . ." Nor does it declare these rights in the affirmative, such as "The right of the people to freedom of speech shall not be abridged. . . ."

There are at least two reasons why the First Amendment was drafted in this manner. First, the framers of the Constitution and the Bill of Rights were keenly aware of the need to respect state sovereignty to the fullest extent possible without impairing the ability of the new central government to serve its national purposes. The framers believed that to declare that no state could make any law infringing on these specified rights would interfere with state sovereignty.

Second, several of the state constitutions already contained Declarations of Rights protecting many of these rights. Those declarations remained in effect for the protection of individual rights from infringement by state government. The Bill of Rights was written to address the need for amendments to the *national* Constitution, not because of any perceived violation of personal rights by the state governments.

In *Barron v. Baltimore* (1833), the Supreme Court confirmed that the Bill of Rights restrains the actions of the United States government, *not* the actions of the state governments. However, with the passage of the Fourteenth Amendment in 1868, which prohibits the *states* from depriving "any person of life, liberty, or property, without due process of law," the argument emerged that the Bill of Rights, previously seen as a limitation only on the federal government, was now incorporated into the concept of "due process of law," and therefore applies to the states as well as the federal government.

In a series of Supreme Court decisions beginning with *Gitlow v. New York* (1927) and continuing for the next 50 years, the essential provisions of the first eight amendments to the Constitution were applied to the states under the *incorporation doctrine.* As Justice Benjamin N. Cardozo wrote in *Palko v. Connecticut* (1937), due process includes those rights "implicit in the concept of ordered liberty," which are so important that "neither liberty nor justice would exist if they were sacrificed." In other words, the first eight amendments were "incorporated" into the Due Process Clause of the Fourteenth Amendment and thereby became applicable to the states.

Consequently, as we examine the First Amendment (and the rest of the Bill of Rights) from the vantage point of the twenty-first century, it is important to recognize that these fundamental rights are protected from *both* federal *and* state interference. Neither Congress, the president, state legislators, governors, nor any official high or low may violate the individual liberties protected by the First Amendment and the rest of the Bill of Rights.

Freedom of Religion

It is no coincidence that the First Amendment opens with two fundamental guarantees regarding religion. Within the same sentence the First Amendment prohibits "an establishment of religion" by government (called the Establishment Clause) *and* prohibits government from interfering with "the free exercise thereof" (the Free Exercise Clause). The Establishment Clause prohibits government from endorsing or supporting religion or from adopting a state religion, while the Free Exercise Clause prevents government from interfering with the right of an individual to practice his or her religion.

These are important and independent rights. On the one hand, government may not designate an official religion or favor one religion over another or favor religion over non-religion. Thus, government must remain neutral when it comes to religion. On the other hand, government may not prevent any person from privately worshiping as he or she sees fit. Thus, government may not be antagonistic toward religion. Again, when it comes to religion, government must remain neutral.

Historical Precedents

The Establishment and Free Exercise Clauses were written against a long and troubled history of religious intolerance and persecution. From the arrival of the Pilgrims at Plymouth in 1620 to Roger Williams' founding of Providence, Rhode Island in 1636, the colonists had preached religious freedom (although they didn't always practice what they preached in regards to others). In the next century, James Madison promoted religious tolerance and freedom of conscience and Thomas Jefferson

coined the phrase "the wall of separation" between church and state. By the time the First Amendment was written, a consensus had emerged that government should be kept out of religion and religion should be kept out of government. Indeed, Article VI of the Constitution expressly prohibites any religious test as a qualification for any office in the new government.

Freedom of conscience means that people are free to profess their own religious beliefs without fear of reprisals. The framers were intent on releasing the grip which religion had exercised over the state for centuries. Enlightened thought emphasized *rationalism,* the use of human reason to solve problems, and left no room for the church to control how people were governed. By the same token, freedom of conscience entitles each person to practice his or her own religion regardless of what the majority believes. Dissenting religious views should be entitled to the same protection as those of the dominant religions.

In writing the opening lines of the First Amendment, Madison sought to express the theme of freedom of conscience in the Establishment and Free Exercise Clauses. It would be left to later generations and the U.S. Supreme Court to refine these fundamental principles and to apply them to the myriad of circumstances which would arise as society became more complex and diverse.

The Establishment Clause

Beyond the prohibition on a state religion, what was the reach of the Establishment Clause? In *Everson v. Board of Education of Ewing Township* (1947), a closely divided Court ruled that under the Establishment Clause, government can neither establish a particular state or national church, prefer one religion over another, nor aid religion. However, it upheld state reimbursements to the parents of parochial school children for the cost of transporting their children to school, analogizing such incidental aid to the cost of publicly financed police or fire protection for religious institutions and buildings.

In 1971, in *Lemon v. Kurtzman,* the Court established a three-part test for courts to use to determine whether a particular government action violates the Establishment Clause:

1. A law must have a non-religious, or *secular,* legislative purpose.
2. The law must have a primary effect that neither advances nor hinders religion.
3. The law must not foster an excessive entanglement between government and religion.

Although the *Lemon* test has been criticized, it survives to this day.

How far must the government go to avoid an establishment of religion? Must it deny a religious club the right to hold its meetings at a public university? In *Widmar v. Vincent* (1981), the court allowed a university to permit such meetings after hours in campus classrooms on equal terms with all other student groups. In *Rosenberger v. University of Virginia* (1995), the Court held that the Establishment Clause does not prevent a public university from paying the cost of a Christian student group's newsletter on the same basis as the university pays for other student publications.

Can public school facilities, including teachers and the public address system, be used to lead students in prayer? In *Engel v. Vitale* (1962), the Court invalidated the practice of having public school children recite prayers composed by state education officials; in *Abington School District v. Schempp* (1963), the Court extended the restriction to readings of the Lord's Prayer and the Bible in public school classrooms; and in *Stone v. Graham* (1980), the court held that posting copies of the Ten Commandments in public school classrooms is unconstitutional. In *Edwards v. Aguillard* (1987), the Court invalidated a Louisiana statute that mandated the teaching of creationism whenever the theory of evolution was taught.

Marking out the boundaries of the Establishment Clause, especially in the context of secondary public schools, the Court has been sensitive to the impact of the prohibited practices on students who do not practice the religion of most of the other students. When a Christian prayer is recited in a public school classroom, the establishment problem is not cured by allowing Jewish, Muslim, Buddhist, or atheist students to step into the hall or to remain silent. The stigma that attaches to the outsider, combined with the seal of approval placed on the Christian prayer, are precisely the burdens and benefits which the First Amendment prohibits under the Establishment Clause.

The Free Exercise Clause

As much as the Court has grappled with the Establishment Clause, it has also had to confront conflicts between individuals seeking to exercise their religious beliefs freely and the enforcement of general laws which may contradict those religious practices. In *Reynolds v. United States* (1879), the Court addressed just such a conflict between anti-bigamy laws (which prohibit

multiple spouses) and the practice of polygamy by members of the Church of Jesus Christ of Latter-Day Saints. Rejecting the Mormon lawyers argument that bigamy laws violate the Free Exercise Clause of the First Amendment, the Court distinguished between religious *beliefs* and religious *practices*. "Congress was deprived of all legislative power over more opinion, but was left free to reach actions which were in violation of social duties or subversive of good order." The Court noted that a devout believer in human sacrifice could not seek refuge in the Free Exercise Clause if charged with murder. In *Davis v. Beason* (1890), the Court went even further and upheld a law which denied the right to vote not only to those who practiced polygamy but to those who merely advocated it or were simply members of the Church of Jesus Christ of Latter-Day Saints.

By the middle of the twentieth century, the Court began exhibiting greater tolerance for religious diversity. In *Sherbert v. Verner* (1963), the Court, in an opinion written by Justice William J. Brennan, Jr., a strong proponent of individual rights, found that the decision of state officials to deny unemployment benefits to a Seventh Day Adventist who refused to work on Saturday, the day of her Sabbath, amounted to a violation of the Free Exercise Clause. And in *Wisconsin v. Yoder* (1972), the Court, in an opinion by Chief Justice Warren E. Burger, exempted Amish children from compulsory school attendance beyond the eighth grade. In these cases, the Court gave preeminence to genuinely held religious beliefs and practices where the government could not establish a compelling state interest to the contrary.

Regrettably, a degree of hypocrisy has pervaded this area. Large religious denominations, with widespread public support and political influence, have been able to secure exemptions for their religious practices, while smaller less mainstream religious groups (often marginalized as "cults") have not. Thus, although from 1919 to 1933, when the Eighteenth Amendment prohibited the sale or transportation of alcoholic beverages, Congress made an exception for the use of sacramental wine at Christian ceremonies, yet many states make no exceptions for the use of the drug peyote in Native American religious ceremonies. Are Native American ceremonies any less deserving of constitutional protection than Christian services?

Yet in *Employment Division v. Smith* (1990), the Supreme Court upheld the denial of unemployment benefits to two Native Americans who were fired from their jobs as drug rehabilitation counselors because they ingested peyote in connection with Native American religious rites. The state of Oregon took the position that they had been fired for job-related misconduct (the use of a controlled substance) and made no exception for the sacramental use of peyote. In an opinion by Justice Antonin Scalia, the Court held there was no violation of the Free Exercise Clause because Oregon's drug law was not targeted at the suppression of religious beliefs or practices but was a law of general application which incidentally had the effect of burdening those beliefs or practices.

The *Smith* decision was roundly criticized by religious and civil liberties groups, which successfully lobbied Congress to pass the Religious Freedom Restoration Act (RFRA) in 1993. The law required exemptions for religious practices from federal, state, or local laws that burdened such practices unless the state could show a compelling reason why the law had to be applied to religious groups and that the law was the least restrictive means of furthering that interest. But in 1997, in response to a legal challenge from state and local governments, the Supreme Court in *Boerne v. Flores* struck down RFRA, finding that Congress had exceeded its power in deciding what was or was not protected by the Free Exercise Clause. Given the power and influence of religion in American life, there is no end in sight to the battles over the Establishment and Free Exercise Clauses.

Freedom of Speech and Press

Ask most people what constitutional right they value most and the answer will be freedom of speech. A close second would be freedom of the press.

Freedom of speech generally refers to the right of individuals to express themselves freely without fear of government restrictions. *Freedom of the press* refers to the right of the publishers of newspapers, magazines, and books; the writers and producers of motion pictures and television productions; and the creators and distributors of records and CDs, and now the Internet, to sell and distribute materials free of government censorship. The two concepts are often referred to together as *freedom of expression*.

Although the First Amendment speaks in absolute terms ("Congress shall make *no* law abridging . . . freedom of speech or of the press"), the question remains, what is meant by "freedom of speech" and "freedom of the press"? First Amendment absolutists cite the unqualified language of the First Amendment itself. The First Amendment means what it says: "Congress shall make *no* law . . ."—not "some laws" or "almost no laws," but "no law."

Most scholars and virtually all Supreme Court Justices however, recognize that at the time the First Amendment was ratified there were certain limited exceptions to freedom of speech and freedom of the press that were already part of the law. There were libel laws in 1791 under which people could be punished for making false and defamatory statements. There were obscenity laws in 1791 under which publishers could be fined or jailed for selling books or pictures deemed obscene. Consequently there are certain limited exceptions that prevent the First Amendment from being taken literally.

On the other hand, no one today seriously argues that First Amendment protection is confined to the printing press as it existed in 1791. The Supreme Court has held that the First Amendment protects motion pictures, radio, television, cable, recordings, and most recently the Internet, regardless of the fact that none of this technology existed when the First Amendment was written. The Supreme Court takes a utilitarian view of freedom of expression to encompass any form of communication that provides information or opinion as books and newspapers did in 1791.

Rationale for Freedom of Expression

Why do we protect freedom of expression? One reason often given is that truth is best discovered by the free and open exchange of ideas. In 1644, in his seminal work *Areopagitica*, John Milton confidently asked, "who ever knew Truth put to the worse, in a free and open encounter?" In 1919, Justice Oliver Wendell Holmes, Jr. wrote that "the best test of truth is the power of the thought to get itself accepted in the competition of the market." Thus, it is believed that people have the best chance of finding the truth in a free and open marketplace of ideas.

Another important reason to protect freedom of expression is to foster human dignity and autonomy. The opportunity to express oneself freely tends to create inner satisfaction and individual fulfillment. Freedom of expression deserves constitutional protection to help realize what Justice Thurgood Marshall called "a spirit that demands self-expression."

Then there is the rationale based on what is good for the community rather than what is good for the individual.

Under this view, freedom of expression is a vital part of self-governance in a democratic society. For citizens to participate fully in their own government, they need to exchange information and express their opinions on pending legislation, candidates, and public policy issues. Only open and unrestricted communication free of government censorship ensures the viability of democracy.

Finally, there is the value of dissent. While the theory of self-governance looks at the role of free expression from *within* the system, the dissent rationale recognizes the value of those who work *outside* the system. Sometimes referred to as the *loyal opposition,* dissident speech is protected because it allows opponents of the established order to express themselves peacefully and openly, thereby reducing the risk of violent opposition. Tolerating, indeed encouraging, dissent serves as a safety valve allowing the system to let off steam.

For the sake of maintaining order and morality, can the expression of certain ideas deemed dangerous or offensive be suppressed? In the early 1970s, American Nazis announced that they intended to march through Skokie, Illinois, a suburb of Chicago and home to a large number of Jewish families, including survivors of the Holocaust. The city took various steps to block the march, but the Nazis, represented by the American Civil Liberties Union, went to court, claiming that they had a constitutional right to express themselves. The ACLU argued that regardless of whether it, the city, or a majority of Americans disagreed with them, the Nazis had a right to speak and march peacefully. Eventually, the federal courts agreed that the First Amendment protected the Nazis' freedom of expression. (Ironically, having won the right to march, the Nazis chose to go elsewhere.)

Can the government deny funding to artists because of the controversial or offensive nature of their work? This issue arose in 1991 when Congress imposed content restrictions on the grants awarded by the National Endowment for the Arts, a federal agency established in 1965 to further the progress of the arts. Civil libertarians argued that once the government decided to provide funds to artists through the NEA, it could not condition those funds on whether the government agreed or disagreed with the artistic or political messages communicated by the art. Eventually, the courts sided with the artists and struck down the congressional restrictions. The Supreme Court held that the NEA could establish goals encouraging "decency" and respect for diverse American values, but could not deny funds for specific works of art based on their controversial or offensive content.

Each new technology renews the debate over freedom of expression. Most recently, the conflict has centered on the Internet. In 1996, Congress passed the Communications Decency Act (CDA) making it a crime to communicate "indecent" material over the Internet to persons under 18 years old. The ACLU challenged the CDA, first before a federal three-judge panel and later in the U.S. Supreme Court. This was the first Supreme Court case involving freedom of expression on the Internet. In the 1998 decision *(Reno v. ACLU)*, the Court found that the Internet is a vast marketplace of ideas entitled to the widest possible constitutional protection. With respect to the CDA, the Court held that material available for adults could not be reduced to what is acceptable only for children. In the absence of effective age verification technology, the Court found that the responsibility for protecting children from indecent material on the Internet rests with their parents, not with the government.

Before the Internet was ever invented, sexually explicit material in books, art, movies, and videos proved a persistent subject for public debate. By 1968, the Supreme Court had adopted a three-part test for defining obscenity: sexually explicit material could not be banned unless it (a) appealed to a prurient, or morbid, interest in sex, (b) exceeded contemporary community standards and (c) was utterly without redeeming social value. In 1973, in the case of *Miller v. California*, the Court recast the third prong in an effort to expand the scope of unprotected obscenity. Under *Miller*, material can be banned if it lacks "serious literary, artistic, political, or scientific value." While one leading First Amendment scholar, Charles Rembar, optimistically called his 1969 book *The End of Obscenity*, federal and state governments continue to prosecute material deemed obscene. The controversy over obscenity is not likely to end in the near future — if ever.

Slander and Defamation

The Supreme Court has held that laws punishing defamation do not violate the First Amendment, except when it comes to public officials and public figures. *Defamation,* which encompasses slander and libel (the written word as well as the spoken word), is defined as a false statement of fact which holds someone up to shame and humiliation. Allowing someone to be punished for criticizing an elected official or famous person tends to suppress the very public debate protected by the First Amendment. In 1964, in the landmark case of *New York Times v. Sullivan,* the Supreme Court faced a historic dispute. At the height of the civil rights movement, a group called the Committee to Defend Martin Luther King took out an ad in the *Times* condemning racism and the actions of the officials in Montgomery, Alabama. One of the officials, L.B. Sullivan, sued for libel and won a $500,000 judgment against the *Times.* Ultimately, the Supreme Court overturned the verdict and established strong protection for freedom of the press.

In an opinion by Justice William J. Brennan, Jr., the Court held that the freedom to criticize the government is so important and the possibility that journalists might make innocent mistakes is so great that defamation suits against public officials cannot succeed unless the official proves that the defamatory statement was made with "actual malice"—knowledge of falsity or reckless disregard for the truth. Nothing less would serve the "profound national commitment to the principle that debate on public issues should be uninhibited, robust, and wide-open."

Freedom of speech also encompasses actions intended to communicate a message, such as burning a draft card to protest a war or burning an American flag to express disagreement over government policy. *Symbolic speech,* as these expressive activities are called, is entitled to constitutional protection so long as it does not involve violence or destruction of private property. In 1989, in *Texas v. Johnson,* Justice Brennan, speaking for a majority of the Court, characterized as "a bedrock principle underlying the First Amendment" that "the Government may not prohibit the expression of an idea simply because society finds the idea itself offensive or disagreeable." He suggested that there is "no more appropriate response to burning a flag than waving one's own."

One of the greatest threats to freedom of expression is *prior restraint,* which means any effort by government to suppress speech even before it is published. The history of England is stained by examples of the monarchy preventing books and newspapers from being printed. It has been suggested that the essential purpose of the First Amendment is to prohibit prior restraints. The Supreme Court has never upheld a prior restraint. In the landmark case involving the Pentagon Papers—a series of secret U.S. Defense Department studies on the Vietnam War—the Supreme Court rejected the request of the Nixon administration to enjoin *The New York Times* and *The Washington Post* from publishing the controversial reports.

Law books bulge with cases dealing with freedom of speech and the press. It seems inevitable that in every generation new battlelines will be drawn over the desire of people to read, create, write, and disseminate books, newspapers, music, paintings, plays, Web sites, and all manner of expression and the impulse of government officials and others to restrict or entirely censor those works deemed a threat to established values of order and morality.

The Right to Peaceably Assemble

The framers of the Constitution and the Bill of Rights remembered only too well the tyranny of King George and his soldiers in breaking up meetings of colonists who gathered to share their hopes and dreams for independence. The founders pledged not to copy that repressive example. Consequently, they included in the First Amendment protection for "the right of the people peaceably to assemble." While the freedom to exercise one's religion or to speak freely generally focus on the rights of the individual, the freedom to assemble peaceably focuses on the rights of a group or community. The framers understood how important it is for like-minded people to come together to exchange ideas, learn from each other, and make plans to advance their common interests. Then, as now, there was a natural desire among citizens to gather together with a sense of community. So basic were these instincts that the framers saw them as fundamental rights deserving constitutional protection.

Closely akin to the right to assemble peaceably is the related "right of association," which is nowhere specifically mentioned in the Constitution or Bill of Rights. The *right of association* goes beyond the right to assemble physically. It encompasses the broader right to form relationships, both intimate and communal, and to establish groups and organizations to further various political, social, religious, educational, charitable, and other ends.

The key qualification to the right of assembly and the right of association is the requirement that it be done "peaceably." No one has a constitutional right to go on a violent rampage, damaging property and injuring passersby.

Throughout American history, labor unions and political protestors have exercised the right to assemble peaceably in order to express their views and gain attention for their causes. In the 1960s and 1970s, marches, demonstrations, and teach-ins were held across the country to oppose the Vietnam War and to push for civil rights. These gatherings attracted widespread attention and reached a vast audience through television coverage. Most observers believe that these protests and demonstrations brought home to the rest of America the moral force of the demands of civil rights workers, pacifists, religious leaders, women's groups, and elected officials for peace and equality, and contributed directly to the end of the Vietnam War and to the passage of historic civil rights laws. The demonstrations also showed that there is strength in numbers, and they gave participants a sense of solidarity. Activists from that time believe that their political protests represented democracy in action and showed that major government policies could be influenced, and indeed reversed, through mass demonstrations. In 1967, 50,000 people protested the Vietnam War at the Pentagon. Between January and June of 1968, 221 demonstrations were held at over 100 colleges and universities, and in November 1969, 750,000 protesters gathered in Boston, New York, Washington, D.C., and other cities, to observe Moratorium Day.

Regrettably, blood was spilled and lives were lost during this period. At the Democratic National Convention in Chicago in August 1968, 5,000 activists staged five days of protest and 1,000 were clubbed by police in what some called a police riot. Tragically, on May 4, 1970, during a campus protest at Kent State University over the U.S. invasion of Cambodia, National Guardsmen opened fire on the crowd, killing four protestors and wounding nine. Meanwhile, draft board offices and Army Reserve installations were repeatedly broken into and vandalized. At the University of Wisconsin, an anti-war activist blew up a laboratory to protest the university's involvement in war research, killing one person and injuring four others.

Violence on both sides inflamed further anger and resentment. In time, as the war came to an end and the public became more accepting of advances in civil rights, public protests and demonstrations began to wane as a method of political expression.

In 1999, protestors staged a massive protest in Seattle, Washington in opposition to the World Trade Organization. In August 2000, major rallies were held in Philadelphia and Los Angeles to protest the Republican and Democratic National Conventions. Civil liberties organizations went to court to defend the constitutional rights of protesters to assemble peaceably. In Los Angeles, a federal court ordered the Los Angeles Police Department to allow demonstrators to gather next to the Democratic Convention in order to ensure that their public messages were seen and heard by the delegates, the press, and the public. Regrettably, on the first night of the convention, the LAPD declared a demonstration an unlawful assembly, and converged on the protestors, journalists, and legal observers, injuring several with rubber bullets.

Clashes between police and protestors in the midst of mass demonstrations will persist until the public and the courts insist that authorities direct their efforts at arresting specific lawbreakers while protecting the right of "the people peaceably to assemble."

Generally, the courts have tried to navigate through this area by seeking to ensure order while simultaneously allowing the use of public streets and parks for peaceful protest, since those places have "immemorially been held in trust for the use of the public for purposes of assembly and discussing public questions," as the Supreme Court stated in *Hague v. Congress of Industrial Organizations* (1939). The courts have sought to distinguish between reasonable "time, place, and manner" regulations (such as prohibiting use of loudspeakers at night in a residential neighborhood) that are enforced even-handedly without discriminating against any particular message or viewpoint versus government restrictions or regulations imposed because "public officials oppose the speaker's view."

When it comes to freedom of association, the Supreme Court has rejected the notion of guilt by association (*Yates v. United States* [1957]) and protected a group's membership rolls from government inspection (*NAACP v. Alabama* [1958]).

On occasion, the right of association comes into conflict with other fundamental rights. Thus, in *Rotary International v. Rotary Club of Duarte* (1987), the Supreme Court upheld a California law that prevented Rotary International from excluding women from membership but in *Boy Scouts of America v. Dale* (2000), the Court upheld the right of the Boy Scouts of American to expel a gay scout leader.

The right of association has also played a pivotal role as a constitutional source for the recognition of the right of privacy, which is not expressly mentioned in the Constitution or Bill of Rights. In *Griswold v. Connecticut* (1965), the Court held that a married couple had a constitutional right, derived from the right of association and the right of privacy, to obtain medical advice regarding birth control, despite a state law to the contrary. The Court observed that the "right to be left alone is the beginning of all freedoms."

The Right to Petition

The final provision of the First Amendment protects the right of the people "to petition the Government for a redress of grievances." This constitutional right, like the others covered by the First Amendment, has a long history, tracing its origins to English law.

The Magna Carta, signed in 1215, protected the right of the barons to petition the Crown for redress of grievances, meaning that their petitions seeking remedies from their government would be received and given fair hearings. The British Bill of Rights of 1689 lists the right to petition the king as one of the rights of the people. And the Declaration of Independence, itself a catalogue of grievances, gives as one of its reasons for rebellion against the king, that "our repeated petitions have been answered only by repeated injury."

Thus, in drafting the First Amendment, the framers were intent on assuring American citizens the right to complain to their government on any matter they deem important. Often overlooked in the First Amendment, overshadowed by the prominence of such vaunted rights as freedom of speech and freedom of religion, the right to petition the government for redress of grievances goes to the very heart of a democracy. People have a direct and unencumbered right to go straight to their government to seek solutions to their problems. People are not limited to simply electing representatives and then leaving governance entirely to them. People have the right—many would say the duty—to address their concerns directly to every branch of government, alerting officials to unfair and unjust conditions.

Of course, the First Amendment does not guarantee that the government will adopt the particular solution offered by any one citizen or group of citizens. Indeed, on most public policy questions, citizens differ dramatically on the appropriate solution. The right to petition covers a host of methods by which people can communicate with their government. The original and most formal method is a written petition signed by individuals seeking a specific goal, such as the passage of a particular bill or support or opposition for a particular action, on any issue from waging war to installing a traffic light at a busy intersection. Formal petitions are also used in many states to place propositions, also known as *initiatives,* on the ballot, which, if passed, become law with the same force and effect as a law passed by the legislature and signed by the governor. In addition, formal petitions are used to seek the *recall,* or removal from office, of elected officials or judges.

The right to petition encompasses far more than such formal written documents. Anything from a telephone call to the mayor, a letter to a senator, or a speech before a local school board, constitutes a petition to the government for redress of grievances. In *Thornhill v. Alabama* (1940), the Supreme Court held that orderly union picketing was protected as a form of petition and assembly. In *Edwards v. South Carolina* (1963), the Court stated that a march by 180 African-American students to protest racial discrimination was protected by the right to petition, despite claims that the presence of a hostile crowd waiting at the end of the march might result in disorderly conduct. And in *United States v. Grace* (1983), the Court overturned a federal law prohibiting picketing and distributing leaflets on the steps of the Court's own building.

So protective of the right to petition is the Court that it held in *Talley v. California* (1960) and *McIntyre v. Ohio Elections Commission* (1995), that ordinances against anonymous leaflets and campaign literature were unconstitutional. More recently, in *Buckley v. American Constitutional Law Foundation* (1999), the Court invalidated a Colorado law that required petition circulators to wear identification badges and meet strict reporting requirements.

In certain circumscribed areas, such as the military, the Court has limited the right to petition. In *Brown v. Gilnes* (1980), the Court held that base commanders could prevent military personnel from sending a petition to Congress and in *Walters v. National Association of Radiation Survivors* (1985), the Court upheld a $10 limit on the amount a veteran could pay an attorney to pursue claims with the Veterans Administration.

The importance of the right to petition then is that it announces that the process of government is open and accessible to the people and that no government may seal itself off, refusing to listen to what the people have to say.

A debate continues to rage over wealthy individuals and corporations enjoying a greater right to petition their government for redress of grievances because they have the money to hire well-paid lobbyists and public relations consultants and to produce flashy television ads and glossy flyers. Generally, the courts have been reluctant to venture into the thicket of economic disparities when it comes to constitutional rights. Efforts to overhaul the way political campaigns are financed have yet to succeed, in part because they raise serious First Amendment problems over whether the regulation of money in the political system constitutes the regulation of speech. Many observers believe that the best solution to removing the taint of money from politics is for the public to fund political campaigns—just as the public pays for sample ballots, legislative summaries, polling places, and the salaries of election officials.

Nevertheless, no one is suggesting that a citizen's right to petition the government for redress of grievances will ever be eliminated. On the contrary, since the days when Thomas Paine distributed his pamphlets in the streets calling for independence, Americans have jealously guarded their right to "complain to City Hall," despite the fact that few know that their right to do so is specifically guaranteed in the closing words of the First Amendment, the protector of so much considered precious in our democracy.

Second Amendment (1791)

The Second Amendment protects the right to keep and bear arms on the basis that a well-regulated militia is necessary to the security of a free state.

II

A well-regulated militia, being necessary to the security of a free State, the right of the people to keep and bear arms, shall not be infringed.

COMMENTARY

To this day, the meaning and intent of the Second Amendment remain controversial. Beginning with "A well regulated militia, being necessary to the security of a free state," the amendment declares that "the right of the people to keep and bear arms shall not be infringed." Were it not for the opening phrase, there would be little doubt that the amendment grants full constitutional protection to the right to keep and bear arms, on a par with the right to free speech or free press or any other constitutional right.

Unraveling the Second Amendment

But the preamble is there. Every part of the Constitution and the Bill of Rights must be given meaning, none of it can be ignored. Consequently, what impact on the right to "keep and bear arms," does the prefatory language, referring to the necessity of a "well regulated militia," have? Is the right to keep and bear arms limited to a citizen's participation in a state militia, thereby giving meaning to the preamble? Or, should the reference to the militia be viewed as an anachronism, thereby ensuring the right to keep and bear arms to all people even those who are not members of a militia?

Proponents of a broad reading of the Second Amendment argue that the amendment assures to the people "their private arms," as stated in an article that received James Madison's approval and was the only analysis available to Congress when it voted in 1789. Where William Blackstone described arms for personal defense as among the "absolute rights of individuals" of common law, his eighteenth-century American editor commented that this right had been constitutionalized in the Second Amendment.

Early constitutional commentators point to Aristotle's observation that basic to tyrants is a "mistrust of the people; hence they deprive them of arms." Political theorists from Cicero to John Locke also believed that the possession of arms was implicit in personal freedom and therefore vital to popular government.

James Madison, in *The Federalist* No. 46, assured Americans that they need never fear the federal government because of "the advantage of being armed, which you possess over the people of almost every other nation," and Patrick Henry declared, "The great principle is that every man be armed. Everyone who is able may have a gun." Samuel Adams proposed that "the Constitution never be construed . . . to prevent the people of the United States who are peaceable citizens from keeping their own arms."

Supporters of a broad right to bear arms argue that it is necessary to remember that in the eighteenth century, the militia embraced the entire adult male citizenry. By colonial law, every household was required to possess arms and every male of military age was required to muster during military emergencies, bearing his own arms.

The supporters also argue that it is impossible to believe that the First Congress used "right of the people" in the First Amendment to describe an individual right but 16 words later, the Second Amendment uses the phrase to describe a "right" vested exclusively in the states. Moreover, "right of the people" is used again to refer to personal rights in the Fourth and Ninth Amendments, and the Tenth Amendment expressly distinguishes "the people" from "the states."

The Second Amendment and the Supreme Court

The U.S. Supreme Court has never addressed these broad issues in interpreting the Second Amendment, but it has reviewed several cases involving gun regulations. In *Presser v. Illinois* (1886), the Court upheld the conviction of Herman Presser under a state law for leading an armed group through the streets of Chicago. Presser argued that the law was superseded by various federal laws, including the Second Amendment, but the Court found that Presser's interpretation would amount to denying the power of the states to disperse mobs.

In 1939, the Court in *United States v. Miller* upheld a federal regulation outlawing shotguns having barrels less than 18 inches long on the grounds that there was no indication that such a weapon "was . . . ordinary military equipment or . . . could contribute to the common defense." *Miller* suggests that the right protected under the Second Amendment must bear a reasonable relationship to the maintenance of a "well-regulated militia."

In *Cases v. United States* (1943), the Court, in declining to review a challenge to a provision of the Federal Firearms Act, noted that "apparently . . . under the Second Amendment, the federal government can limit the keeping and bearing of arms by a single individual as well as by a group . . . but it cannot prohibit the possession or use of any weapon which has any reasonable relationship to the preservation of efficiency of a well-regulated militia."

Most recently, in *Quilici v. Village of Morton Grove* (1983), the Court let stand a lower court decision upholding a municipal ordinance banning possession of handguns. While it is risky to try to tell what the Supreme Court is thinking when it declines to hear a case, the *Village of Morton Grove* decision suggests that there was not a majority of the Justices who believed that the ban on handguns violated the Second Amendment.

Limitations?

No one, including the National Rifle Association, seriously argues that the Second Amendment prohibits any and all gun controls. The ownership of firearms by minors, felons, and the mentally impaired may be limited or banned. Moreover, the government may limit the types of arms that may be kept; there is no recognized right in the Second Amendment, for example, to own artillery or automatic weapons or sawed-off shotguns. Gun controls in the form of registration and licensing requirements are also permissible.

The debate over the Second Amendment has become emblematic of a broader question: Has the government gone too far in restricting individual rights? Liberals think the answer is yes when it comes to the First Amendment and conservatives think so when it comes to the Second Amendment. Suspicion of big government runs across the political spectrum.

Third Amendment (1791)

The Third Amendment provides that no soldier shall, in time of peace, be quartered at any house without the owner's consent, nor in time of war except as prescribed by law.

III

NO soldier shall, in time of peace be quartered in any house, without the consent of the owner, nor in time of war, but in a manner to be prescribed by law.

COMMENTARY

Vitally important to the founding generation, the Third Amendment is of little consequence today, except as a warning against the risks of an unchecked military.

Although the British government conveniently ignored its own history during its occupation of the American colonies, there was a long tradition in English law against troops forcibly using private houses as barracks and shelter, also known as *quartering*. Illegal quartering was condemned in the Petition of Right in 1628 and the English Bill of Rights in 1689.

When the American colonies resisted taxation without representation in 1765, British troops were sent over, and under the English Quartering Act, if barracks were insufficient, private houses and buildings could be commandeered over the owner's objections.

Indeed, this was one of the grievances listed in the Declaration of Independence, which specifically accuses the King of keeping standing armies in the colonies in time of peace without the consent of the colonial legislatures and "quartering large bodies of armed troops among us."

Consequently, it was not surprising that during the debates over the ratification of the Constitution between 1787 and 1789, several state conventions urged an amendment to prohibit the quartering of troops in private homes in times of peace. It was one of James Madison's original proposals for the Bill of Rights and easily passed the Congress.

In affirming the sanctity of private property, today the Third Amendment serves a primarily symbolic purpose. It reinforces the notion that government cannot make use of one's home without one's consent.

So fundamental is this proposition that Congress has never proposed any quartering law and the Supreme Court has had no occasion to address the Third Amendment.

Fourth Amendment (1791)

The Fourth Amendment declares that the right of the people to be secure in their persons, houses, papers, and effects against unreasonable searches and seizures shall not be violated. Warrants can be issued only with probable cause, must be supported by oath or affirmation, and must describe the place to be searched and the persons or things to be seized.

IV

THE right of the people to be secure in their persons, houses, papers, and effects, against unreasonable searches and seizures, shall not be violated, and no warrants shall issue, but upon probable cause, supported by oath or affirmation, and particularly describing the place to be searched, and the persons or things to be seized.

COMMENTARY

Few rights are more important than the right of privacy, and few invasions of that right are more intrusive than an illegal search and seizure of one's person, house, papers, or effects. These rights were as important to Americans when the Bill of Rights was written as they are today, which explains why the entire Fourth Amendment is devoted to searches and seizures.

History of the Amendment

The Fourth Amendment was drafted in reaction to the old English practice of *general warrants,* which were issued for the lifetime of the monarch and could be used by the authorities to search at will. No specific person or place had to be named, no probable cause was necessary, and the warrant could be issued on the basis of rumor or speculation, without any statement made under oath. In 1763, a typical general warrant called for a diligent search for an unidentified author, printer, and publisher of a satirical journal, *The North Briton* No. 45, and the seizure of their papers. Eventually, the warrant led to the search of five different houses, the arrest of 49 persons, and the seizure of thousands of books and papers.

Abuses of this sort had long prompted demands for reform. As early as 1589, Robert Beale charged that the general search warrant used by the High Commission against Puritans violated the Magna Carta of 1215.

Although general warrants had been used in the American colonies, they were the target of criticism. After the colonies declared independence, between 1776 and 1784 eight states included a guarantee against general

warrants in their constitutions. During the debates over the ratification of the Constitution, four state conventions urged amendments to address the problem. Consequently, what became the Fourth Amendment was readily included by James Madison when he drafted the Bill of Rights in 1789 in the First Congress.

Unfortunately, Madison introduced an ambiguity when he inserted the qualification that the people were secure in their persons, houses, papers, and effects against *"unreasonable"* searches and seizures. Without that phrase, there would have been a clear demarcation: No search without a search warrant, describing the person and place to be searched and the things to be seized. Madison's qualifier raised another possibility: a search *without* a warrant so long as it was not "unreasonable." The courts, police, and civil libertarians have been grappling with what is "unreasonable" ever since.

Limits to the Fourth Amendment

What has emerged is a series of exceptions: Police do not need a warrant for a search made in connection with an arrest; or in connection with stop-and-frisk situations; when illegal or stolen items are in plain view (or plain feel) during a legal search. In addition, no warrant is required for administrative, consensual, and border searches or searches involving exigent circumstances such as automobile searches.

In *Chimel v. California* (1969), the Supreme Court held that a search made in connection with an arrest included occasions when the suspect might reach to grab a weapon or an item of evidence. In *Minnesota v.*

Kickerson (1993), the Court held that if an officer, while patting down the outside of a suspect's clothing, feels what seems to be evidence of a crime or contraband (something illegal), the items can be seized without a warrant.

Given our mobile society and the risks of flight, as early as 1925 in *Carroll v. United States*, the Court made clear that an automobile would not justify the same privacy protections as one's home or person. Whether it is reasonable to search a passenger, trunk, glove box, or other containers in the car without a warrant has led to complicated litigation that often depends on the particular facts of each case.

Although a search may be conducted without a warrant if the individual or owner consents, serious disputes arise over whether such consent is voluntary; whether it is freely and knowingly given; whether it has been coerced; and whether it is the product of trickery, fear, or a promise of reward. Consent may be withdrawn at any time, and a refusal to give consent cannot later be used against a suspect to establish probable cause—"He didn't give consent, so he must be hiding something."

The Fourth Amendment also applies to wiretapping and other forms of police surveillance. In *Katz v. United States* (1967), the Court expressed the view that a person's "expectation of privacy" includes personal mail and telephone conversations. Consequently, absent emergency circumstances, the seizure of one's words requires a search warrant.

Governmental agencies other than the police, such as health, fire, housing, welfare, and safety agencies, may also conduct searches that comply with the Fourth Amendment, but they are subject to a lesser standard than probable cause. Controversy persists over whether certain occupations or categories of individuals may be required to submit to drug tests. In *National Treasury Employees Union v. Von Raab* (1989), the Court upheld mandatory urinalysis for promotions on the grounds that employees would have access to firearms and secret information. And in *Vernonia School District v. Acton* (1995), the Court upheld a program of drug testing all student athletes, regardless of whether there was any suspicion of particular students.

Although the Fourth Amendment prohibits illegal searches and seizures, it is silent on the consequences if one occurs. Common law at the time the Bill of Rights was written prescribed the remedy as a lawsuit against the police for trespass, but the illegally obtained evidence could still be introduced as evidence at an individual's criminal trial.

This changed in 1914 when the Court held in *Weeks v. United States* that illegally obtained evidence, seized in violation of the Fourth Amendment, must be excluded as evidence at a subsequent trial. Known as the *Exclusionary Rule,* it both preserves the integrity of the judiciary and deters police misconduct. Since a civil suit for damages could prove costly and time-consuming, it serves as a weak remedy to stop police from illegally seizing evidence which they know will still get into evidence. Only by putting police on notice that illegally obtained evidence will be excluded automatically will officers be deterred from acting improperly and encouraged to play by the rules.

Initially, the Exclusionary Rule applied only to agents of the federal government, but in 1949 in *Wolf v. Colorado*, the Court applied the Fourth Amendment to the states. And in *Mapp v. Ohio* (1961), the remedy of the Exclusionary Rule was applied to all state, as well as federal, authorities.

Subsequently, the Exclusionary Rule has been restricted. In *United States v. Calandra* (1974), the Court held that it did not apply to grand jury proceedings. In *United States v. Havens* (1980), the Court held that illegally seized evidence can be used to impeach the credibility of a defendant at trial, if he or she chooses to testify. In *Nix v. Williams* (1984), the Court held that such evidence can be admitted if the police would have inevitably discovered it by lawful means. And in *United States v. Leon* (1984) and *Massachusetts v. Sheppard* (1984), the Court significantly limited the Exclusionary Rule by holding that illegally obtained evidence can be admitted in evidence if the police error was made in objective good faith.

The erosion of the Exclusionary Rule has been justified as a means of separating police misconduct from the exclusion of reliable evidence that a crime has been committed. Opponents of the Exclusionary Rule complain that criminals should not get off scot-free just because an overworked patrolman made a mistake. Supporters of the Exclusionary Rule argue that unless there is a test clearly warning police that illegally obtained evidence will be excluded automatically, the precious rights protected by the Fourth Amendment will be sacrificed in the name of fighting crime, and police will conveniently claim a good faith error whenever they are caught illegally seizing evidence.

The Fourth Amendment and the continuing controversies over its interpretation and application exemplify just how seriously the American system takes the right of privacy and the desire to prohibit unwarranted government intrusion into the lives and homes of Americans. Even balanced against the important societal goal of convicting criminals, the Fourth Amendment errs on the side of protecting innocent people and insists that the government adhere strictly to the requirements of the Constitution. In a world filled with authoritarian regimes that don't think twice about the rights of their citizens, America's high standards of protecting the right of privacy represent a model in which the sanctity of the individual takes precedence over the demands of the criminal justice system. Indeed, it could well be said that it is the Fourth Amendment and the rest of the Bill of Rights that put the "justice" in the criminal justice system.

Fifth Amendment (1791)

The Fifth Amendment provides that 1) no person may be charged with a *capital crime* (one punishable by death) or other infamous crime unless indicted by a Grand Jury (except in time of war); 2) no person may be charged with the same crime twice; 3) no person may be compelled in any criminal case to be a witness against him- or herself; 4) no person may be deprived of life, liberty, or property without due process of law and 5) private property may not be taken for public use without just compensation.

V

NO person shall be held to answer for a **capital**, or otherwise infamous crime, unless on a presentment or indictment of a Grand Jury, except in cases arising in the land or naval forces, or in the Militia, when in actual service in time of War or public danger; nor shall any person be subject for the same offense to be twice put in jeopardy of life or limb; nor shall be compelled in any criminal case to be a witness against himself, nor be deprived of life, liberty, or property, without due process of law; nor shall private property be taken for public use without just compensation.

NOTE

capital (crime): a crime punishable by death.

COMMENTARY

Despite the importance of each of these rights, when most people think of the Fifth Amendment they think of the right against self-incrimination. The expressions "taking the Fifth" and "pleading the Fifth" have entered the popular culture through movies and television shows.

Unfortunately, all too often people assume that an individual must be guilty if he or she invokes, the Fifth Amendment, when in truth there may be a variety of legitimate reasons an innocent person would do so, including protecting others; advice of legal counsel because of other pending proceedings; or a highly principled refusal to allow the government to pry into one's affairs.

The right against self-incrimination can be traced to early English law. By the seventeenth century, the principle had begun to take hold that "no man is bound to accuse himself" (*nemo tenetur seipsum accusare*). In 1641, in reaction to the conviction of John Lilburne, a Puritan agitator who refused to testify against himself, the Parliament prohibited religious courts (known as "ecclesiastical courts") from administering any oath which forced one "to confess or to accuse himself or herself of any crime."

In England, the emergence of the right against self-incrimination was tightly linked to the origins of freedom of conscience, freedom of religion, and freedom of speech. The right against self-incrimination (sometimes erroneously referred to as merely a privilege against self-incrimination) goes hand-in-hand with the right to hold unorthodox religious and political beliefs.

The right against self-incrimination soon took hold in the American colonies. In 1776, the Virginia Constitution and Declaration of Rights stated that in criminal prosecutions the accused cannot "be compelled to give evidence against himself." All eight states that prefaced their constitutions with a bill of rights included virtually the same provision. During the debate over the ratification of the Constitution, all four states that recommended amendments included the right against self-incrimination among them.

When James Madison wrote the Bill of Rights during the First Congress in 1789, he included what became the Fifth Amendment, although his broader language was changed to limit the right against self-incrimination to criminal cases only. Thus the Fifth Amendment joined the rest of the Bill of Rights in underscoring the founders' conviction that the powers of the government are

Senator Joseph McCarthy
© Bettmann/CORBIS

subordinate to personal rights and that, when it comes to prosecuting crime, the government has the burden of proving guilt and the accused is under no obligation to assist in that endeavor. The fundamental principle that a person is innocent until proven guilty pervades the entire Bill of Rights, although it is not spelled out in any of the amendments.

Courts in the United States have spent considerable time interpreting the Fifth Amendment. In *McCarthy v. Arndstein* (1924), the Supreme Court held that the right against self-incrimination protected witnesses as well as the accused. And in *Griffin v. California* (1965), the Court prohibited prosecutors or the court from commenting adversely on the failure of a criminal defendant to testify since such a comment "is a remnant of the inquisitorial system."

Faced with the constitutional right against self-incrimination, police tended to rely on confessions. But in 1931, the Wickersham Commission documented widespread use of violent police tactics to extract involuntary confessions, especially from members of minority groups. In *Brown v. Mississippi* (1936), the Court threw out the convictions of three African Americans based on involuntary confessions extracted by brutal police whippings.

The Supreme Court finally stepped in and imposed fixed rules defining when a confession could be considered voluntary. In the landmark case *Miranda v. Arizona* (1966), the Court found that since the police interrogation room is inherently coercive and intimidating, no incriminating statements could be used unless the suspect was first read what has come to be known as the *Miranda*

warnings, popularized in police shows on television and in the movies: "You have the right to remain silent. If you give up that right, anything you say can and will be used against you in a court of law. You have the right to an attorney, who shall be present during your interrogation. If you cannot afford an attorney, one will be appointed for you at taxpayers' expense. Do you understand these rights?"

The *Miranda* decision represents a hallmark of the American criminal justice system. However, the Supreme Court has subsequently issued several opinions which have cut back on the *Miranda* doctrine. In *Harris v. New York* (1971), the Court held that incriminating statements made without the Miranda warnings could still be introduced into evidence to attack a defendant's credibility if he or she chooses to take the witness stand. In *Michigan v. Tucker* (1974), the Court held that, depending on the facts of each case, the failure to advise a suspect of the right to an appointed counsel before interrogation could be harmless error. In *New York v. Quarles* (1984), the Court held that, when a danger to public safety exists, the police may ask questions to remove the imminent danger before giving the Miranda warnings. In *Illinois v. Perkins* (1990), the Court held that Miranda warnings are not required when the suspect does not know that he or she is being officially interrogated in custody (as when the defendant unwittingly speaks to an undercover agent in his or her jail cell), with Justice Anthony Kennedy writing that "*Miranda* forbids coercion, not mere strategic deception." And in *Arizona v. Fulminante* (1991), the Court conceded that the defendant's confession was coerced by the threat of physical violence, but held that the conviction based on the confession need not be overturned if sufficient independent evidence supports a guilty verdict.

Double Jeopardy

The Fifth Amendment also protects against *double jeopardy,* which is an effort by the government to make more than one attempt to convict an individual for the same crime. Double jeopardy comes into play only if a person is acquitted. If the first jury is unable to reach a verdict or is discharged or if an appellate court returns a case to trial because of defects in the original indictment, the defendant may be tried a second time. The prohibition against double jeopardy is not violated when a person is prosecuted for the same act under both federal and state law. This rule was used against several members of the Los Angeles Police Department who were first acquitted on state charges of beating Rodney King, but then were convicted on separate federal charges.

Eminent Domain

At the other end of the spectrum from criminal rights, the Fifth Amendment also protects property rights by providing that "private property [shall not] be taken for public use without just compensation." This provision grows out of the framers' deep and abiding respect for the sanctity of private property, which many of them believed was the foundation for all personal liberties. Despite the elitism implicit in that concept (where do the propertyless derive their personal liberties?), constitutional respect for private property was taken for granted among the founders.

This provision of the Fifth Amendment is known as the Takings Clause. It simultaneously protects private property and recognizes the government's legitimate need from time to time to acquire private property for public use. Thus, the cornerstone of the Takings Clause is the constitutional requirement that if government elects to take private property, it must pay for it.

This is called *eminent domain*—the principle that since the existence of the state is the very precondition to the existence and protection of private property, the state may on occasion take such property for the benefit of the common good. In a state of nature, without a government and without laws, there is no private property, only the opportunity to stake a temporary claim to certain land for so long as one is powerful enough to defeat the efforts of others to steal it.

Yet there is something potentially dangerous in the notion that all private property is held at the pleasure of the state. Indeed, it is the opposite of the companion idea that all personal rights existed before there was a government. The Taking Clause is meant to temper the government's power to seize private property for public use by requiring that it pay "just compensation."

The legal procedure by which the government—local, state, or federal—exercises eminent domain is known as *condemnation*. For example, the government may condemn private property to build a highway or to construct a state office building or to do any number of things typically done by government. In the condemnation proceedings, the *fair market value*—what a willing buyer would pay to a willing seller—is established and the property is sold to the government at that price. So long as the court fixes the fair market value, the owner must

sell at that price. Otherwise, a single homeowner could block a multi-billion dollar freeway project designed to benefit millions of motorists.

Yet sometimes actions by the government, far short of taking property let alone destroying it, have run afoul of the Fifth Amendment. In *Causby v. United States* (1946), the Court held that flights of military aircraft just above the surface of adjacent privately owned farmland caused so much noise that the farm was rendered virtually worthless for agricultural purposes, and constituted a taking, thereby entitling the farmer to compensation.

As early as 1922 in *Pennsylvania Coal Co. v. Mahon*, Justice Oliver Wendell Holmes addressed the issue of when regulations, short of the government taking possession, sufficiently diminishes the value of private property so as to require the payment of just compensation. Holmes ruled that citizens must accept some impairment of the value of their property as part of the cost of living in a modern society, but that when such impairment results in the near total destruction of the value of such property, the public must bear the cost by paying just compensation.

Consequently, in *Euclid v. Ambler Realty Co.* (1926), the Court found that a zoning ordinance which banned industrial development in a particular area was a valid exercise of the government's powers and required no compensation, despite the claim of a landowner that the law reduced the potential uses of his land. However, in *Nectow v. City of Cambridge* (1928), the Court held that a similar restriction did constitute a taking requiring compensation, where the land was under a contract to be sold for industrial development and there were no other practical uses. In *Agins v. City of Tiburon* (1980), the Court adopted a test to balance the public benefit against the private loss: Does a land use restriction advance a legitimate state interest while still permitting an economically viable use of the property?

In applying the *Agins* test, the Court has not slighted the importance of private property even when it comes to such universally recognized concerns as protecting the environment. Thus, in *Kaiser Aetna v. United States* (1980), the Court found that requiring a landowner to provide public access to a private pond amounted to a taking justifying just compensation and in *Nollan v. California Coastal Commission* (1987), the Court held that the requirement of a coastal easement on private beachfront property constituted a regulatory taking deserving of just compensation.

The Supreme Court has demonstrated the Fifth Amendment's protection of private property and the framers foresight in anticipating the inevitable tension that arises as government expands to meet the needs of society.

Due Process

At the core of the Fifth Amendment is the phrase "due process of law," considered by one of the leading scholars of the U.S. Constitution to be "the most important and influential term in American constitutional law." The amendment provides that "no person may be deprived of life, liberty, or property without due process of law."

The first appearance of the term in America was in the Massachusetts Act of 1692, endorsing the Magna Carta. All of the state constitutions, however, used the more ancient formulation of "the law of the Land." The first American constitution to use the term "due process of law" was the U.S. Constitution in the Fifth Amendment. All four states that ratified the Constitution with recommendations for amendments urged that this concept be included, although only New York referred to it as "due process of law," which is the formulation James Madison preferred. (The phrase is repeated verbatim in the Fourteenth Amendment, extending constitutional protection for "due process of law" to the states.)

Due process of law applies to both civil and criminal matters and has both a procedural and substantive aspect. Overall, *due process* is a repository of all of the fundamental rights enjoyed by every individual in the face of the awesome power and authority possessed by the government. As Justice Felix Frankfurter put it in *Joint Anti-Fascist Committee v. McGrath* (1951): "No better instrument has been devised for arriving at truth than to give a person in jeopardy of serious loss notice of the case against him and an opportunity to meet it. Nor has a better way been found for generating the feeling, so important to a popular government, that justice has been done."

The essential task in deciding whether one is entitled to due process of law under the Fifth Amendment is first to determine whether "life, liberty, or property" is at stake and, if so, then to decide what process is due. No doubt exists over when life is at risk at the hands of the state, but the concepts of liberty and property have generated considerable debate.

In its narrowest sense, *liberty* means freedom from incarceration. Consequently, any act or threat by the state with the potential of putting someone behind bars or of limiting his or her liberty triggers a due process analysis. However, the notion of liberty has a broader meaning; it also encompasses and includes a constellation of personal interests, which are not entirely definable, but which represent what it means to be a free and autonomous individual. Viewed in this light, liberty can mean such things as a school child's security against corporal punishment, protected in *Ingraham v. Wright* (1977), or a parent's retention of child custody, protected in *Santosky v. Kramer* (1982).

For purposes of the Fifth Amendment, *property* means real estate and personal possessions which one owns or to which one has a lawful right and which one expects not to be arbitrarily taken away.

Assuming life, liberty, or property are at risk, how much process of law is due? The Fifth Amendment itself is of little or no help in answering this question. On the first occasion that the Supreme Court addressed the due process clause, in *Murray's Lessee v. Hoboken Land & Improvement Co.* (1856), it lamented that the "Constitution contains no description of those procedures which it was intended to allow or forbid. It does not even declare what principles are to be applied to ascertain whether it be due process."

Time and again when faced with the question of whether a safeguard in a civil or criminal proceeding is required by the Due Process Clause or whether the denial of a particular procedure violates the Due Process Clause, the Court has struggled to articulate an appropriate standard. The Court asks whether it was "of the very essence of a scheme of ordered liberty," or whether a "fair and enlightened system of justice would be impossible without it," or whether "liberty and justice" would exist if it were sacrificed, or whether it is among those "immutable principles of justice, acknowledged . . . wherever the good life is a subject of concern."

On other occasions, particularly when it comes to protecting the rights of persons accused of a crime, the Court asks whether the government's actions have violated a "principle of justice so rooted in the traditions and conscience of our people as to be ranked as fundamental," or whether it subjected a person to "a hardship so acute and shocking that our policy would not endure it," or whether it offended "those canons of decency and fairness which express the notions of justice of English-speaking peoples even toward those charged with the most heinous offenses," since due process "embodies a system of rights based on moral principles so deeply imbedded in the traditions and feelings of our people as to be deemed fundamental to a civilized society as conceived by our whole history."

Yet, there are still some things that can be said about due process with a high degree of certainty. The essence of due process of law is made up of three essential concepts: notice, an opportunity to be heard, and a fair and independent decision-maker. In both the civil and criminal realms, it is indefensible to deprive someone of life, liberty, or property without *at least* giving sufficient notice of the claims or charges being made, an adequate opportunity to present one's side of the case, and a determination by an unbiased, detached decision-maker who is independent of both sides and owes allegiance only to the truth.

On the substantive level, the Court has found that certain rights not spelled out in the Constitution or Bill of Rights are protected by the due process clause. Ironically, a principle which has led to the expansion of *personal* rights was first used in the service of *economic* rights. In *Allgeyer v. Louisiana* (1897), the Court, dominated by justices who believed strongly in *laissez-faire* capitalism (which favors the free marketplace over government regulations) found that part of "fundamental liberty" protected by the due process clause is the right to make contracts without governmental interference. While at first glance this appears to be an unassailable proposition, the Court used it to strike down legislation enacted to improve working conditions of employees in large factories and elsewhere. For example, in *Lochner v. New York* (1905), over a vigorous dissent by Justice Oliver Wendell Holmes, the majority of the Court declared unconstitutional a New York law restricting the number of hours per day that bakers could work because it violated the due process right of the bakers and their

employers to make contracts as they saw fit. Eventually Justice Holmes' dissent prevailed and in *Morehead v. New York ex rel. Tipaldo* (1936), Washington state's minimum wage law was upheld against a due process challenge.

The next time the concept of substantive due process emerged from the Supreme Court, 60 years after *Lochner*, the times and the Court had changed. In *Griswold v. Connecticut* (1965), the Court, by a 7-2 vote, struck down a statute prohibiting the use of birth control devices and the giving of birth control information, based in part on the due process clause of the Fifth Amendment. And in the historic decision in *Roe v. Wade* (1973), the Court, in another 7-2 decision, upheld a pregnant woman's right to an abortion during the first trimester, again, in part, on the grounds of substantive due process which Justice Harry Blackmun found was "broad enough to encompass a woman's decision whether or not to terminate her pregnancy." In dissent, Justice William Rehnquist, joined by Justice Byron White, maintained that there was no "fundamental" right to an abortion and that the Court should defer to the wishes of the majority, as expressed in state laws banning or restricting abortion.

The battle over *Roe v. Wade* and the controversy over substantive due process continues. Opponents of abortions believe that with new appointments to the Supreme Court, *Roe v. Wade* will be overruled, while defenders of women's reproductive rights urge that that decision was correctly decided and must be respected as a precedent of the Court.

On abortion and a multitude of other important issues affecting the life, liberty, and property of Americans, the debate over the meaning and the application of the due process clause shows no signs of abating.

Sixth Amendment (1791)

The Sixth Amendment is a catalogue of fundamental constitutional rights protecting persons accused of a crime.

VI

IN all criminal prosecutions, the accused shall enjoy the right to a speedy and public trial, by an impartial jury of the State and district wherein the crime shall have been committed, which district shall have been previously ascertained by law, and to be informed of the nature and cause of the accusation; to be confronted with the witnesses against him; to have **compulsory process** for obtaining witnesses in his favor, and to have the assistance of counsel for his defense.

NOTE

compulsory process: lawful means of requiring a person to testify or produce evidence.

COMMENTARY

The six rights protected in the Sixth Amendment are 1) the right to "a speedy and public trial"; 2) the right to "an impartial jury" chosen from people who live near the crime scene; 3) the right "to be informed of the nature and cause of the accusation"; 4) the right "to be confronted with the witnesses against him"; 5) the right "to have compulsory process for obtaining witnesses in his favor"; and 6) the right "to have the assistance of counsel for his defense."

The Right to a Speedy and Public Trial

The framers understood the risks posed to personal liberty if trials were endlessly delayed. For defendants held in jail awaiting trial, every day is a punishment. Unwarranted delays jeopardize a defendant's ability to present an effective defense: Witnesses die. Evidence is lost. Memories fade.

The Sixth Amendment does not define "speedy" and sets no specific time limits by which the accused must be brought to trial. In 1974, Congress passed the Speedy Trial Act which set a general deadline of 100 days between arrest and trial in federal courts. Many states have passed similar laws.

The framers also understood that trials should be public. English history is marked by dark periods when trials were held in secret. Government abuse, politically motivated prosecutions, and gross denial of basic rights can too easily be hidden from scrutiny when trials are not held in public.

The Supreme Court has held that the "public trial" clause of the Sixth Amendment was solely for the benefit of the defendant, who could waive it and that neither the press nor members of the public had any standing to challenge such a ruling. But it also found that excluding the press from a criminal trial was unconstitutional. Today, most states allow cameras in the courtroom, although federal courts, including the U.S. Supreme Court, still do not.

Trial by Jury

Trial by an impartial jury has come to be seen as essential to both the criminal justice system and self-government.

By the time of the Revolution, trial by jury had taken on a political dimension as a means of checking the unlimited power of the King. Consequently, the right to a jury trial appears once in the Constitution and twice in the Bill of Rights, in the Sixth and Seventh Amendments.

Today, the jury system serves what the Supreme Court in *Witherspoon v. Illinois* (1968) called "the conscience of the community." There is a widespread belief that when presented with evidence offered by both sides and when instructed by the judge on the applicable law, a jury assembled from the community will generally figure out who is telling the truth, what actually happened, and what the proper outcome should be.

The Court in the case of *In re Winship* (1970) confirmed that jurors must find criminal defendants guilty "beyond a reasonable doubt" (a standard found nowhere in the Constitution). In criminal cases, the Court held in *Burch v. Louisiana* (1979) that a jury must render a unanimous verdict, while civil juries can generally reach decisions by a 9-3 vote. The Court has held that neither side in a trial may exclude a potential juror solely on the basis of race (*Batson v. Kentucky* [1986]) or gender (*J.E.B. v. Alabama ex rel. T.B.* [1994]).

Due Process of the Law

Elaborating on the Due Process clause of the Fifth Amendment, the Sixth Amendment expressly guarantees the right "to be informed of the nature and cause of the accusation." No system worthy of calling itself fair and just can convict a defendant of a crime unless that defendant is informed in advance what crime is being charged. In order to mount a defense, present an alibi, identify witnesses, accumulate evidence, and assert an adequate defense, a defendant must be informed of the accusation. The framers were all too familiar with politically-motivated prosecutions in which suspects were held incommunicado without any idea of why they had been arrested or with what crimes they had been charged. This part of the Sixth Amendment was intended to prevent that from happening in America. Unfortunately, there have been occasions when alleged concerns over national security or terrorism have superseded this constitutional right.

The Right to Call and Confront Witnesses

The right to be confronted by adverse witnesses guaranteed by the Sixth Amendment was intended by the framers to prevent the government from convicting a defendant on the basis of the testimony of witnesses the defendant had never had the chance to observe. Obviously, defendants cannot defend themselves or assist their counsel without knowing what witnesses will be called by the prosecution. The only area in which the Court has qualified the right to confront adverse witnesses is in cases involving child victims.

In addition to having the right to confront witnesses, the Sixth Amendment guarantees the accused the right to compel witnesses to appear in court. This is accomplished through the issuance of "compulsory process" generally in the form of a *subpoena*, which requires an individual to come to court or risk a contempt citation, involving a potential fine or jail sentence. The prosecution can subpoena all the witnesses it wants. Under this amendment, the defendant can do likewise. There's no guarantee that the witnesses will be found or will appear—only that the accused has the opportunity to invoke the same subpoena power as the state.

The Right of Legal Counsel

Last but hardly least of the indispensable rights guaranteed in the Sixth Amendment is the right "to have the assistance of counsel." Some scholars believe that when this amendment was ratified in 1791, this provision only meant that the government could not prevent a criminal defendant from hiring an attorney to assist in his or her defense, but did *not* mean that the government had to provide an attorney if the defendant could not afford one.

The Supreme Court first seriously addressed the constitutional right to counsel in the celebrated case of *Powell v. Alabama* (1932), in which nine illiterate young black men, who would come to be known as the "Scottsboro Boys," were charged with raping two white women. When no lawyer volunteered to represent any of them, the trial judge facetiously appointed "all the members of the bar." Three separate trials were held, each lasting only a day, and eight of the defendants were convicted and sentenced to death. Eventually, the Supreme Court held that in the "special circumstances" of this case the defendants' Sixth Amendment right to have counsel appointed for them had been violated. In *Johnson v. Zerbst* (1938) the Supreme Court abandoned the case-by-case approach and squarely held that in serious criminal cases the Sixth Amendment encompassed not only the right of a defendant to hire private legal counsel, but the companion right to have counsel appointed by the state if the defendant could not afford one.

Having settled the right to counsel at a criminal trial, the issue remained whether a suspect was entitled to appointed counsel at any time *prior* to trial. In *Escobedo v. Illinois* (1964), a closely divided Court, in a 5-4 decision, held that as soon as police interrogation focused on a suspect, even before he or she is charged with a crime, the suspect has the right to appointed counsel. And in the landmark case of *Miranda v. Arizona* (1966), the Court stated that whenever a suspect is taken into custody he or she must be given the famous Miranda warnings (discussed in connection with the Fifth Amendment), including the right to appointed counsel.

The final issue regarding the right to counsel is whether a defendant has a constitutional right to a *good* lawyer. The Court has held that a defendant's Sixth Amendment rights are violated if he or she receives ineffective assistance of counsel resulting in reversible error at trial.

In the end, all the Bill of Rights can do is guarantee fundamental rights. It is the men and women who act as lawyers, judges, jurors, prosecutors, and police officers who must see to it that the constitutional rights of those charged with crimes are fully respected and conscientiously implemented. Indeed, that is the duty of all citizens.

Seventh Amendment (1791)

The Seventh Amendment guarantees a jury trial in civil cases and ensures that the facts decided by a jury may not be re-examined by a federal court.

VII

IN suits at common law, where the value in controversy shall exceed twenty dollars, the right of trial by jury shall be preserved, and no fact tried by a jury shall be otherwise re-examined in any court of the United States, than according to the rules of the common law.

COMMENTARY

Few delegates to the Constitutional Convention anticipated the controversy over the provision in Article III giving the Supreme Court jurisdiction "both as to law and fact." Anti-Federalists argued that the provision would deny the right of trial by jury in civil cases.

The purpose of the Seventh Amendment was not to expand the right to a jury trial but to preserve it as it then existed. Existing common law made two distinctions when it came to the right to a jury trial. Cases in *equity* were tried exclusively by judges without a jury, while cases in *law* were tried before both a judge and a jury—the judge having the sole power to decide the law and the jury having the sole power to decide the facts. Generally, cases in *law* result in verdicts for money damages, while cases in *equity* result in court-ordered decrees such as injunctions preventing (or mandating) certain actions, or declaratory judgments, in which a judge decides the respective rights and duties of the parties under a contract or a statute.

It was vitally important to the Founders that the right to a jury trial be protected. After all, King George's denial of a trial by a jury of one's peers (or equals) was a major cause of the Revolutionary War. The founding generation saw the jury, made up of common folks, as a shield against overzealous prosecutors or corrupt judges. In a very real sense, the jury was seen as an integral part of "self government," keeping as much decision-making power in the hands of the people as possible.

Consequently, the fact that Article III of the Constitution gives the Supreme Court jurisdiction "both as to Law and Fact, with such Exceptions, and under such Regulations as the Congress shall make" posed twin threats for those who valued the right of the jury to be the final arbiter of questions of fact. First, Article III suggested that the Supreme Court could reverse factual findings made by a jury. Second, the fact that Article III gave Congress the power to make "Exceptions" and enact "Regulations" raised the possibility of partisan political squabbles, further jeopardizing the rights of individual litigants. Since the Seventh Amendment has not been made applicable to the states, state courts are free, under federal constitutional law, to dispense with juries altogether in civil cases.

The U.S. Supreme Court has jealously guarded the right to a jury trial. In *Beacon Theatres Inc. v. Westover* (1964), Justice Black stated that only "under the most imperative circumstances," could the right to a jury trial be lost due to the fact that the court had previously decided related equitable claims.

Eighth Amendment (1791)

Three separate issues are covered by the Eighth Amendment: 1) that "excessive bail shall not be required," 2) that "excessive fines" shall not be imposed, and 3) that "cruel and unusual punishment" shall not be inflicted.

VIII

EXCESSIVE bail shall not be required nor excessive fines imposed, nor cruel and unusual punishments inflicted.

COMMENTARY

The Eighth Amendment is the third time that the Bill of Rights devotes an amendment to issues involving the criminal justice system, demonstrating just how seriously the framers felt about protecting the individual rights of persons accused of crimes. That the amendment prohibits only "excessive bail" leaves open the question of whether there is a constitutional right to bail at all. Surely if a criminal defendant cannot be constitutionally required to post an "excessive bail," it follows that he or she is therefore entitled to a "reasonable bail," although curiously that is not the way the Eighth Amendment is written.

The language of the bail clause was taken verbatim from the Virginia Declaration of Rights of 1776 drafted by George Mason, who had in turn taken it directly from the 1689 English Bill of Rights. Mason saw bail as a means of protecting civil liberties. Having been charged with a crime, given the presumption of innocence (an ancient principle so well-established that it is not spelled out in either the Constitution or the Bill of Rights), a person should remain free so long as he or she promises to return to court for trial and posts financial assets *(bail)* to secure that promise. Presumably, Mason borrowed the language believing a right to bail was assumed but that the abuse of "excessive" bail had to be prohibited.

Mason's assumptions, apparently shared by James Madison when he wrote the Bill of Rights, have been borne out by statements by the U.S. Supreme Court to the effect that bail reflects the "traditional right to freedom before conviction" lest "the presumption of innocence, secured only after centuries of struggle, would lose its meaning" (*Stack v. Boyle* [1951]) and that bail "is basic to our system of law" (*Schilb v. Kuebel* [1971]).

At times, however, the Court has carved out exceptions to the right to bail. In *Carlson v. Landon* (1951), the very same year in which the Court in *Stack* was applauding bail as a "traditional right," it ruled that alien communists could be held without bail pending deportation, and in *Schall v. Martin* (1984), the Court ruled that an accused juvenile could be held in "preventive detention" without bail pending the outcome of a family court hearing.

The right to bail was seriously limited by the 1984 federal Bail Reform Act and several state constitutions and statutes which permit preventive detention of those charged with *non-capital* crimes (crimes that do not qualify for the death penalty) if a court finds that pretrial release poses a danger of future criminal activity.

As for the definition of "excessive" bail, the courts simply apply a reasonable rule based on the amount normally imposed for the same crime in the same geographical area.

Excessive Fines

The second prohibition covered by the Eighth Amendment is against "excessive fines." This provision has generated little controversy or Supreme Court review in the area of criminal law. Generally, so long as a fine is proportionate to the crime and in keeping with fines imposed for the same or similar crimes, no constitutional issue is raised. Ironically, in the civil area, large corporations have attempted (unsuccessfully) to invoke the "excessive fines" clause to strike down punitive damages in class-actions and other tort claims.

Cruel and Unusual Punishment

The most important provision in the Eighth Amendment is the prohibition on "cruel and unusual punishment." Derived from the English Bill of Rights of 1688, the prohibition against cruel and unusual punishment is intended to prevent shockingly barbarous punishments, including an array of horrible torture methods associated with the Middle Ages.

As thumbscrews and beheadings became a thing of the past, American law viewed the prohibition against cruel and unusual punishment more flexibly in order to adapt to the "evolving standards of decency" of a maturing society (*Trop v. Dulles* [1958]). As early as 1910, in *Weems v. United States*, the Court held that a conviction for being an accessory to the falsification of a public document did not justify a sentence of 12 to 20 years at hard labor in chains and permanent deprivation of civil rights.

By any measure, the most controversial issue under the Eighth Amendment is whether the prohibition against cruel and unusual punishment outlaws the death penalty. It is difficult to make the case that when the Bill of Rights was written the framers intended the prohibition against cruel and unusual punishment to ban capital punishment. After all, the death penalty is referred to three times in the Fifth Amendment, which specifically acknowledges capital crimes and prohibits a defendant being "put in jeopardy of life and limb" twice for the same offense or being "deprived of life, liberty, or property without due process of law."

The Supreme Court held in *Furman v. Georgia* (1972) that capital punishment is cruel and unusual. Justice William O. Douglas read an equality element into the prohibition against cruel and unusual punishment given how disproportionately the death penalty is applied to the poor and socially disadvantaged. Justices Potter Stewart and Byron White found that the death penalty was used so rarely that it is cruel and unusual to impose it in those few cases.

In reaction to the *Furman* decision, 35 states revised their death penalty statutes in an effort to overcome the defects identified by the Court, and in *Gregg v. Georgia* (1976) the Court upheld capital punishment laws which required a trial separating the guilt from the penalty phase, in which aggravating circumstances are weighed against mitigating circumstances. Subsequent challenges to the death penalty have centered on other provisions of the Constitution including the Due Process and Equal Protection Clauses, in light of evidence that capital punishment is applied disproportionately against the poor and people of color.

If a majority on the Supreme Court comes to adopt the view that the prohibition on cruel and unusual punishment has evolved to adapt to modern circumstances, the United States may some day join most other civilized countries and abolish the death penalty.

Ninth Amendment (1791)

The Ninth Amendment provides that the fact that certain rights are specifically set forth in the Constitution shall not deny or disparage other rights retained by the people.

IX

THE enumeration in the Constitution, of certain rights, shall not be construed to deny or disparage others retained by the people.

COMMENTARY

When in 1789 James Madison, a freshman Congressman, set about to draft the Bill of Rights, he had a problem. How could he take it upon himself to list *every* fundamental personal right enjoyed by the citizens of the new nation? While the Declaration of Independence spoke boldly of certain "unalienable rights" enjoyed by every person, it did not attempt to list all of them. Indeed, at the Constitution Convention in 1787, one of the most powerful arguments *against* including a Bill of Rights was that there was a serious risk that if a fundamental right were overlooked, its omission could later be cited as evidence that no such constitutional right existed.

Designing an Amendment

Eventually, Madison found a solution to this problem, as he had so often in his role as the key draftsman of the Constitution and Bill of Rights. Faced with drawing up a complete list of fundamental personal rights, he included a catch-all clause, which eventually became the Ninth Amendment.

It rather straight-forwardly states that the *enumeration,* or listing, "of certain rights in the Constitution" (including presumably its amendments, such as the rest of the Bill of Rights) "shall not be construed to deny or disparage others retained by the people."

In other words, the Ninth Amendment candidly recognizes that there are other rights which belong to the people which are *not* enumerated or listed in the Constitution. Consequently, the Ninth Amendment dispels the notion that the only rights citizens enjoy are the ones expressly spelled out in the Constitution. It ensures that the Constitution is not seen as a rigid document frozen in 1787.

The Ninth Amendment confirms something else vitally important about the relationship between the people and their government: It refers to these "other" rights as being "retained by the people." The word "retained" is very important. It underscores that the *source* of our constitutional rights resides with the people themselves, not with the government. Consistent with the idea clearly articulated in the Preamble to the Declaration of Independence that the people are "endowed" with "certain unalienable rights," the Ninth Amendment speaks of unenumerated rights as being "retained" by the people.

Therefore, it is beyond dispute in the American system that we begin with the image of the individual possessing all of the rights he or she was born with. The individual is "endowed" with these rights, they are not granted or bestowed by any government. These rights are "unalienable"; they cannot be taken away without the consent of the individual or through constitutionally established laws. And the fact that some of these rights may be explicitly set forth in the Constitution or its amendments in no way means that all other rights "retained" by the people are not entitled to equal protection.

Given the importance of the Ninth Amendment in the entire constitutional scheme, it may come as a surprise that no U.S. Supreme Court decision has yet been based squarely on an interpretation of the Ninth Amendment.

It was not until 1965 that the Ninth Amendment became the focus of any Supreme Court attention. After two decades of not enforcing a law that prohibited the use of contraceptives, Connecticut prosecuted a doctor for giving contraceptive advice to a married couple in a family planning clinic. He was charged with "aiding and abetting" a violation of the state law which prohibited the use of contraceptives.

The case, *Griswold v. Connecticut* (1965), presented a difficult problem for a majority of the Justices who believed that only arbitrary, capricious, or invidiously dis-criminatory laws, or those that violated a specific consti-tutional right, could be invalidated. All of the Justices agreed that in regulating the conjugal affairs of married couples, the law was ill advised. But the Court had to identify the provision of the Constitution that prohibits a state legislature from attempting to discourage extra-marital sexual relations. Connecticut claimed that in order to achieve the objective of deterring sex outside of mar-riage, the state could constitutionally prohibit the use of *all* contraceptives—including contraceptives for married people—thus making them less available. If no specific constitutional right had been violated, could Connecticut constitutionally make its own laws, leaving it to the peo-ple, through their elected representatives, to change them by electing other representatives through the demo-cratic process?

The Supreme Court's answer, in an opinion by Justice William O. Douglas, was to recognize a constitutional right of marital privacy which was found in "penumbras, formed by emanations" from other guarantees found in enumerated rights, specifically those in the First, Third, Fourth, and Fifth Amendments. Justice Douglas was say-ing that surrounding each amendment there are addi-tional margins or zones that enhance and enlarge the rights expressly stated in the amendment. The Ninth Amendment was also mentioned, but the constitutional approach of the majority was to expand *existing* enu-merated rights in order to establish a new right of mari-tal privacy.

Chief Justice Earl Warren and Justices Arthur Gold-berg and William J. Brennan, Jr., in a concurring opinion by Justice Goldberg, relied specifically on the Ninth Amendment as an additional basis for striking down the Connecticut law. Justice Goldberg's standard for defin-ing rights "retained by the people" referred to funda-mental rights and to the "traditions" and "conscience of our people." This language prompted a vigorous dissent from Justice Hugo L. Black, who accused the majority and concurring Justices of engaging in unprincipled per-sonal jurisprudence.

The Decision's Aftereffects

The *Griswold* case might have been regarded merely as a slight and unique broadening of enumerated rights to encompass the basic right to decide whether or not to conceive a child were it not for the impact of the emerg-ing women's rights movement emerging throughout the country during the 1960s and 1970s. Women were moving steadily toward equality of opportunity to participate in American life. Attitudes about private sexual behavior, marriage, cohabitation, and family relationships were all showing a greater respect for individual choice.

In the 1970s, the Court responded by recognizing some of these new attitudes and guaranteeing them as consti-tutionally protected rights. In *Eisenstadt v. Baird* (1972), for example, the principles of *Griswold* were extended to include the right of *unmarried* persons to obtain and use contraceptives. And in the historic decision *Roe v. Wade* (1973), the Court guaranteed constitutional protection for a woman's right to procure an abortion, particularly dur-ing the first 26 weeks of pregnancy.

The Ninth Amendment was mentioned in *Roe v. Wade*, but only as one of a number of constitutional provisions to support the Court's conclusion that "liberty" encom-passed a woman's decisions about childbearing. Justice Douglas, who had written the majority opinion in *Griswold*, based his concurrence in *Roe v. Wade* prima-rily on the Ninth Amendment and suggested a broad range of personal autonomy rights such as "control over development and expression of one's intellect, interest, tastes, and personality," "freedom of choice in the basic decisions of one's life respecting marriage, divorce, pro-creation, contraception, and the education and upbring-ing of children," "freedom to care for one's health and person, freedom from bodily restraint or compulsion, free-dom to walk, stroll, or loaf."

The Supreme Court deals with unenumerated rights primarily through the technique employed in *Griswold* and in similar cases that followed. The Court generally tries to base its decisions on one or more *specific* constitu-tional provisions, and then expands those provisions to include new rights.

The Ninth Amendment was the original safety net to compensate for the imperfection of language and the impossibility of anticipating changing circumstances. Such an approach leaves room for a gradual expansion of rights, but does it require some grounding for each newly recognized right in the constitutional text?

It remains to be seen how the Supreme Court will interpret the Ninth Amendment in light of *Griswold*, *Roe*, and related cases. Is it a mere footnote to the rest of the Bill of Rights with little meaning or importance? Is it a helpful but limited adjunct to the rights already set forth in the Constitution? Or, is it the repository of other funda-mental rights waiting to be enlisted in future battles?

Tenth Amendment (1791)

The Tenth Amendment reserves to the states all powers not delegated to the Congress by the Constitution.

X

THE powers not delegated to the United States by the Constitution, nor prohibited by it to the States, are reserved to the States respectively, or to the people.

COMMENTARY

As the Ninth Amendment guarantees that the people possess all other *rights* not spelled out in the Constitution, the Tenth Amendment guarantees that all *powers* not delegated to the federal government in the Constitution or prohibited to the States are "reserved to the states respectively, or to the people."

The Reasons for the Amendment

The Tenth Amendment reveals just how suspicious of the new federal government most of the Founders were. Having recently fought a bloody war to rid themselves of an all-powerful King and an overbearing Parliament, the last thing the Founders wanted was to create an all-powerful national government to usurp the powers of the state governments, which saw themselves as sovereign and independent and far closer to the will and desire of the people.

Indeed, the Articles of Confederation, which were entirely thrown out to make way for the Constitution, explicitly provided that "each state retains its sovereignty," and many state constitutions contained provisions declaring the primacy of the states over the Confederation. Yet the new Constitution contained none of this. On the contrary, after listing the specific powers granted to Congress, the Constitution in Article I, Section 8, gives *Congress* the power to enact laws to carry out those powers. And on top of that, Article VI requires state judges to uphold the Constitution and the "supreme Law of the Land."

Consequently, it comes as no surprise that when the new Constitution was sent to the States for ratification, the most popular amendment was a clause reserving to the states all powers not delegated to Congress. That clause eventually became the Tenth Amendment. Defenders of the Constitution could not see what all the fuss was about. Writing in No. 39 of *The Federalist* (1788), James Madison, an ardent supporter of the Constitution, tried to reassure critics that each state remained "a sovereign body." Other Federalists, such as Alexander Hamilton and John Marshall, argued that the new government was a creature of *limited* authority confined only to the specific powers granted by the Constitution.

In the end, the Federalists decided that a "reserved power amendment" would do no harm and would actually help gather support for ratification of the Constitution. After all, it was useless to argue over the powers of Congress if the Constitution was never ratified. Therefore, Madison assured his opponents that if the Constitution were ratified, appropriate amendments would be offered in the First Congress. A man of his word, in 1789 Madison proposed the Bill of Rights, which ended with the Tenth Amendment.

Having won ratification and viewing the Tenth Amendment as innocuous, proponents of a robust and energetic federal government, such as Hamilton, set about the business of building a new nation equipped to play an ambitious role in the world. Among other things, Hamilton pushed for the adoption of a national bank. He was met with opposition from a powerful figure, Thomas Jefferson, who had advised President George Washington that he viewed the incorporation of a national bank as unconstitutional on the grounds that it exceeded the powers delegated to Congress, even before the Tenth Amendment had been ratified.

The Supreme Court Weighs In

The conflict between states' rights and the supremacy of the federal government reached the U.S. Supreme Court in 1819 in the landmark case of *McCulloch v. Maryland*, in which the national bank was upheld as constitutional, even though it is not mentioned anywhere in the Constitution. The case arose when the state of Maryland imposed a tax on the Second National Bank, which its employee, McCulloch, refused to pay. The United States justified the bank under the Necessary and Proper Clause in Article I of the Constitution. Maryland argued that this clause did not expand the powers of Congress, but merely gave Congress very limited authority to do only what was absolutely necessary to carry out its enumerated powers, which is precisely what the Federalists had assured everyone during the ratification debates.

But, in an opinion by Chief Justice John Marshall (who had been an outspoken supporter of the Constitution during the ratification debates 31 years earlier), the Court adopted a broad interpretation of the Necessary and Proper Clause, finding that it contained "implied powers," which included the power to establish the national bank. Marshall theorized that the Constitution envisioned that Congress would be authorized to pursue a limited set of national ends or purposes. However, the framers did not and could not spell out all of the various legislative means appropriate to achieving these constitutional ends, especially given changing historical, economic, political, and social circumstances.

Consequently, so long as an act of Congress is in pursuit of a purpose set forth in the Constitution, any legislation that furthers that end is constitutional. According to Marshall, this line of reasoning did not contradict the Tenth Amendment, which the First Congress had drafted without limiting itself to those powers "expressly granted," as had the Articles of Confederation.

The decision in *McCulloch* came at a pivotal moment in American history. Had Congress' powers been truncated in favor of state sovereignty, the United States might have been hobbled in its role as a world economic player, returning to the disunity that existed under the Articles of Confederation. On the other hand, *McCulloch* and an endless stream of subsequent decisions that generally upheld an expansive view of Congress' power to enact legislation in a vast array of areas touching almost every facet of life have been criticized as granting far too much power to the federal government.

With the Civil War, Reconstruction, industrialization, and two World Wars, the authority and influence of the federal government expanded greatly, while the authority of the states shrank, due in part to a series of Supreme Court decisions that paid little or no attention to the Tenth Amendment. In *Champion v. Ames* (1903), the Supreme Court upheld a federal law prohibiting the sale of lottery tickets across state lines, despite the fact that gambling had traditionally been regulated by the states. In *United States v. Darby Lumber Co.* (1941), the Court held that Congress, regardless of its underlying purposes, could stop any goods from moving in interstate commerce, regardless of whether they were manufactured in conformity with state law. Writing for the majority, Justice Harlan Fiske Stone discredited the Tenth Amendment as "redundant" and a "constitutional tranquilizer and empty declaration." Stone dismissed the amendment as a "truism," merely expressing the obvious notion that Congress could only exercise the powers granted to it in the Constitution though the amendment does not identify or limit those powers.

Changes in Interpretation

Interpretation of the Tenth Amendment has seesawed in the Supreme Court in the last part of the twentieth century. In *Fry v. United States* (1975), the Court revived the Tenth Amendment, holding that it "expressly declares the constitutional policy that Congress may not exercise power in a fashion that impairs the States' integrity or their ability to function effectively in a federal system." And the very next year, in *National League of Cities v. Usery* (1976), the Court invalidated federal usage and hour standards for state employees, comparing states' rights "regarding the conduct of integral governmental functions" to the rights of individuals protected by the Bill of Rights.

But the *Usery* decision threatened to impede the development of uniform nationwide standards in the areas of civil liberties and environmental protection, and it was overruled in *Garcia v. San Antonio Metropolitan Transit Authority* (1985), with the Court preferring to protect state interests through legislation enacted by elected representatives in Congress, instead of judicial intervention.

The *Garcia* decision appeared to have settled the matter until the Tenth Amendment was given renewed importance in a series of unanticipated Supreme Court decisions in the 1990s. In *United States v. Lopez* (1995), the Court, in a 5-4 decision written by Chief Justice William H. Rehnquist, found that the Gun-Free School Zone Act, making it a federal crime to possess a gun within 1,000 feet of a school, violated the Tenth Amendment. Rehnquist stated that Congress could regulate only "those activities that have a substantial relationship to interstate commerce," and that since gun laws were traditionally a concern of local police power, the possession of guns near a school had nothing to do with interstate commerce.

Although some observers treated the *Lopez* decision as an aberration, two years later, in *Printz v. United States* (1997), another 5-4 decision, the Court struck down a key provision of the Brady Handgun Violence Prevention Act of 1993, which required state officials to conduct background checks on gun buyers. Justice Antonin Scalia, writing for the majority, held that the Constitution established a system of dual sovereignty and that the states, as an essential attribute of their "retained" powers under the Tenth Amendment, are "independent and autonomous within their proper sphere of authority."

In his dissenting opinion, Justice John Paul Stevens argued that the commerce clause in the Constitution authorized Congress to regulate the interstate commerce in handguns and that nothing in the Tenth Amendment prohibits Congress from delegating enforcement to the states.

Notes

AMERICAN WORDS OF FREEDOM

SUBSEQUENT AMENDMENTS

More Work to be Done 111

Eleventh Amendment (1798) 113

Twelfth Amendment (1804) 114

Thirteenth Amendment (1865) 116

Fourteenth Amendment (1868) 120

Fifteenth Amendment (1870) 123

Sixteenth Amendment (1913) 127

Seventeenth Amendment (1913) 128

Eighteenth Amendment (1919) 129

Nineteenth Amendment (1920) 130

Twentieth Amendment (1933) 132

Twenty-First Amendment (1933) 134

Twenty-Second Amendment (1947) 136

Twenty-Third Amendment (1961) 137

Twenty-Fourth Amendment (1964) 138

Twenty-Fifth Amendment (1967) 139

Twenty-Sixth Amendment (1971) 141

Twenty-Seventh Amendment (1992) 142

More Work to be Done

With the ratification of the Bill of Rights on December 15, 1791, most of the framers believed they had accomplished the twin goals of designing a new national government and guaranteeing personal liberties. No doubt they were proud of their work, yet they had no illusions that the process of amending the Constitution was at an end.

The framers had included in Article V of the Constitution a workable means to amend the national charter. It was a two-step procedure involving separate super-majorities in order to maintain both stability *and* flexibility. First, either two-thirds of both Houses of Congress or two-thirds of the state legislatures have to propose an amendment and then three-fourths of the state legislatures or three-fourths of special state conventions must ratify it.

Given the struggles and triumphs marking American history, the Constitution has proven to be remarkably stable, helping the country to navigate through times of unrest and division. Since 1789, 5,000 bills proposing constitutional amendments have been introduced in Congress, but only 33 have received the necessary two-thirds vote of both Houses of Congress to be sent to the states for ratification, resulting in 27 amendments which were ratified and 6 which were not.

With a few exceptions, all of the amendments have been adopted and ratified during four brief periods in American history. From 1789 to 1804, the Bill of Rights (the first ten amendments) and the Eleventh and Twelfth Amendments were approved. More than a half century would pass before the Thirteenth, Fourteenth, and Fifteenth Amendments, known as the Civil War Amendments, were adopted between 1865 and 1870. Another half century intervened before the Populist and Progressive movement from 1913 to 1920 prompted the Sixteenth, Seventeenth, Eighteenth, and Nineteenth Amendments. Finally, between 1961 and 1978, the Twenty-Third, Twenty-Fourth, Twenty-Fifth, and Twenty-Sixth Amendments were approved.

By far the largest proportion of the amendments deal with elections and voting rights. Ten of the seventeen amendments after the Bill of Rights (the Twelfth, Fifteenth, Seventeenth, Nineteenth, Twentieth, Twenty-Second, Twenty-Third, Twenty-Fourth, Twenty-Fifth, and Twenty-Sixth) address these issues, while two (the Thirteenth and Fourteenth) deal with civil rights, two (the Eighteenth and Twenty-First) with imposing Prohibition and then repealing it, and one each on the judicial system (the Eleventh), income taxes (the Sixteenth), and compensation of senators and representatives (the Twenty-Seventh).

Failed Amendments

Almost 10,000 amendments have been proposed at one time or another, but have never gotten through Congress. Some of the failed amendments include the abolition of the Senate (1876), replacing the president with an Executive Council of Three (1818), renaming the country the "United States of the Earth" (1893), abolishing the U.S. Army and Navy (1893), acknowledging that the Constitution recognizes God and Jesus Christ as the supreme authorities in human affairs (1894), making marriage between races illegal (1912), making divorce illegal (1914), requiring a national vote on declaring war (anyone voting yes would be required to volunteer for the Army) (1916), limiting personal wealth to $1,000,000 (1933), limiting income taxes for an individual to 25 percent (1947), guaranteeing the right of citizens to segregate themselves from others (1948), and assuring all American citizens the right to an environment free of pollution (1971).

Six amendments have been approved by Congress but never ratified by the states, including amendments to strip any American who accepts a title of nobility or a gift, pension, office, or emolument from a foreign power of citizenship; to prohibit any amendment to the Constitution which would authorize Congress to abolish or interfere with slavery; and authorizing Congress to limit, regulate, and prohibit the labor of persons under 18 years of age.

In 1972, Congress proposed the Equal Rights Amendment which simply stated that: "Equality of rights under the law shall not be denied or abridged by the United States or by any State on account of sex." Over 750 variations of this amendment had been proposed since 1928. The Equal Rights Amendment failed to be ratified and expired on June 20, 1982.

Recently, unsuccessful amendments have been proposed to balance the federal budget, to allow prayers in public schools, and to ban the desecration of the American flag.

More to Come?

The subsequent amendments are a testament to the resilience of the Constitution and the genius of the system devised by the framers that provides a "safety valve" for the will of the people to alter the structure of government without reducing the Constitution to a mere ordinance to be changed cavalierly or in response to the fickle winds of temporary crises.

Eleventh Amendment (1798)

Under the Eleventh Amendment, federal courts do *not* have jurisdiction over suits brought against a state by the citizens of another state or foreign country.

XI

The judicial power of the United States shall not be construed to extend to any suit in law or equity, commenced or prosecuted against one of the United States by citizens of another state, or by citizens or subjects of any foreign state.

COMMENTARY

The conflict over whether individual states would maintain their sovereignty and independence in the face of the new energetic federal government created by the U.S. Constitution did not disappear with its ratification in 1788. The issue triggered both the first constitutional law case decided by the U.S. Supreme Court and, in retaliation the Eleventh Amendment.

Article III of the Constitution extends the judicial power of the United States to all cases and controversies "between a State and citizens of another State" and gives the Supreme Court jurisdiction in all cases in which a state is a party. Anti-Federalists, who opposed ratification of the Constitution, warned that Article III would destroy state sovereignty by giving federal judges the authority to issue judgments and decrees against individual states. Supporters of the Constitution, including James Madison and Alexander Hamilton, eager to win ratification, countered that Article III covered only suits in which a state had consented to be sued or had filed the case itself. These reassurances carried the day and the Constitution was ratified.

Yet fears over state sovereignty persisted, the states' and the Anti-Federalists' worst nightmare came true in 1793 when Article III was tested in the Supreme Court in the case *Chisholm v. Georgia.* A South Carolinian executor of the estate of a man whose lands had been confiscated by Georgia during the Revolutionary War sued the state of Georgia in federal court for restitution of the value of the property. In a 4 to 1 decision (at that time there were only 5 justices), the Supreme Court upheld the lawsuit. Chief Justice John Jay and Associate Justice James Wilson delivered forceful opinions endorsing a broad interpretation of federal jurisdiction.

The *Chisholm* decision ignited a firestorm of controversy. Anti-Federalists were outraged that the Constitution had been ratified under the false pretense that states could *not* be sued in federal court without their consent. Now the Supreme Court ruled the very opposite. Consequently, in March 1794, with lopsided majorities of 23–2 in the Senate and 81–9 in the House of Representatives, Congress proposed the Eleventh Amendment. By February 1795, the legislatures of three-fourths of the states had ratified it, but due to administrative delays, adoption of the Eleventh Amendment was not proclaimed until 1798.

The Eleventh Amendment overturned the *Chisholm* decision by declaring that the judicial power of the United States did not extend to lawsuits filed against a state by a citizen of another state or foreign country.

The Eleventh Amendment does not preclude a state from being sued in federal court by another state or by the United States, nor does it prevent a state from filing suits in federal courts. In addition, a state may waive its immunity from suit in federal court, and while generally such waivers must be explicit, on occasion implied waivers have been upheld.

The immunity afforded by the Eleventh Amendment extends to state governments and their agencies, but not to political subdivisions, such as counties, cities, or towns. Likewise, state officials may be sued in federal court for acts performed or threatened under unconstitutional state legislation, provided the official knew or reasonably should have known that the statute was unconstitutional based on prior binding judicial interpretation, under the doctrine of "qualified immunity."

Twelfth Amendment (1804)

The Twelfth Amendment provides that electors vote for president and vice president in separate ballots. If no candidate receives a majority of electoral votes for president, the House of Representatives (voting by states) selects the president and if no candidate receives a majority of electoral votes for vice president, the Senate selects the vice president.

XII

The **electors** shall meet in their respective states and vote by ballot for President and Vice-President, one of whom, at least, shall not be an inhabitant of the same state with themselves; they shall name in their ballots the person voted for as President, and in distinct ballots the person voted for as Vice-President, and they shall make distinct lists of all persons voted for as President, and of all persons voted for as Vice-President, and of the number of votes for each, which lists they shall sign and certify, and transmit sealed to the **seat of the government** of the United States, directed to the President of the Senate;—The President of the Senate shall, in the presence of the Senate and House of Representatives, open all the certificates and the votes shall then be counted;—the person having the greatest number of votes for President, shall be the President, if such number be a majority of the whole number of electors appointed; and if no person have such majority, then from the persons having the highest numbers not exceeding three on the list of those voted for as President, the House of Representatives shall choose immediately, by ballot, the President. But in choosing the President, the votes shall be taken by states, the representation from each state having one vote; a quorum for this purpose shall consist of a member or members from two-thirds of the states, and a majority of all the states shall be necessary to a choice. And if the House of Representatives shall not choose a President whenever the right of choice shall **devolve** upon them, before the fourth day of March next following, then the Vice-President shall act as President, as in the case of the death or other constitutional disability of the President. The person having the greatest number of votes as Vice-President, shall be the Vice-President, if such number be a majority of the whole number of electors appointed, and if no person have a majority, then from the two highest numbers on the list, the Senate shall choose the Vice-President; a quorum for the purpose shall consist of two-thirds of the whole number of senators, and a majority of the whole number shall be necessary to a choice. But no person constitutionally ineligible to the office of President shall be eligible to that of Vice-President of the United States.

COMMENTARY

Article II of the Constitution established the indirect election of the president and vice-president through the Electoral College. Each state was allocated electors equal to the total number of its senators and representatives.

What the framers did not anticipate was the emergence of political parties. Or more precisely, what the framers sought to avoid was the emergence of political parties. The Constitution makes no reference to political parties whatsoever. In *Federalist* No. 10, James Madison applauded the Constitution because it served as an antidote to the "mischiefs of faction." No sooner had the Constitution been signed in Philadelphia in 1787 than the first American political parties were organized during the ratification debate. Soon, instead of the Electoral College fielding an array of nominees, political parties began to pre-screen candidates even before the electors cast their votes. As a consequence, the Electoral College almost immediately, and with only a few exceptions over the next 200 years, assumed the role of simply choosing between party slates rather than from a group of individual candidates.

Problems Arise

The elections of 1796 and 1800 led to the adoption of the Twelfth Amendment, which was quickly ratified on July 27, 1804.

In the election of 1796, the Electoral College chose John Adams, a Federalist, as president and Thomas Jefferson, a Republican, as vice president. The prospect of the executive branch being headed by members of different political parties was disturbing and fraught with potential for divisiveness.

The election of 1800 caused a different problem. Straight party voting resulted in a tie between Jefferson and his Republican running mate Aaron Burr. It took 35 separate ballots in the House of Representatives—until January 17, 1801—to select Jefferson as president and Burr as vice president. People feared that there might not even be a president to be sworn in on inauguration day.

Eventually, all but two of the states adopted rules for "unit voting" by which all of a state's electoral votes would go to a particular slate. Unit voting favors a dominant party, makes it hard on second parties, and virtually excludes third parties from gaining the White House.

Problems Remain

Despite the Twelfth Amendment, the Electoral College remains a target of criticism. Three presidents, (Rutherford B. Hayes, Benjamin Harrison, and George W. Bush) have been chosen in elections in which their opponents received *more* popular votes. The 2000 election, in which Al Gore received approximately 550,000 more popular votes than Bush, has prompted renewed calls for the elimination of the Electoral College, but the requirement of ratification of a constitutional amendment by three-fourths of the states makes that unlikely. In the alternative, if states replaced the winner-take-all rules with proportionate voting, by which electors are sent to the Electoral College in proportion to the popular vote in each state, the result would more closely approximate the will of the people.

Thirteenth Amendment (1865)

The Thirteenth Amendment prohibits slavery or involuntary servitude and authorizes Congress to enforce that prohibition.

XIII

Section 1. Neither slavery nor involuntary servitude, except as a punishment for crime whereof the party shall have been duly convicted, shall exist within the United States, or any place subject to their jurisdiction.

Section 2. Congress shall have power to enforce this article by appropriate legislation.

COMMENTARY

Abraham Lincoln's election as president in 1860 to preside over a nation deeply divided on the issue of slavery was achieved with support only from the free states and with no support from the slave states. The cancer of slavery, sustained in the Constitution and left intact by the Bill of Rights, had infected the body politic, spreading into new states and territories, threatening the health of the nation and risking its doom.

The Civil War and the Foundations of an Amendment

By December 1860, South Carolina had seceded from the Union, followed within weeks by Florida, Alabama, Georgia, Mississippi, Louisiana, and Texas. The Confederacy quickly raised an army of over 100,000 soldiers and on April 12, the first shots of the Civil War were fired at Fort Sumter in Charleston Harbor.

The irreconcilable differences over slavery, bequeathed to another generation by the Founding Fathers, erupted into armed rebellion pitting American citizens against one another less than a hundred years after the Declaration of Independence was signed. Despite all the enlightened ideas and thoughtful deliberations that had gone into the Constitution, the Bill of Rights, and the building of a new nation, no one had been able to resolve the issue of slavery peacefully. Instead, America reverted to the barbarism of war to decide whether it would mend its broken promise of equality or would persist half slave, half free.

On September 22, 1862, Lincoln, utilizing the presidential war powers under the Constitution, announced the Emancipation Proclamation. Lincoln proclaimed that unless slaveowners in those Confederate states which had not yet been occupied by Union forces publicly renounced the rebellion by January 1, 1863, their slaves

President Abraham Lincoln.
© CORBIS

"shall be then, thenceforward, and forever free." The Proclamation required all Union military personnel to assist runaway slaves. With respect to slave states that had not seceded, Lincoln encouraged immediate or gradual emancipation by state initiative, with compensation to owners loyal to the Union and the colonization abroad of freedmen.

The bitter and bloody Civil War ended on April 9, 1865, with the surrender of General Robert E. Lee to General Ulysses S. Grant at Appomattox Court House in Virginia.

By then Lincoln and Congress had already adopted policies, in December 1863 and July 1864, providing for emancipation as a prerequisite for Confederate states to be readmitted to the Union.

The Battle Over the Thirteenth Amendment

In 1865, Congress approved the Thirteenth Amendment (the first amendment in 61 years) formally abolishing slavery. In Section 1 it declares slavery and involuntary servitude illegal, except as punishment for a crime. Section 2 granted Congress enforcement powers.

There was virtually no debate on the amendment in Congress; in reality the debate had been going on for a century.

The Thirteenth Amendment applied to the American people directly, not through their elected representatives. Members of Lincoln's party, the Republicans, vigorously campaigned in favor of the ratification of the Thirteenth Amendment. They pointed out that the Emancipation Proclamation was a wartime measure and left slavery undisturbed in the border states that did not secede and in some Confederate areas occupied by the Union army. Only a constitutional amendment would reach every state and territory, clearly announcing to the world that the abomination of slavery had been abolished.

The Democratic party, centered in the South, vehemently opposed ratification. Despite the fact that the Union had won the war, Democrats argued that that did not change the structure of the Constitution. They asserted that no amendment could alter one's property rights and that slave property remained exclusively subject to the authority of the states, not the federal government.

In one respect, however, the Thirteenth Amendment posed a risk for Republicans and an opportunity for Democrats. Everyone agreed that if the amendment were ratified, any provision of the Constitution to the contrary

Robert E. Lee
© Hulton-Deutsch Collection/CORBIS

would be nullified. In particular, the amendment would void the Constitution's infamous Three-Fifths Clause. Consequently, every black person in the South would count as a *whole* person in determining the size of a state's congressional delegation, and therefore its number of electoral votes. Ironically, having seceded from the Union, declared war, fought for four years, and lost, the South would *increase* its voting strength in Congress and in presidential elections. By supporting the Thirteenth Amendment, from a purely political standpoint, the Republican party was cutting off its nose to spite its face.

Following the assassination of Lincoln, Vice President Andrew Johnson became president and pushed for ratification. He required former Confederate states, now known as *reconstructing states,* to ratify the Thirteenth Amendment under threat of continuing military control by Union armies. Eventually southern states ratified the amendments in sufficient numbers to meet the three-fourths requirement of Article V of the Constitution, thereby averting a constitutional crisis.

On December 15, 1865, eight months after the surrender at Appomattox, the Thirteenth Amendment went into effect. The word "slavery" was officially added to the Constitution on the occasion of its legal abolition.

Yet a constitutional declaration that slavery was abolished was hardly the same as making it disappear from the lives of the men and women who suffered under it and those who prospered from it. After more than 250 years on American soil, slavery had become deeply woven into the fabric of the social, economic, political, sexual, cultural, and spiritual life of the United States.

The ownership of slaves was not confined to the first generation of American leaders. Historian William Lee Miller makes the point powerfully by observing that "(F)ive of the first seven presidents were slaveholders; for thirty-two of the nation's first thirty-six years, forty of its first forty-eight, fifty of its first sixty-four, the nation's president was a slaveholder." He also notes that "The majority of cabinet members and—very important—of Justices on the Supreme Court were slaveholders. The slaveholding Chief Justice Roger Taney, appointed by the slaveholding President Andrew Jackson to succeed the slaveholding John Marshall, would serve all the way through the decades before the war into the years of the civil war itself."

The Supreme Court and Slavery

So it was that in 1857 Chief Justice Taney, slaveholder, announced the Supreme Court's infamous decision in *Dred Scott v. Sandford*, which excluded free African Americans from citizenship. Scott, a Missouri slave owned by an army medical officer, lived at military posts in Illinois and in federal territory, where slavery was prohibited by the Missouri Compromise. In 1846, Scott brought suit claiming he had been emancipated by his residence on free soil. The majority of the Supreme Court held that blacks, free and slave, were not citizens when the Constitution was written because, in the Court's notorious words, they "had no rights which the white man was bound to respect." Taney treated all African Americans as a degraded class of beings who "had been subjugated by the dominant race, and, whether emancipated or not, yet remained subject to their authority."

That the Thirteenth Amendment was ratified only eight years after a Chief Justice expressed such racist views in a Supreme Court opinion suggests how daunting a task the United States faced in truly eradicating the consequences of slavery from society. No parchment amendment could accomplish such a task overnight, especially with proponents of slavery dragging their feet and placing innumerable obstacles in the way of genuine emancipation.

As soon as the Thirteenth Amendment was ratified, Republicans in Congress set about using their new-found authority to enforce the prohibition on slavery and involuntary servitude. Over President Johnson's veto, Congress passed the Civil Rights Act of 1866, which not only confirmed the citizenship of freed slaves, but also protected them against racial discrimination in the form of *Black Codes,* which were adopted in Southern states to disqualify blacks from owning property, making contracts, or serving on juries.

Differing Interpretations

From the outset, there was a conflict between those who read the Thirteenth Amendment *narrowly* to mean that the owning of one person by another was unconstitutional, or *broadly* to mean that any act, private or public, which imposed any "incident" of slavery was also unconstitutional.

In the 1883 *Civil Rights Cases*, the Supreme Court, over a strong dissent by Justice John Marshall Harlan, struck down the Civil Rights Act of 1875, which prohibited racial discrimination in public accommodations, such as hotels, theaters, and railroads. Although the majority said it agreed with Justice Harlan that the Thirteenth Amendment was designed to prohibit the "incidents" of slavery as well as slavery itself, the decision held that racially based refusals of access to public accommodations did not amount to "badges of slavery and servitude."

In 1906 in *Hodges v. United States*, the Supreme Court reversed the convictions of a group of white workers at a lumber yard for ordering black laborers to stop working, assaulting them, and violently driving them from their workplace. The Court held that under the Thirteenth Amendment, Congress could prohibit the "entire subjection" of one person to another, but could not eliminate merely the "badges" or "incidents" of slavery.

Tragically, stymied by the Court's restrictive rulings, Congress was powerless to remedy racial discrimination for the next six decades, and passed no civil rights legislation from the time of Reconstruction to the late 1950s.

Finally, prompted by new appointments to the Supreme Court and the demands voiced by the emerging civil rights movement, Congress passed the Civil Rights Act of 1964. In *Heart of Atlanta Motel v. United States*

(1964) and *Katzenbach v. McClung* (1964), the Court upheld the prohibitions on racial discrimination in public accommodations (although the decisions were based on the Commerce Clause of the Constitution, not the Thirteenth Amendment).

Four years later, in *Jones v. Alfred H. Mayer* (1968), the Court reclaimed the spirit of the Thirteenth Amendment and interpreted the Civil Rights Act of 1866 to prohibit all racial discrimination in the sale of property. The Court overruled the *Hodges* decision and essentially adopted the dissenting views of Justice Harlan in the *Civil Rights Cases* to the effect that under the Thirteenth Amendment Congress had the power to prohibit slavery *and* its "badges and incidents." According to *Jones*, it is for Congress itself "rationally to determine what are the badges and incidents of slavery" and to enact laws to eradicate any "relic of slavery."

Because the Thirteenth Amendment prohibits the enslavement of anyone of any race, in *McDonald v. Santa Fe Trail Transportation Co.* (1976), the Court upheld the use of the 1866 Act to prohibit racial discrimination against whites. And in *Runyon v. McCrary* (1976), the Court relied on the Thirteenth Amendment and the 1866 Act to prohibit a private school from accepting applicants from the entire general public, except blacks.

As the scope of persons protected by the Thirteenth Amendment extended beyond African Americans or former slaves, some commentators suggest that the broad reading in *Jones* means that Congress can define a given right—any right—as one essential to freedom, define its impairment as an incident of slavery, and enact federal legislation to protect that right from both public and private interference.

It remains to be seen how Congress and the Court will continue to apply and interpret the Thirteenth Amendment, born from the blood spilled in the Civil War, stunted in its growth for a century, but later raised as a healthy defender of civil rights.

Fourteenth Amendment (1868)

The Fourteenth Amendment guarantees due process and equal protection of the laws to all persons.

XIV

Section 1. All persons born or naturalized in the United States, and subject to the jurisdiction thereof, are citizens of the United States and of the state wherein they reside. No state shall make or enforce any law which shall abridge the privileges or immunities of citizens of the United States; nor shall any state deprive any person of life, liberty, or property, without due process of law; nor deny to any person within its jurisdiction the equal protection of the laws.

Section 2. Representatives shall be apportioned among the several states according to their respective numbers, counting the whole number of persons in each state, excluding Indians not taxed. But when the right to vote at any election for the choice of electors for President and Vice President of the United States, Representatives in Congress, the executive and judicial officers of a state, or the members of the legislature thereof, is denied to any of the male inhabitants of such state, being twenty-one years of age, and citizens of the United States, or in any way abridged, except for participation in rebellion, or other crime, the basis of representation therein shall be reduced in the proportion which the number of such male citizens shall bear to the whole number of male citizens twenty-one years of age in such state.

Section 3. No person shall be a Senator or Representative in Congress, or elector of President and Vice President, or hold any office, civil or military, under the United States, or under any state, who, having previously taken an oath, as a member of Congress, or as an officer of the United States, or as a member of any state legislature, or as an executive or judicial officer of any state, to support the Constitution of the United States, shall have engaged in insurrection or rebellion against the same, or given aid or comfort to the enemies thereof. But Congress may by a vote of two-thirds of each House, remove such disability.

Section 4. The validity of the public debt of the United States, authorized by law, including debts incurred for payment of pensions and bounties for services in suppressing insurrection or rebellion, shall not be questioned. But neither the United States nor any state shall assume or pay any debt or obligation incurred in aid of insurrection or rebellion against the United States, or any claim for the loss or emancipation of any slave; but all such debts, obligations and claims shall be held illegal and void.

Section 5. The Congress shall have power to enforce, by appropriate legislation, the provisions of this article.

COMMENTARY

Despite the fact that slavery and involuntary servitude were formally abolished by the Thirteenth Amendment, racial segregation persisted and Congress' efforts to eliminate the "badges and incidents" of slavery were rebuffed by the Supreme Court's narrow interpretation of the amendment.

Although the Republicans in Congress overrode President Andrew Johnson's veto and passed the Civil Rights Act of 1866, doubts remained about whether the legislation would be upheld without a further constitutional amendment explicitly granting Congress broader powers to eradicate state laws and practices which perpetuated the vestiges of slavery.

Ironically, with the ratification of the Thirteenth Amendment, which eliminated the Three-Fifths Clause in the Constitution, Republicans feared that southern representation in Congress would *increase*, making it even harder to pass effective civil rights legislation.

The Republicans would have to simultaneously protect the rights of newly freed slaves, force the southern states to be loyal to the Union, and prevent former insurrectionists, who had served the Confederacy, from holding any state or federal elective office.

In the opening days of the Thirty-Ninth Congress, a Joint Committee on Reconstruction was convened to address these critical issues.

An omnibus measure was presented to both houses of Congress on April 30, 1866. Section 1 contained today's Privilege and Immunities, Due Process, and Equal Protection Clauses, while Section 2 reduced the representation of states who denied the right to vote to males over the age of 21. Section 3 deprived all persons who had voluntarily supported the Confederate cause the right to vote in federal elections prior to 1870, while Section 4 dealt with the war debt. Section 5 gave Congress power to enforce the other four sections.

The omnibus amendment passed the House as proposed, but it met serious resistance in the Senate. When it emerged from the Senate, it had been changed in two significant respects: A definition of citizenship was added to Section 1. That was appropriate; however the Senate also weakened Section 3. Instead of disenfranchising those who had supported the Confederacy, it merely barred from federal office those Confederate supporters who prior to the Civil War, had taken an oath to support the Constitution.

After the House concurred on June 13 with the Senate's changes, the amendment was sent to the states for ratification. Twelve days later, on June 25, Connecticut became the first state to ratify. Five additional states ratified the amendment in 1866, and eleven added their ratification in January 1867. By June of 1867, one year after the amendment had been approved by Congress, a total of 22 states had ratified it.

However, ratification by six more states was needed, which finally occurred in July, 1868. But, by that time two of the states that had previously ratified the amendment—New Jersey and Ohio—voted to withdraw their approval. In response, Congress ruled that their ratifications survived the subsequent efforts at withdrawal and remained valid. On July 28, 1868, the Fourteenth Amendment became part of the Constitution.

The Fourteenth Amendment contains several powerful and far-reaching provisions. Section 1 begins by defining citizens as everyone born in or made a naturalized citizen of the United States. This is the first time that American citizenship is defined in the Constitution.

Section 1 also contains three very important constitutional protections. First, it sets a national standard of citizenship and ensures that no state can violate the "privileges or immunities" that are attendant to national citizenship.

Next, Section 1 provides a wellspring of constitutional protection for a wide range of personal rights, launching a continuing debate down to the present day over the meaning and scope of the phrase "due process of law."

Finally, Section 1 establishes another constitutional lightening rod, drawing everyone's attention to the key phrase "equal protection of the laws," which like "due process" has engendered numerous Supreme Court conflicts and mountains of scholarly commentary.

Section 2 of the Fourteenth Amendment codifies what had been implicit in the abolition of slavery under the Thirteenth Amendment, namely that representation in Congress be apportioned to states according to their population (but still excluding Native Americans). Without saying so explicitly, this provision nullified the ignominious Three-Fifths Clause which treated a slave as less than a whole person. Regrettably, "Indians not taxed" retained that second-class status for Native Americans.

The second portion of Section 2 was intended to punish any state for disenfranchising (male) voters. It provides that if a state denies or limits any male inhabitant the right to vote, that state's representation in Congress is reduced proportionately.

This is the first mention of a right to vote in the Constitution or the Bill of Rights, but it is only an indirect reference. (Constitutional protection for the right to vote would have to wait until the Fifteenth Amendment.) The Fourteenth Amendment assumes that a right to vote exists and then creates a disincentive for any state that denies or abridges that right by reducing its representation in Congress. The amendment assumes that states will not want to lose their power in Congress.

Section 3 of the Fourteenth Amendment punishes certain individuals who were disloyal to the Union during the Civil War. Any person who had previously taken an oath to support the Constitution of the United States as a member of Congress, or as an officer of the United States, or as a member of any state legislature, or as an executive or judicial officer of any state, and had "engaged in insurrection or rebellion" against the United States or "given aid or comfort to the enemies thereof," is forever prohibited from serving as a senator or representative in Congress, or an elector of the president or vice president, or holding any office, civil or military, unless Congress removes such disability by a two-thirds vote of the Senate and the House of Representatives. Although obviously written with the Civil War in mind, Section 3 of the Fourteenth Amendment is not limited to that conflict and applies to *any* "insurrection or rebellion."

Section 4 of the Fourteenth Amendment guarantees that federal debts incurred by suppressing insurrection or rebellion shall not be questioned, presumably by any state or private individual or institution. On the other hand, debts incurred in aid of insurrection or rebellion against the United States are not legal, nor can states make claim for any compensation due to the loss or emancipation of a slave. To the victor belongs the spoils and to the vanquished the debts. Having defeated the rebellious southern states, the last thing the Union would do (or allow readmitted states to do) was bear the debts created by that rebellion. Likewise, this section makes it a matter of constitutional law that no former slave owner could

seek payment from anyone for the loss or emancipation of his or her former slaves. Any claim that emancipation constituted the taking of private property without just compensation, in violation of the Fifth Amendment, was trumped by the Fourteenth Amendment.

Section 5, like Section 2 of the Thirteen Amendment, grants Congress the power to enforce the Fourteenth Amendment through appropriate legislation.

Despite the compromises necessary to enact the Fourteenth Amendment, it represented a major advancement in the struggle for equality and personal liberty, coming at a time of deep national division and domestic unrest. It is equal to the best of the Constitution and the Bill of Rights, and indeed it has strengthened both of those documents, adding in explicit terms vital protections previously only hinted at.

In his 1865 State of the Union address, President Johnson credited the Fourteenth Amendment with guaranteeing "equal and exact justice to all men, special privileges to none." Representative John Bingham, one of the architects of the amendment, referred to it as enforcing the "equal rights of every man" and "the absolute equality of all men before the law."

The Fourteenth Amendment empowers advocates of civil rights and equality to condemn the historically myopic, racist rhetoric of bigots like Garrett Davis, a Democratic senator from Kentucky, who contrasted the "superior race" composed of "the Caucasian race, the highest type of man," with the "four million negroes, the lowest type, of which race, no nation or tribe, from the first dawning of history to the present day, has ever established a polity that could be denominated a Government, or has elaborated for itself any science or literature or arts or even an alphabet . . . "

Republicans labeled such a diatribe as "prejudice" which "belong[ed] to an age of darkness and violence," and "a poisonous, dangerous exotic when suffered to grow in the minds of republican institutions."

In a real sense, the Fourteenth Amendment (in partnership with the Thirteenth and Fifteenth) cleansed the Constitution of the stain of legal subjugation which had diminished its grandeur for almost a century.

Fifteenth Amendment (1870)

The Fifteenth Amendment guarantees that the right to vote shall not be denied on account of race, color, or previous condition of servitude.

XV

Section 1. The right of citizens of the United States to vote shall not be denied or abridged by the United States or by any state on account of race, color, or previous condition of servitude.

Section 2. The Congress shall have power to enforce this article by appropriate legislation.

COMMENTARY

In a democracy, it is inconceivable to think of citizenship without the right to vote. A citizen may participate in democratic life in a variety of ways, but none is more vital than casting a ballot in elections for everything from local school board to president of the United States. The right to vote, also known as *suffrage* or *the franchise*, is at the center of any political system worthy of being called a democracy.

It is remarkable, then that as originally written, the Constitution did not grant anyone the right to vote. In Sections 1 and 2 of Article I, the Constitution obliquely refers to the selection of electors to choose the president and Article IV entrusts to the national government the vague duty to "guarantee to every State in this Union a Republican Form of Government." By "Republican" the Constitution meant the form of government by which decisions are made through the election of representatives who in turn make laws and conduct the business of government.

The founding generation, of course, was familiar with voting because the individual states for many years had been writing their own suffrage laws prior to the adoption of the new Constitution—that is to say, free adult white males who owned property were familiar with voting. Women, Native Americans, and slaves had no right to vote.

Working Out the Language

In 1866, Congress began to confront the issue of suffrage directly by passing a law ending racial qualifications for voting in the District of Columbia. President Andrew Johnson vetoed the legislation, claiming that it was wrong to enfranchise "a new class, wholly unprepared" for democracy "by previous habits and opportunities." Congress overrode his veto; it prohibited racial bars in any existing or future federal territories and to require Nebraska and Colorado to adopt impartial suffrage as a prerequisite for their admission to statehood.

This energetic push for voting reforms led by the Radical Republicans and opposed by southern Democrats, culminated in the Reconstruction Act of March 1867 which denied recognition to existing state governments in the South unless and until they ratified the Fourteenth Amendment and adopted a state constitution that permitted blacks to vote on the same terms as whites. Again President Johnson vetoed the bill and again Congress overrode his veto.

In 1867 and 1868, African Americans took full advantage of their new-found political power. New state governments were elected, new state constitutions were adopted, the Fourteenth Amendment was ratified, and seven states were readmitted to the Union.

These achievements generated intensive opposition and white hostility, exemplified by a petition to Congress from Alabama conservatives which argued that "Negroes" had no right to vote because they were "ignorant generally, wholly unacquainted with the principles of free Governments, improvident, disinclined to work, credulous yet suspicious, dishonest, untruthful, incapable of self-restraint, and easily impelled . . . into folly and crime."

The racist rhetoric of the petition was matched by violence against blacks and Republicans throughout the South, often instigated by the Ku Klux Klan. Opposition to black suffrage also damaged Republicans at the polls. Democrats began gaining seats, so in the 1868 presidential election, the Republican Party nominated a safe candidate, Civil War hero General Ulysses S. Grant, who was elected by a narrow margin.

Realizing that the Democrats' popularity was growing and that their control of Congress was slipping, Republicans decided to push for a constitutional amendment to guarantee the right to vote to African Americans. Motivated by the high moral purpose of making blacks full citizens and by the practical political motive of enlarging their own voting base in both the North and the South, Republicans were convinced this was the time to do good for the cause of equality and to do well for their own political fortunes.

The first version of the amendment was offered by Representative George S. Boutwell of Massachusetts. It guaranteed that the right to vote "shall not be denied or abridged . . . by reason of race, color, or previous condition of slavery of any citizens or class of citizens of the United States." It was met by opposition from Democrats and a few conservative Republicans, who claimed blacks were not qualified to vote and that the amendment infringed states' rights.

In the Senate, proponents of black suffrage, such as Henry Wilson of Massachusetts, fearing that the Boutwell amendment could be circumvented by southern states through the use of poll taxes, literacy tests, or property requirements, offered an amendment which prohibited discrimination in voting or the right to hold office in any state "on account of race, color, maturity, property, education, or creed." Wilson declared: "Let us give to all citizens equal rights, and then protect everybody in the United States in the exercise of those rights."

Senator Simon Cameron of Pennsylvania supported Wilson's amendment "because it invites into our country everybody: the Negro, the Irishman, the German, the Frenchman, the Scotchman, the Englishman, and the Chinaman."

The battlelines over the amendment began to form between supporters of the *narrow* House version authored by Representative Boutwell and the *broader* Senate version sponsored by Senator Wilson. A conference committee of the two Houses met to hammer out an acceptable compromise. With time running out before a Congressional adjournment and Republicans fearing that they might end up with nothing if they insisted on the broader Wilson amendment, the conference committee agreed to a draft very similar to Boutwell's, which made no mention of office holders or discrimination on the basis of property, education, or creed.

On February 26, 1869, Congress passed the Fifteenth Amendment, which simply states that the right to vote cannot be denied "on account of race, color, or previous conditions of servitude" and authorized Congress to enforce the article by appropriate legislation.

Ratification

The battle for ratification of the Fifteenth Amendment lasted for 13 months and the outcome was hardly a foregone conclusion. Not surprisingly, ratification came quickly in New England and most of the Middle West, as well as in the South where Republican legislators had control. But there were fierce battles in Indiana and Ohio, where new black voters were likely to decide future elections, and on the Pacific Coast, especially California, where anti-Chinese prejudice ran deep. Indeed, all the legislatures in the western states, except Nevada, rejected ratification of the amendment.

President Grant actively supported the Fifteenth Amendment. Ratification was made a condition for readmission to the Union for four southern states. In the end, Republicans won most of the contested battles and on March 30, 1870, the Fifteenth Amendment became part of the Constitution.

It was an occasion for celebrating. African Americans marched in enthusiastic parades throughout the country. President Grant, in a message to Congress, optimistically wrote that the amendment "completes the greatest civil change and constitutes the most important event that has occurred since the nation came to life." Abolitionist Frederick Douglas, announced that the amendment "means that we are placed upon an equal footing with all other men . . . that liberty is to be the right of all."

While the passage of the Fifteenth Amendment, enfranchising more than a million former slaves, was, in the words of historian Alexander Keyssar, "a landmark in the history of the right to vote," the celebrations proved premature, and later events would make a mockery of the amendment's historic promise. By 1875, a Republican newspaper referred to the Fourteenth and Fifteenth Amendments as "dead letters," suggesting they had no further practical force or effect.

An Empty Promise

A combination of public interference with the right to vote, through poll taxes, literacy tests, and property requirements, and private intimidation through vigilante violence and lynchings, frustrated the enforcement of the Fifteenth Amendment. In 1870 alone, hundreds of freedmen were killed and scores of others were wounded by the Ku Klux Klan and other segregationists.

In reaction, Congress passed the Enforcement Act, which made it a federal crime, punishable in federal court, to interfere with the right to vote. It also passed the Ku Klux Klan Act, which authorized the president to deploy federal troops to protect the electoral process. These measures provided some temporary assistance, and violence dropped off for a few years, but soon resistance to the Civil War Amendments resumed. By then President Grant had lost interest, devoting his attention to the economic depression and labor unrest in the North.

In the South, the Redemption Movement was emerging, which sought to restore the glory of antebellum society—before the Civil War and before the humiliations imposed by the federal government. Systematic segregation under Jim Crow laws (named after a minstrel song) denied blacks the enjoyment of their constitutional rights.

Tragically, instead of enforcing the Civil War Amendments to the fullest extent of the law, the Supreme Court showed little or no interest in advancing justice and equality. The Court reversed convictions for private interference with voting rights in state or local elections and rejected civil actions against a state official for refusing to register blacks.

In 1890, the Republicans made another effort to enforce the Fifteenth Amendment by proposing the Federal Elections Bill, which would authorize the appointment of federal supervisors in congressional elections with the power to overturn election results, even if those results had been certified by state officials. Senator Henry Cabot Lodge of Massachusetts, speaking on the floor of the Senate, urged that the "Government which made the black man a citizen is bound to protect him in his rights as a citizen of the United States, and it is a cowardly Government if it does not do it! No people can afford to write anything into their Constitution and not sustain it." Despite such eloquent pleas, the Democrats defeated the Federal Election Act, ironically claiming it was "a scheme to rob the people of the States of the dearest right of American citizenship."

Without federal enforcement, the prediction that the Fourteenth and Fifteenth Amendments would be "dead letters" came true. Defiantly, the states quickly passed laws imposing poll taxes, literacy tests, secret ballot laws, lengthy residence requirements, elaborate registration procedures, confusing multiple voting-box systems, and eventually, Democratic primaries restricted to white voters.

While Republicans condemned these onerous laws, nothing was done to enforce the Fifteenth Amendment, and the Supreme Court provided no assistance. It upheld the legality of all of the major schemes used to disenfranchise black and poor voters. As just one example, in 1898, the Supreme Court upheld a Mississippi literacy test because the law creating the test was not, on its face, directed at blacks.

Decades passed and freedmen and their children lived under these discriminatory laws, which frustrated their ability to exercise one of their fundamental rights as citizens.

The Tide Finally Turns

In the twentieth century, the tide finally began to change. In *Nixon v. Herndon* (1927) and *Nixon v. Condon* (1932), NAACP attorneys successfully attacked statutes that barred blacks from voting in elections, and that permitted political parties to exclude blacks from voting in primaries. In *Smith v. Allwright* (1944) and *Terry v. Adams* (1953), the Court found that primary and general elections were "fused" and that a whites-only "pre-primary" in Texas violated the Fifteenth Amendment.

No longer able to manipulate primaries, white segregationists had far less success in blocking black voters. While in the nineteenth century these obstructionist measures had reduced black registrations by a third, by the 1950, they had only a limited effect. Black literacy rates had improved and only Alabama, Mississippi, and Louisiana retained discriminatory literacy tests. Eventually the Court not only struck down all these tests, but went further and nullified tests that did not appear discriminatory but that in reality penalized black students who had been segregated in inferior schools.

In the 1960s, in response to the growing civil rights movement, Congress returned to the historic role it had played a century earlier when it wrote the Thirteenth, Fourteenth, and Fifteenth Amendments. Congress expanded judicial protection for voting rights in the Civil Rights Acts of 1957, 1960, and 1964, and the Voting Rights

Act of 1965. Black voter registration in the South, which had been only 5 percent in 1940, climbed to 63 percent by 1976, narrowing the gap between black and white registrations to only 5 percent.

African Americans continued to expand their role in electoral politics at the local, state and national levels.

Modern Backsliding

Unfortunately, the steady progress in the expansion of voting rights for African Americans was recently placed in doubt by the controversy surrounding the 2000 presidential election. The race between Democratic candidate Al Gore and Republican candidate George W. Bush was so close that no winner was announced on election night. Attention turned to the state of Florida, where Bush had a slim lead of only a few hundred votes out of over six million. The Gore campaign contested the election in court, leading to a controversial 5-4 Supreme Court decision on December 12, 2000, and resulting in the certification of Bush as the 43rd President of the United States.

While most of the attention in the Florida election was devoted to disputes over the hand-counting of paper ballots (popularizing such terms as "hanging chads" and "pregnant chads"), the NAACP and other civil rights leaders accused Florida officials of systematically interfering with African American voters through the use of outdated voting machines in historically black precincts and the intimidation of black voters.

The events in Florida in the 2000 election remind us that constitutional rights, including the right to vote, are always at risk and require eternal vigilance.

Sixteenth Amendment (1913)

The Sixteenth Amendment provides Congress the power to impose and collect income taxes.

XVI

The Congress shall have power to lay and collect taxes on incomes, from whatever source derived, without apportionment among the several states, and without regard to any census of enumeration.

COMMENTARY

At the time the Constitution was written, there were no income taxes as we know them (only too well) today. At the Constitutional Convention, the framers included two clauses in Article I regarding taxes: that taxes be "uniform throughout the United States" (Section 2) and that any tax be proportional to population (Section 9). The Constitution contains no definition of a direct tax. Apparently, delegate Gouverneur Morris added the term, almost as an afterthought, to contrast "indirect" taxes (such as those levied on exports, imports, and consumption) from other "direct" taxes (such as those imposed on land or buildings).

Shortly after the ratification of the Constitution, the U.S. Supreme Court provided some guidance. In the case of *Hylton v. United States* (1796), the Court limited "direct" taxes to taxes on earnings from land and ruled that if a tax could not be apportioned, then it was not a "direct" tax subject to the restrictions of Article I, Section 9.

The first federal income tax was enacted by Congress in 1864 to help finance the Civil War. It was upheld by the Supreme Court in 1881 in *Springer v. United States*, which ruled that it was an indirect tax, which could be levied without apportioning it among the several states.

In 1894, Congress imposed an income tax of 2 percent on all income above $4,000, which affected only the richest 1 percent of the population. That tax was challenged in *Pollack v. Farmers' Loan and Trust Co.* (1895) and in a highly controversial decision, the U.S. Supreme Court struck it down as a "direct" tax prohibited by the Constitution. The ruling was criticized because the Court voided the *entire* income tax, even though only part of it included a tax on earnings from the lease of real estate.

The Sixteenth Amendment was designed to overrule the decision in *Pollock*. Following *Pollock*, powerful political forces continued to urge an income tax to replace the regressive consumption taxes (taxes on goods that are consumed) which was then employed to finance the federal government.

Although there was support for overturning *Pollock* by re-enacting a personal income tax, President William Howard Taft urged a constitutional amendment, which was ratified in 1913. Armed with the authority granted by the Sixteenth Amendment, Congress promptly passed a new income tax statute the same year.

Only one Supreme Court decision has found an income tax provision unconstitutional. *Eisner v. Macomber* (1920) held that a stock dividend on common stock in the form of common stock was not "income" because the element of "realization" was lacking. *Macomber* has been severely limited by subsequent cases, such as *Helvering v. Bruun* (1940), which went so far as to hold that the return of a lessor's property at the termination of a lease is a realization of income. While *Macomber* defined "income" for constitutional purposes as "the gain derived from capital, from labor, or from both combined," in *Commissioner v. Glenshaw Glass Co.* (1955), the Court rejected all considerations of source, holding that even a windfall is constitutionally taxable as income.

The Sixteenth Amendment is an example of an amendment to the Constitution to keep pace with changing times and the financial needs of the expanding national government.

Seventeenth Amendment (1913)

The Seventeenth Amendment provides for direct election of United States senators by the people of the states.

XVII

The Senate of the United States shall be composed of two Senators from each state, elected by the people thereof, for six years; and each Senator shall have one vote. The electors in each state shall have the qualifications requisite for electors of the most numerous branch of the state legislatures.

When vacancies happen in the representation of any state in the Senate, the executive authority of such state shall issue writs of election to fill such vacancies: Provided, that the legislature of any state may empower the executive thereof to make temporary appointments until the people fill the vacancies by election as the legislature may direct.

This amendment shall not be so construed as to affect the election or term of any Senator chosen before it becomes valid as part of the Constitution.

COMMENTARY

Selection of United States senators had been criticized for many years. For 124 years, under the first clause of Article I, Section 3, of the Constitution, senators had been chosen by the state legislatures. Direct election of senators was first proposed in 1826; and beginning in 1893, a constitutional amendment to establish direct election was proposed in Congress every year. By 1912, 29 of the 48 state legislatures provided for either nomination by party primaries, with the individual legislators bound to vote for their party's nominee, or a statewide general election, the result of which was binding on the legislature.

Many reasons were advanced for direct election, including reducing corruption, eliminating national party domination of state legislatures, and direct representation of the people in the Senate. Most observers see little difference in the types of persons elected to the Senate or in the proceedings of the Senate or state legislatures as a result of the Seventeenth Amendment.

The Seventeenth Amendment has not required much judicial review. In 1915, the Supreme Court held that the right to vote for United States senators was a privilege of United States citizenship, protected by the privileges and immunities clause of the Fourteenth Amendment; and in 1946 it held that that right could not be denied on account of race. The Court has also held that the Seventeenth Amendment does not require that a candidate receive a majority of the votes cast in order to be elected; a plurality will suffice.

Eighteenth Amendment (1919)

The Eighteenth Amendment was written to provide a peacetime constitutional basis for the national prohibition of alcoholic beverages, which had begun during World War I.

XVIII

Section 1. After one year from the ratification of this article the manufacture, sale, or transportation of intoxicating liquors within, the importation thereof into, or the exportation thereof from the United States and all territory subject to the jurisdiction thereof for beverage purposes is hereby prohibited.

Section 2. The Congress and the several states shall have concurrent power to enforce this article by appropriate legislation.

Section 3. This article shall be inoperative unless it shall have been ratified as an amendment to the Constitution by the legislatures of the several states, as provided in the Constitution, within seven years from the date of the submission hereof to the states by the Congress.

COMMENTARY

The Supreme Court, in the *National Prohibition Cases* (1920), upheld the 18th amendment, despite the claim that "ordinary legislation" cannot be made part of the Constitution and the assertion that the Constitution cannot be amended so as to diminish the residual sovereignty of the states (states' rights).

Prohibition proved very difficult to enforce. The widespread disregard of federal law undermined the high-minded morality that prompted its adoption. In 1933, the Eighteenth Amendment became the only constitutional amendment ever to be entirely reversed when it was repealed by passage of the Twenty-First Amendment.

Prohibition, and the Eighteenth Amendment that prompted it, sparked a debate that continues to this day on the role of the law and the Constitution in enforcing a particular view of morality.

Nineteenth Amendment (1920)

The Nineteenth Amendment guarantees that the right to vote may not be denied on the basis of gender.

XIX

The right of citizens of the United States to vote shall not be denied or abridged by the United States or by any state on account of sex.

Congress shall have power to enforce this article by appropriate legislation.

COMMENTARY

As the Fifteenth Amendment sought to correct the failure of the Constitution to guarantee African Americans the right to vote, the Nineteenth Amendment, half a century later, remedied that defect for women of all races. The struggle for women's suffrage pre-dated the Civil War and was marked by setbacks and disappointments, not the least of which was the lack of national will in 1870 to include women along with African American males when the Fifteenth Amendment was adopted.

Some trace the movement for equal rights for women to the earliest days of the republic and the influence of women such as Abigail Adams, the wife of John Adams, who was a drafter of the Declaration of Independence and second president of the United States. However, the pivotal political event did not occur until 1848, when the first women's rights convention was held in Seneca Falls, New York. Organized by Elizabeth Cady Stanton and Lucretia Mott, the convention adopted the Seneca Falls Declaration of Sentiments and Resolution which declared that woman was man's equal and labeled the right to vote as one of the "inalienable rights" to which women were entitled. Of the 260 women and 40 men who attended the convention, only one, Charlotte Woodward, lived to see the adoption of the Nineteenth Amendment, seventy-two years later in 1920.

The Fifteenth Amendment prohibiting the denial of the right to vote "on account of race, color, or previous condition of servitude," did not specifically apply to women. Some proponents of women's suffrage argued that the Fourteenth Amendment's prohibition on any state abridging "the privileges or immunities of citizens of the United States," did in fact guarantee a women's right to vote. But

Susan B. Anthony, suffragette.
© Bettmann/CORBIS

the Supreme Court unanimously rejected that argument in 1875 in *Minor v. Happersett*.

Undaunted, supporters of women's suffrage continued their campaign. As declining birth rates and greater educational and employment opportunities due to industrialization prompted more and more women to enter the workforce and become active in public life, they supported such progressive causes as the abolition of slavery, birth control, and prohibition. Opponents warned that women's suffrage would lead to immorality, free love, divorce, socialism, and anarchism.

As with other social and political movements, the struggle for women's suffrage was hampered by internal dissension and factionalism as different leaders spoke in favor of and against different tactics and strategies. The increasing role of women in education, social welfare, and the war effort during World War I helped strengthen their cause. This coincided with women's enfranchisement in several Western nations and eventually in a majority of the United States.

The suffrage movement gained strength with the formation of the National Woman's Suffrage Association and the National Women's Party, which organized more than two million women to participate in almost 1,000 campaigns targeting state and federal legislators, party officials, and referendum voters. Eventually Congress adopted the Nineteenth Amendment guaranteeing that the "right of citizens of the United States to vote shall not be denied or abridged by the United States or by any state of account of sex."

On August 18, 1920, Tennessee became the 36th state to ratify the Nineteenth Amendment. Harry Burns, at 24 years old the youngest member of the Tennessee House of Representatives, cast the deciding vote after receiving a note from his mother telling him not to "forget to be a good boy."

Twentieth Amendment (1933)

The Twentieth Amendment provides that the president, vice president, and members of Congress begin their terms in the January following their election.

XX

Section 1. The terms of the President and Vice President shall end at noon on the 20th day of January, and the terms of Senators and Representatives at noon on the 3d day of January, of the years in which such terms would have ended if this article had not been ratified; and the terms of their successors shall then begin.

Section 2. The Congress shall assemble at least once in every year, and such meeting shall begin at noon on the 3d day of January, unless they shall by law appoint a different day.

Section 3. If, at the time fixed for the beginning of the term of the President, the President elect shall have died, the Vice President elect shall become President. If a President shall not have been chosen before the time fixed for the beginning of his term, or if the President elect shall have failed to qualify, then the Vice President elect shall act as President until a President shall have qualified; and the Congress may by law provide for the case wherein neither a President elect nor a Vice President elect shall have qualified, declaring who shall then act as President, or the manner in which one who is to act shall be selected, and such person shall act accordingly until a President or Vice President shall have qualified.

Section 4. The Congress may by law provide for the case of the death of any of the persons from whom the House of Representatives may choose a President whenever the right of choice shall have devolved upon them, and for the case of the death of any of the persons from whom the Senate may choose a Vice President whenever the right of choice shall have devolved upon them.

Section 5. Sections 1 and 2 shall take effect on the 15th day of October following the ratification of this article.

Section 6. This article shall be inoperative unless it shall have been ratified as an amendment to the Constitution by the legislatures of three-fourths of the several states within seven years from the date of its submission.

COMMENTARY

Congress proposed the Twentieth Amendment on March 2, 1932 and ratification was completed on January 23, 1933. Under the old scheme of Article I, Section 4, representatives did not take their seats until 13 months after their election, and a short lame duck session in election years included members who had been defeated. The amendment also makes provisions for presidential succession and authorizes Congress to provide for a situation in which a president-elect or vice-president-elect does not qualify by inauguration day. (For more information on presidential qualifications, see Article II of the Constitution.)

The Twentieth Amendment has not been reviewed by the U.S. Supreme Court and has engendered little or no controversy.

Twenty-First Amendment (1933)

The Twenty-First Amendment repealed the Eighteenth Amendment and rescinded the constitutional prohibition on alcoholic beverages in effect during the 13 years of the Prohibition Era.

XXI

Section 1. The eighteenth article of amendment to the Constitution of the United States is hereby repealed.

Section 2. The transportation or importation into any state, territory, or possession of the United States for delivery or use therein of intoxicating liquors, in violation of the laws thereof, is hereby prohibited.

Section 3. This article shall be inoperative unless it shall have been ratified as an amendment to the Constitution by conventions in the several states, as provided in the Constitution, within seven years from the date of the submission hereof to the states by the Congress.

COMMENTARY

Congress proposed the Twenty-First Amendment in February 1933 and it was swiftly ratified by December 1933.

The second clause of the Twenty-First Amendment retains the prohibition on transportation or importation of intoxicating liquors into states or territories that have laws forbidding those activities. The clause appears to give the states power to regulate interstate commerce in alcoholic beverages, thus freeing them, as far as liquor is concerned, from commerce clause restrictions. The Supreme Court has upheld that interpretation in several cases, notably *State Board v. Young's Market* (1936). The Court suggested an even broader scope for state regulatory power in *California v. LaRue* (1972), when it upheld a regulation banning sexually explicit entertainment in licensed taverns, and in *Elks' Lodge v. Ingraham* (1973), when it upheld a statute denying liquor licenses to private clubs that practiced racial discrimination.

Opposition to the Eighteenth Amendment came not only from those who believed that the federal government had no business regulating, let alone prohibiting, the sale of alcoholic beverages, but also from critics who were alarmed that the Supreme Court was relying on the Eighteenth Amendment to uphold dangerously expansive police powers that Congress used to enforce Prohibition.

In *United States v. Lanza* (1922), the Court found that under the Eighteenth Amendment both state and federal governments possessed independent authority to punish violations of Prohibition laws, thereby raising the risk that individuals could be convicted and punished *twice* for the same act. In *Carroll v. United States* (1925), the Court upheld warrantless searches of automobiles transporting liquor due to the risk of flight, thus generally expanding the search and seizure authority of the police. In *Olmstead v. United States* (1928), the Court held that the use of wiretapping by law enforcement agencies constituted lawful search and seizure.

These Supreme Court decisions, expanding the methods used by police to enforce Prohibition laws, fueled support to repeal the Eighteenth Amendment and led to the formation of such organizations as the Association Against the Prohibition Amendment and the Women's Organization for National Prohibition Reform.

The groundswell against the Eighteenth Amendment came to a head in 1933, when Congress proposed the Twenty-First Amendment and specified that the amendment be submitted for ratification to state conventions instead of state legislatures, which were believed to be dominated by anti-liquor representatives from rural areas.

Between April and November, 1933, 37 states held elections on whether to retain or repeal the Eighteenth Amendment. Nearly 21 million Americans voted, and 73 percent favored repeal. On December 5, 1993, the Twenty-First Amendment was ratified and the Eighteenth Amendment was repealed.

The Twenty-First Amendment is the only constitutional amendment to be ratified by voters at state conventions rather than by state legislatures.

Twenty-Second Amendment (1947)

The Twenty-Second Amendment limits the president to two four-year terms.

XXII

Section 1. No person shall be elected to the office of the President more than twice, and no person who has held the office of President, or acted as President, for more than two years of a term to which some other person was elected President shall be elected to the office of the President more than once. But this article shall not apply to any person holding the office of President when this article was proposed by the Congress, and shall not prevent any person who may be holding the office of President, or acting as President, during the term within which this article becomes operative from holding the office of President or acting as President during the remainder of such term.

Section 2. This article shall be inoperative unless it shall have been ratified as an amendment to the Constitution by the legislatures of three-fourths of the several states within seven years from the date of its submission to the states by the Congress.

COMMENTARY

Although the president, as Alexander Hamilton wrote in *Federalist* No. 69, was "to be re-eligible as often as the people of the United States shall think him worthy of their confidence," by a tradition dating back to President George Washington, the president served no longer than two terms in office.

In 1940, however, with World War II raging, President Franklin D. Roosevelt sought and won election to a third term. He was subsequently elected to a fourth term, but died two months after that term began.

The Twenty-Second Amendment makes the earlier tradition of a two-term limit an official part of the Constitution. Congress proposed the amendment in March 1947 and ratification was complete four years later.

Since the ratification of the Twenty-Second Amendment in 1947, four presidents—Dwight D. Eisenhower, Richard M. Nixon, Ronald Reagan, and Bill Clinton—have each been elected to the maximum of two terms of office.

The Twenty-Second Amendment has not been challenged in court. Instead, the movement to impose term limits on other elective offices has spread through many states.

Twenty-Third Amendment (1961)

The Twenty-Third Amendment provides that residents of the District of Columbia must be included in the process of electing the president and vice president by allowing them to choose members of the Electoral College.

XXIII

Section 1. The District constituting the seat of government of the United States shall appoint in such manner as the Congress may direct:

A number of electors of President and Vice President equal to the whole number of Senators and Representatives in Congress to which the District would be entitled if it were a state, but in no event more than the least populous state; they shall be in addition to those appointed by the states, but they shall be considered, for the purposes of the election of President and Vice President, to be electors appointed by a state; and they shall meet in the District and perform such duties as provided by the twelfth article of amendment.

Section 2. The Congress shall have power to enforce this article by appropriate legislation.

COMMENTARY

As originally introduced, the Twenty-Third Amendment would have allocated to the District of Columbia as many electoral votes as a state with the same population, and would have allowed the District to elect representatives to Congress on the same basis. There was some opposition to the Twenty-Third Amendment from Republicans, who predicted that the District would inevitably support Democratic candidates, and from southerners, who feared that the amendment would increase the political power of blacks.

The influence of the District is limited by the provision permitting it no more electoral votes than the least populous state, which in practice caps the District's electoral votes at three.

The Twenty-Third Amendment, which became effective on March 29, 1961, has not been the subject of any U.S. Supreme Court case.

Twenty-Fourth Amendment (1964)

The Twenty-Fourth Amendment provides that the right of United States citizens to vote in federal elections cannot be denied or abridged for nonpayment of a poll tax or other tax.

XXIV

Section 1. The right of citizens of the United States to vote in any primary or other election for President or Vice President, for electors for President or Vice President, or for Senator or Representative in Congress, shall not be denied or abridged by the United States or any state by reason of failure to pay any **poll tax** or other tax.

Section 2. The Congress shall have power to enforce this article by appropriate legislation.

NOTE

poll tax: a payment made to the government in order to be allowed to vote.

COMMENTARY

Poll taxes, which had to be paid before a person was allowed to vote, were enacted by southern states in the mid-1800s to disenfranchise African Americans, most of whom lived in poverty and could ill afford to pay for anything but the bare necessities of life. In *Breedlove v. Sattles* (1937), the Supreme Court unanimously upheld a Georgia poll tax despite claims that it violated the Equal Protection and Privileges and Immunities Clauses of the Fourteenth Amendment. Ironically, the claimant in *Breedlove* was a white male voter who was challenging exceptions to the poll tax for persons over sixty, the blind, and women who had not registered to vote. The Court found the exceptions reasonable and held that the use of poll taxes as a condition for voting had long been an accepted tradition.

Legislation to abolish the poll tax was introduced every year beginning in 1939, and a constitutional amendment was proposed every year from 1949 on. The Twenty-Fourth Amendment was proposed by Congress on August 27, 1962, and became part of the Constitution on February 4, 1964. By 1964, only five states continued to impose a poll tax as a qualification for voting. Because the Twenty-Fourth Amendment governed only federal elections, four states divided their elections, stubbornly continuing to require poll taxes in state elections. However, in *Harper v. Virginia Board of Elections* (1966), the Supreme Court, in an opinion by Justice William O. Douglas for a 6-3 majority, held that this remaining poll tax violated the Constitution by denying equal protection of the laws.

A cruel vestige of slavery and inequality, the poll tax disenfranchised generations of poor and minority voters. Its prohibition, 173 years after the adoption of the Bill of Rights, is bittersweet proof that while the original Constitution was an incomplete document, when it came to the rights of the disenfranchised, America has moved in the direction of greater freedom and equality for all, however slowly.

Twenty-Fifth Amendment (1967)

The Twenty-Fifth Amendment designates who shall discharge the duties of the presidency should the president be unable to carry them out due to illness, death, removal, or resignation and also provides for filling the office of vice president should a vacancy occur.

XXV

Section 1. In case of the removal of the President from office or of his death or resignation, the Vice President shall become President.

Section 2. Whenever there is a vacancy in the office of the Vice President, the President shall nominate a Vice President who shall take office upon confirmation by a majority vote of both Houses of Congress.

Section 3. Whenever the President transmits to the President pro tempore of the Senate and the Speaker of the House of Representatives his written declaration that he is unable to discharge the powers and duties of his office, and until he transmits to them a written declaration to the contrary, such powers and duties shall be discharged by the Vice President as Acting President.

Section 4. Whenever the Vice President and a majority of either the principal officers of the executive departments or of such other body as Congress may by law provide, transmit to the President pro tempore of the Senate and the Speaker of the House of Representatives their written declaration that the President is unable to discharge the powers and duties of his office, the Vice President shall immediately assume the powers and duties of the office as Acting President.

Thereafter, when the President transmits to the President pro tempore of the Senate and the Speaker of the House of Representatives his written declaration that no inability exists, he shall resume the powers and duties of his office unless the Vice President and a majority of either the principal officers of the executive department or of such other body as Congress may by law provide, transmit within four days to the President pro tempore of the Senate and the Speaker of the House of Representatives their written declaration that the President is unable to discharge the powers and duties of his office. Thereupon Congress shall decide the issue, assembling within forty-eight hours for that purpose if not in session. If the Congress, within twenty-one days after receipt of the latter written declaration, or, if Congress is not in session, within twenty-one days after Congress is required to assemble, determines by two-thirds vote of both Houses that the President is unable to discharge the powers and duties of his office, the Vice President shall continue to discharge the same as Acting President; otherwise, the President shall resume the powers and duties of his office.

COMMENTARY

Concerns over presidential disability and succession date back to the founding of the nation. The first succession law was signed by President George Washington in 1792, declaring that the vice president would succeed the president, followed by the president pro tempore of the Senate, and the Speaker of the House.

On June 19, 1886, the succession law was revised after Chester A. Arthur became president following the assassination of James Garfield. No president pro tempore or Speaker was in office at the time. The 1886 law put the Secretary of State in line behind the vice president, followed by other cabinet heads.

Prompted by the death of President Franklin D. Roosevelt, his successor, Harry S Truman, expressed doubts over unelected cabinet members holding the highest office in the land. A bill placing the Speaker and the president pro tempore in line after the vice president was passed into law on July 18, 1947.

The assassination of President John F. Kennedy in 1963 reopened the succession debate as the Speaker of the House at that time was quite elderly. The Twenty-Fifth Amendment was formally signed and proclaimed by President Lyndon B. Johnson in a White House ceremony on February 23, 1967.

Under the amendment, in case of the removal of the president from office or in case of his or her death or resignation, the vice president becomes president. Whenever there is a vacancy in the office of the vice president, the president nominates a vice presidential candidate who takes office upon confirmation by a majority vote of both Houses of Congress.

The Amendment Comes into Play

Six years after ratification, the amendment was called into play. In 1973, Spiro Agnew resigned the vice-presidency and Gerald R. Ford assumed that office. Shortly thereafter, the Supreme Court ordered President Richard Nixon to turn over tapes as possible evidence in the Watergate scandal. Nixon announced his resignation on August 8, 1974, and Ford assumed the presidency the next day. Using the Twenty-Fifth Amendment, Congress continued Nelson A. Rockefeller as vice president, the first time two unelected officials held the highest offices in the nation.

Presidential Disability

Also under the amendment, whenever the president transmits to the president pro tempore of the Senate and the Speaker of the House of Representatives his or her written declaration that he or she is unable to discharge the powers and duties of office, and until the president transmits to them a written declaration to the contrary, such powers and duties are discharged by the vice president as acting president. President Ronald Reagan was the first president to employ the disability provisions of this amendment when he was shot during an attempted assasination.

The vice president assumes the powers and duties of the office as acting president when he and a majority of either the Cabinet or another body of Congress' choice provide a written declaration to the president pro tempore of the Senate and the Speaker of the House of Representatives that the president is unable to perform the duties of the office.

Afterwards, the president may resume his other duties by submitting to the president pro tempore of the Senate and the Speaker of the House of Representatives a written declaration that no inability exists, unless the vice president and other specified officials dispute the president's claim. If this happens, Congress must decide the issue, assembling within 48 hours for that purpose if not already in session. A two-thirds vote of both chambers must rule that the president is unable to discharge the powers and duties of the office in order for the vice president to remain as Acting President; otherwise, the president shall resume the powers and duties of the office.

Twenty-Sixth Amendment (1971)

This amendment sets the minimum voting age at 18 years old for all federal, state, and local elections.

XXVI

Section 1. The right of citizens of the United States, who are 18 years of age or older, to vote, shall not be denied or abridged by the United States or any state on account of age.

Section 2. The Congress shall have the power to enforce this article by appropriate legislation.

COMMENTARY

In great part, the lowering of the voting age was driven by the realization that in the Vietnam War, then raging in Southeast Asia, young people between 18 and 21 years of age were risking their lives to defend their country but could not vote.

In the wake of the passage of the Voting Rights Act of 1965, which extended equal voting rights to all racial and ethnic minorities, Congress passed the Voting Rights Act Amendment of 1970, which lowered the minimum voting age in federal, state, and local elections to 18.

Later in 1970, however, the U.S. Supreme Court in Oregon v. Mitchell (1970) by two separate 5-4 votes, upheld the constitutionality of the new law for federal elections but struck down the law for state elections. In response, on March 23, 1971, Congress proposed the Twenty-Sixth Amendment standardizing the voting age in all federal, state, and local elections at 18. Ratification was completed in 107 days, the shortest time ever required to complete the amendment process.

Under the Constitution, the power to establish qualifications for voting in all elections was left to the states, except that the qualifications to vote for representatives in Congress (and, after the Seventeenth Amendment, for senators) had to be the same as the qualifications to vote for members of the most numerous branch of the state legislature. The Fourteenth Amendment set 21 as the highest minimum age a state could require for voters. Before 1970, only four states had enacted a minimum voting age lower than 21.

The *Oregon* decision threatened to throw the 1972 elections into chaos, because in most states the voting age for *federal* officials would have been different from the voting age for *state* races. The speed with which the amendment was ratified is attributable to a general desire to avoid such a crisis.

Congress, in proposing the Twenty-Sixth Amendment, expressed confidence in the "idealism and concern and energy" the new young voters would bring to the political system. However, studies have shown that even after the adoption of the Twenty-Sixth Amendment, 18- to 21-year-olds have the lowest rate of voter turnout of any age group; and those who do vote do not differ markedly from the rest of the population concerning political parties or issues.

On the other hand, the activism of young people in various political movements, including opposition to the Vietnam War, support for civil rights and the environment, and the struggle for economic justice, suggests that many young people are searching for political candidates to support enthusiastically. As young people learn more about the political system and the impact elected officials have on their lives, and when they realize—as many did in the controversial 2000 Presidential election—that the outcome of a race can turn on a handful of votes, participation by young people in electoral politics is likely to increase.

Twenty-Seventh Amendment (1992)

A Congressional pay raise will not take effect until after the next congressional election.

XXVII

No law varying the compensation for the services of the Senators and Representatives shall take effect until an election of Representatives shall have intervened.

COMMENTARY

The Twenty-Seventh Amendment states that any pay raise senators and representatives approve for themselves cannot take effect until after an intervening congressional election (such elections are held every two years).

As difficult as it may be to believe, the Twenty-Seventh Amendment, adopted in 1992, was originally proposed by the First Congress in 1789, over two hundred years earlier.

The Bill of Rights, drafted by James Madison, approved by Congress, and sent to the states for ratification contained twelve, not ten, amendments. During the ratification process the first two amendments were *not* ratified, while the last ten were. The amendments were renumbered, thereby becoming the Bill of Rights as it stands today. Indeed, the First Amendment, sitting atop the Bill of Rights, protecting such fundamental rights as freedom of religion, speech, press, and assembly, originally was the third amendment.

It is unclear why this amendment was not ratified as part of the Bill of Rights in 1791. Surely concerns about elected officials increasing their own compensation were as serious then as they are today.

REVIEW

Use this review to gauge what you've learned and to build confidence in your understanding of the original text. After you work through the review questions, the problem-solving exercises, and the suggested activities, you're well on your way to understanding and appreciating America's freedom documents.

IDENTIFY THE QUOTATION

1. "When in the Course of human events, it becomes necessary for one people to dissolve the political band which have connected them with another, and to assume, among the Powers of the earth, the separate and equal station to which the Laws of Nature and of Nature's God entitle them, a decent respect to the opinions of mankind requires that they should declare the causes which impel them to the separation."

2. "We hold these truths to be self-evident, that all men are created equal, they are endowed by their Creator with certain unalienable Rights, that among these are Life, Liberty, and the pursuit of Happiness."

3. "We the people of the United States, in Order to form a more perfect Union, establish Justice, insure domestic Tranquility, provide for the common defense, promote the general Welfare, and secure the Blessings of Liberty to ourselves and our Posterity, do ordain and establish this Constitution for the United States of America."

4. "To regulate Commerce with foreign Nations, and among the several States, and with the Indian Tribes."

5. "To promote the Progress of Science and useful Arts, by securing for limited Times to Authors and Inventors, the exclusive Right to their respective writings and Discoveries."

6. "To make all Laws which shall be necessary and proper for carrying into Execution the foregoing Powers, and all other Powers vested by this Constitution in the Government of the United States, or in any Department or Officer thereof."

7. "The Migration or Importation of such Persons as any of the States now existing shall think proper to admit, shall not be prohibited by the Congress prior to the Year one thousand eight hundred and eight, but a Tax or Duty may be imposed on such importation, not exceeding ten dollars for each Person."

8. "The Privilege of the Writ of Habeas Corpus shall not be suspended, unless when in Cases of Rebellion or Invasion the public Safety may Require it."

9. "The Citizens of each State shall be entitled to all Privileges and Immunities of Citizens in the several States."

10. "The United States shall guarantee to every State in this Union a Republican Form of Government, and shall protect each of them against Invasion; and on application of the Legislature, or of the Executive (when the Legislature cannot be convened) against domestic Violence."

11. "This Constitution, and the Laws of the United States shall be made in Pursuance thereof, and all Treaties made, or which shall be made, under the Authority of the United States, shall be the supreme Law of the Land; and the Judges in every State shall be bound thereby, any Thing in the Constitution or Laws of any State to the Contrary notwithstanding."

12. "Congress shall make no law respecting an establishment of religion, or prohibiting the free exercise thereof; or abridging the freedom of speech, or of the press, or the right of the people peaceably to assemble, and to petition the Government for a redress of grievances."

13. "A well-regulated militia, being necessary to the security of a free State, the right of the people to keep and bear arms, shall not be infringed."

14. "The enumeration in the Constitution, of certain rights, shall not be construed to deny or disparage others retained by the people."

15. "Neither slavery nor involuntary servitude, except as a punishment for crime whereof the party shall have been duly convicted, shall exist within the United States, or any place subject to their jurisdiction."

16. "No state shall make or enforce any law which shall abridge the privileges or immunities of citizens of the United States; nor shall any state deprive any person of life, liberty, or property, without due process of law; nor deny to any person within its jurisdiction the equal protection of the laws."

17. "The right of citizens of the United States to vote shall not be denied or abridged by the United States or by any state on account of race, color, or previous condition of servitude."

18. "The right of citizens of the United States to vote shall not be denied or abridged by the United States or by any state on account of sex."

TRUE/FALSE

1. T F The Senate has the sole power to try all impeachments under the U.S. Constitution.

2. T F No bill vetoed by the president can become a law during the term of that president.

3. T F The president can make treaties with the concurrence of two-thirds of the senators present.

4. T F The Constitution provides that the U.S. Supreme Court shall have nine members.

5. T F No person may be convicted of treason under the Constitution except on the testimony of two witnesses to the same overt act or by a confession in open court.

6. T F Thomas Jefferson wrote the Preamble to the U.S. Constitution.

7. T F George Mason was a delegate to the Constitutional Convention, but refused to sign the Constitution because it failed to guarantee women the right to vote.

8. T F The Constitution provided that slavery would be abolished in 1808.

9. T F One of the stated purposes of the Constitution was to provide for the common defense.

10. T F The only state which did not send a delegation to the Constitutional Convention was New Hampshire.

11. T F The Twenty-First Amendment repealed the Eighteenth Amendment.

12. T F Slavery was abolished by the Fourteenth Amendment.

13. T F As originally written, the Constitution provides that senators are chosen by the president, with the advice and consent of the House of Representatives.

14. T F Every amendment to the Constitution has been ratified by the requisite number of state legislatures.

15. T F By amendment, the newly elected president is sworn in at noon on January 20.

MULTIPLE CHOICE

1. The Declaration of Independence begins with the following words:

 a. "We the people of the United States . . ."

 b. "We hold these truths to be self-evident . . ."

 c. "When in the course of human events . . ."

 d. "Congress shall make no law . . ."

2. The Declaration of Independence was signed on:

 a. July 4, 1765

 b. July 4, 1776

 c. July 4, 1789

 d. July 4, 1791

3. Due process of law is guaranteed in:

 a. The First Amendment

 b. The First and Fourth Amendments

 c. The Fifth and Fourteenth Amendments

 d. The Fifth and Sixteenth Amendments

4. No person shall be convicted of an impeachable offense under the U.S. Constitution without a vote of:

 a. Two-thirds of senators present

 b. Two-thirds of representatives present

 c. Three-fourths of senators present

 d. Three-fourths of representatives present

5. The Writ of Habeas Corpus may be suspended:

 a. In cases of rebellion

 b. In cases of invasion when the public safety may require it

 c. Upon a two-thirds vote of both Houses of Congress

 d. By the unanimous vote of the U.S. Supreme Court

6. Each state is entitled to the following number of representatives in Congress:

 a. Two

 b. Four

 c. Six

 d. None of the above

7. U.S. Supreme Court Justices are appointed by:

 a. A majority vote of both Houses of Congress.

 b. The president, with the advice and consent of a majority of the Senate.

 c. The president, with the advice and consent of a majority of the House of Representatives.

 d. None of the above.

8. The President may be removed from office on impeachment for, and conviction of:

 a. Treason

 b. Bribery

 c. Other high crimes and misdemeanors

 d. All of the above

9. Federal judges hold office:

 a. For twelve years

 b. During good behavior

 c. For the term approved by Congress

 d. For the term approved by the president

10. The Constitution may be amended when:

 a. Two-thirds of both Houses of Congress propose an amendment, which is ratified by the legislatures of two-thirds of the states.

 b. Two-thirds of the state legislatures propose an amendment, which is ratified by conventions in three-fourths of the states.

 c. Three-fourths of both Houses of Congress propose an amendment, which is ratified by the legislatures of two-thirds of the states.

 d. All of the above.

11. The Constitutional Convention was held in:

   a. Philadelphia in 1776

   b. New York in 1787

   c. Washington, D.C. in 1787

   d. Philadelphia in 1787

12. The First Amendment protects:

   a. The right to legal counsel

   b. The right to bear arms

   c. The right against self-incrimination

   d. The right to peaceably assemble

13. Thomas Jefferson's phrase "a wall of separation" referred to the separation of:

   a. The executive and legislative branches

   b. The Senate and the House of Representatives

   c. Church and state

   d. Federal Courts and the Electoral College

14. Women were guaranteed the right to vote in:

   a. Article II of the Constitution

   b. The First Amendment

   c. The Fourteenth Amendment

   d. The Nineteenth Amendment

15. The poll tax, which had to be paid in order to vote, was abolished by the ratification of:

   a. The Constitution in 1789

   b. The Bill of Rights in 1791

   c. The Fourteenth Amendment in 1868

   d. The Twenty-Fourth Amendment in 1964

FILL IN THE BLANK

1. "We hold these truths to be self-evident, that all men are _____."

2. Ratification of the U.S. Constitution required the approval of ___ states.

3. Members of the House of Representatives serve for ___ years and senators serve for ___ years.

4. Each state is entitled to ___ senators.

5. The minimum age for each of the following officials is as follows: president, ___ years old; senator, ___ years old; representative, ___ years old.

6. A House of Congress can override a presidential veto by a vote of _____.

7. A law directed at a specific person is known as a _____.

8. Under the Constitution, the United States is required to guarantee every state a _____ form of government.

9. The Bill of Rights was submitted to the First Congress by _____.

10. The group opposed to the ratification of the U.S. Constitution was called _____.

11. In the Bill of Rights, the _____ Amendment protects freedom of speech and freedom of the press.

12. The rule that a person may not be prosecuted for the same crime twice is called the prohibition against _____.

13. The group of individuals selected by each state to cast votes for the president and vice president is known as the _____.

14. The Eighth Amendment prohibits _____ punishments.

15. The system in the Constitution of allowing different branches of government to exercise certain authority so that no branch becomes too powerful is known as _____.

16. The Thirteenth, Fourteenth, and Fifteenth Amendments are known as the _____ Amendments because of the historical event that preceded their ratification.

17. Laws passed in southern states after the abolition of slavery to interfere with African Americans enjoying equal rights were known as _____ Laws.

18. A person can only serve __ terms as president, under the Constitution.

19. Since the Twenty-Sixth Amendment was passed in 1971, the minimum age to vote has been __ years old.

ACTIVITIES

1. Hold a press conference following the signing of the U.S. Constitution on September 23, 1787. Choose one person to be James Madison and another to be George Mason. Have several reporters ask them questions about their reactions to the new Constitution.

2. Conduct a Supreme Court argument on whether the Eighth Amendment prohibition against "cruel and unusual punishment" should be interpreted to ban the death penalty. Select a lawyer for each side and up to nine Supreme Court Justices.

3. The trial of King George III is set for July 4, 1776. Select someone to be Thomas Jefferson, as prosecuting attorney and others to be King George (to testify in his own defense), defense counsel, a judge and witnesses to be called by each side. Use the Declaration of Independence as the indictment.

4. Prepare a series of newspaper accounts, headlines and all, on a) the convening of the Constitutional Convention; b) an investigative story from inside the Convention; c) the day the new Constitution was announced, and d) the ratification debates.

5. It is the closing arguments in the trial of *United States v. Patrick Henry*. The defendant has been charged with treason for publicly attacking the U.S. Constitution. Select someone to present the argument for the United States and someone to be Patrick Henry, who is serving as his own attorney. Chose a three-judge panel to pose questions to the lawyers and to render a decision.

6. Conduct a confirmation hearing for Robert Bork to be a Supreme Court Justice. Select someone to be Bork, who has written and spoken widely in support of the view that the Constitution does not protect the right of privacy. Select several people to serve as members of the Senate Judiciary Committee, some supporting Bork and some opposing him, to question Bork and each other, following his opening statement to the Committee.

7. It is September 10, 1787. The place is the Philadelphia State House, location of the Constitutional Convention. Select someone to portray George Mason who presents a proposal to include a Bill of Rights in the proposed Constitution. Select someone else to portray Alexander Hamilton to argue that no Bill of Rights is necessary. If you like, select others to be additional delegates with differing points of view.

8. A legislative hearing has been called in your state capital to debate a proposed law to ban abortions. Select several people to serve as members of the legislative committee and several more to appear as witnesses, including representatives of Planned Parenthood, the National Organization of Women, the Right to Life Foundation, and the Christian Coalition. The agenda specifies that each witness is to address the issue of whether the right to an abortion is protected by the Constitution, and if so by what provisions or amendments and why this matter should not be left up to the state legislatures as the representatives of the people.

9. The president of the United States is about to address the American people on her position regarding the pending bill to amend the First Amendment to ban the burning of the American flag. The president has asked two representatives on each side of the issue to join her in the Oval Office, together with her Attorney General and several key aides. Select people to play all the parts and to explore the issue.

10. *Nightline* host Ted Koppel has invited representatives of the National Rifle Association and Handgun Control, Inc. to debate whether or not the Second Amendment prohibits a new bill introduced in Congress to ban all handguns, except those stored at shooting ranges and in ranger stations in wilderness parks for use by sportsmen while on those premises. Select people to play each of the parts. The show lasts 30 minutes and Koppel is always careful to give each side equal time.

Answers

TRUE / FALSE ANSWERS

1. T 2. F 3. F 4. F 5. T 6. F 7. F 8. F 9. T 10. F 11. F 12. F 13. F 14. F 15. T

MULTIPLE CHOICE ANSWERS

1. C 2. B 3. C 4. A 5. B 6. D 7. B 8. D 9. B 10. B 11. D 12. D 13. C 14. C 15. D

FILL IN THE BLANK ANSWERS

1. created equal 2. nine 3. two; six 4. two 5. thirty-five; thirty; twenty-five 6. two-thirds 7. bill of attainder 8. Republican 9. James Madison 10. Anti-Federalists 11. First 12. double jeopardy 13. Electoral College 14. cruel and unusual 15. checks and balances 16. Civil War 17. Jim Crow 18. two 19. eighteen

RESOURCES

The learning doesn't need to stop here. These resources give you the best of the best: great links to information in print, on film, and online.

BOOKS

Abraham, Henry J. and Perry, Barbara A., *Freedom and the Court: Civil Rights and Liberties in the United States*, New York: Oxford University Press, 1994.

Ackerman, Bruce, *We the People: Foundations*, Cambridge, MA: The Belknap Press of Harvard University Press, 1991.

Ackerman, Bruce, *We The People: Transformations*, Cambridge: The Belknap Press of Harvard University Press, 1998.

Amar, Akhil Reed, *The Bill of Rights: Creation and Reconstruction*, New Haven: Yale University Press, 1998.

Banning, Lance, *The Sacred Fire of Liberty: James Madison and the Founding of the Federal Republic*, Ithaca: Cornell University Press, 1995.

Belz, Herman, *Abraham Lincoln, Constitutionalism and Equal Rights in the Civil War Era*, New York: Fordham University Press, 1998.

Bradford, M.E., *Founding Fathers: Brief Lives of the Framers of the United States Constitution*, Lawrence: University Press at Kansas, 1994.

Cogan, Neil H. Editor, *The Complete Bill of Rights: The Drafts, Debates, Sources and Origins*, New York: Oxford University Press, 1997.

Hickok, Jr., Eugene W. Editor, *The Bill of Rights: Original Meaning and Current Understanding*, Charlottesville: University Press of Virginia, 1991.

Irons, Peter, *A People's History of the Supreme Court: The Men and Women Whose Cases and Decisions Have Shaped Our Constitution*, New York: Viking, 1999.

Kaminski, John P., Editor, *A Necessary Evil? Slavery and the Debate Over the Constitution*, Madison, WI: Madison House, 1995.

Keyssar, Alexander, *The Right to Vote: The Contested History of Democracy in the United States*, New York: Basic Books, 2000.

Levy, Leonard W. *Seasoned Judgments: The American Constitution, Rights and History*, New Brunswick: Transaction Publishers, 1997.

Lieberman, Jethro K., *A Practical Companion to the Constitution: How the Supreme Court Has Ruled on Issues from Abortion to Zoning*, Berkeley: University of California Press, 1999.

Miller, William Lee, *Arguing About Slavery: The Great Battle in the United States Congress*, New York: Alfred A. Knopf, 1996.

Presser, Stephen B., *Recapturing the Constitution: Race, Religion and Abortion Reconsidered*, Washington, DC: Regnery Publishing Inc. 1994.

Schecter, Stephen L., Editor, *Roots of the Republic: American Founding Documents Interpreted*, Madison WI: Madison House, 1990.

Smith, Page, *The Constitution: A Documentary and Narrative History*, New York: Morrow Quill Paperbacks, 1980.

Wood, Gordon S., *The Radicalism of the American Revolution: How a Revolution Transformed a Monarchical Society into a Democratic One Unlike Any That Had Ever Existed*, New York: Alfred A. Knopf, 1992.

Internet

http://www.cs.indiana.edu/statecraft/magna-carta.html

Find the text of the Magna Carta, a document that provided guidance to the framers of the Constitution.

http://www.cr.nps.gov/history/inde1.htm

Who would have thought that The National Parks Service would have such a great Web site devoted to the Declaration of Independence, the Articles of Confederation, and the Constitution? Most questions you have about any of these documents can probably be answered here.

http://www.nara.gov/exhall/charters

The National Archives and Records Administration handles this site, which gives a lot of useful information about the Declaration of Independence, the Constitution, and the Bill of Rights. The essay "The Stylistic Artistry of the Declaration of Independence" discusses the Declaration as a literary work.

http://www.toptags.com/aama/docs/doi.htm

This site discusses the omitted passage condemning slavery in Jefferson's original Declaration of Independence.

http://odur.let.rug.nl/~usa/GOV/chap1.htm

A series of well-written essays discuss the Constitution throughout its history.

http://www.constitutioncenter.org

According to its Web site, the National Constitution Center (NCC) is "an independent, nonpartisan, nonprofit organization. NCC was established to "increase awareness and understanding of the U.S." Constitution, the Constitution's history, and the Constitution's relevance to our daily lives so that all of us—'We the People'—will better understand and exercise our rights and our responsibilities."

http://www.aclu.org/library/pbp9.html

A brief history of The Bill of Rights is featured, appropriately enough, on the ACLU's Web site.

http://www.unitedstates-on-line.com/billofrights.htm

In addition to the accepted amendments to the Constitution, this site includes all of the amendments that were not ratified.

Films

1776. Directed by Peter Hunt. Columbia Tri-Star Home Video, 1972.

A musical(!) based on the events dealing with the drafting and signing of the Declaration of Independence. Parts of the dialogue and songs are actually taken from letters and journals of the participants.

Jefferson in Paris. Directed by James Ivory. Touchstone Video. 1995.

The movie chronicles Thomas Jefferson's stint as the Ambassador to France, focusing on his affair with slave Sally Hemings.

READING GROUP DISCUSSION GUIDE

Use the following questions and topics to enhance your reading group discussions. The discussions can help get you thinking—and hopefully talking—about the Declaration of Independence and the U.S. Constitution in a whole new way!

DISCUSSION QUESTIONS

1. Throughout American history, the debate has persisted over the true nature of the relationship between the people and their government. Does the government grant rights to the people or do their rights exist prior to the formation of a government? How does the text and the structure of the Constitution inform this debate? Does the Declaration of Independence illuminate this issue?

2. Several groups in American life were left out of the Constitution when it was written in 1787. Who were they and where in the text was their exclusion set forth, directly and indirectly? Did the Bill of Rights address these exclusions? Do any of the subsequent amendments do so?

3. Some observers see the Constitution and its amendments as part of a progression expanding individual rights. Is there support for this view? Trace the rights of minorities, women, and dissenters through the Constitution, the Bill of Rights, and the Subsequent Amendments to see if this theory is borne out.

4. Did the Constitution live up to the promise of the Declaration of Independence? Did the two documents have different purposes? Did the Constitution betray any of the ideals in the Declaration of Independence? Should laws be judged not only by whether they violate the Constitution, but also whether they offend the Declaration of Independence?

5. The president has the authority to nominate justices of the Supreme Court with the advice and consent of the Senate. Why did the framers include the Senate in this process? Given its advice and consent role, how should the Senate evaluate a Supreme Court nominee? Should a president have the prerogative to appoint a justice who reflects the president's ideology? Should the Senate reject a nominee because it disagrees with that ideology?

6. Article VI provides that the Constitution, the laws of the United States, and Treaties shall be "the supreme Law of the Land" and that state judges shall be bound thereby. The provision represents the triumph of one view of the national government over a competing view. What were those views and who represented them at the Constitutional Convention and during the ratification debates? How would America be different today if the competing view had prevailed?

7. The delegates to the Constitutional Convention in 1787 finished their work without including a Bill of Rights in the Constitution. George Mason and others urged that a Bill of Rights was necessary given the powers granted to Congress. Alexander Hamilton and others argued that no Bill of Rights was needed and could even be dangerous. How could such divergent views emerge from the Convention? Who had the better side of the argument? With perfect historical hindsight, who was right?

8. Under the First Amendment, the United States affords wider protection for freedom of speech and freedom of the press than any other country in the world when it comes to the protection of hate speech, offensive speech, or speech that espouses racist, sexist, homophobic, or other bigoted views. Does the language of the First Amendment support such broad constitutional protection for speech which many other countries restrict or ban? What values in the American system are furthered by protecting ideas most people find repulsive?

9. Controversy continues to rage over capital punishment. Under the Constitution and the Bill of Rights, what case can be made that the death penalty is unconstitutional and what case can be made upholding the constitutionality of capital punishment? Does the debate turn on the meaning of "cruel and unusual punishment?" What other provisions of the Constitution and Bill of Rights are relevant to the debate over the death penalty?

10. Many Americans hold deeply held opinions on the right to bear arms and gun control. Inevitably the debate centers on the Second Amendment. Does the Bill of Rights guarantee a constitutional right to own guns free of any governmental regulations? Can the right to bear arms be reconciled with the preamble to the Second Amendment? What did the framers mean by "a well-regulated militia?" To preserve the integrity of the Constitution, should gun control advocates concede that the Second Amendment protects the right to bear arms and seek a national consensus to repeal the Second Amendment?

11. In 1919, America prohibited the manufacture and sale of intoxicating liquors in the Eighteenth Amendment, but in 1933 that ban was repealed in the Twenty-First Amendment. What does this exercise say about the amendment process? Did the issue of Prohibition deserve to be regulated by constitutional amendment or should it have been dealt with by statute? How does an issue rise to the level of becoming a constitutional amendment?

12. Women have served vital roles in American society from the founding of the first colonies, yet they were not guaranteed the right to vote until 300 years later in the Nineteenth Amendment. How do you explain this? Why weren't women included with former slaves in gaining the right to vote 50 years earlier in the Fifteenth Amendment? Was this a function of prejudice, social convention, or something else?

13. The Twenty-Second Amendment limits an individual to no more than two terms as president. What constitutional values does this provision support? Does society lose anything because of this limitation? There's no limit on the number of terms a Senator or Representative can serve, yet the movement to impose term limits has spread to state and local offices. How do you explain this? Which is more important when it comes to elective officials: experience and continuity or fresh ideas and new blood?

Index

A

Abington School District v. Schempp, 79
abolition of slavery, 14, 25
Abraham Lincoln, Constitutionalism and Equal Rights in the Civil War Era (Belz), 149
ACLU Web site, 150
acting president, 140
Adams, Abigail, 130
Adams, John, 9, 53, 115, 130
Adams, John Quincy, 50
Adams, Samuel, 86
administrative agencies, 53
Agins v. City of Tiburon, 94
Agnew, Spiro, 140
Albany Congress, 8
Albany Plan of Union, 8, 9
Allgeyer v. Louisiana, 96
amendments, 25, 61, 111
    designing, 103–104
    failed, 111–112
    not permitted, 62
    process questions, 61–62
America
    aspiring to perfection, 34
    building nation of, 7–8
    direct trade with other nations, 9
    disunity, 21
    history tied to England, 7
    as loose confederation of states, 21
    seeds of identity and consciousness of, 7
American citizenship, definition of, 121
American Civil Liberties Union (ACLU), 81
American colonies. *See* colonies
American Revolution, 9
Americans
    declaring equality, 14
    dependence on themselves for survival, 7–8
    as distinct people, 9
    as one people, 34
    patterns of discrimination, 14
Anthony, Susan B., 130
Anti-Federalists, 27, 28, 29, 30, 31, 45, 71–74, 75, 76, 77, 100, 113
Anti-Terrorism and Effective Death Penalty Act, 46
appellate jurisdiction, 55
Areopagitica, 80

Arguing About Slavery: The Great Battle in the United States (Miller), 150
Aristotle, 29, 86
Arizona v. Fulminante, 93
armed forces, 45
army, 43, 45
Arthur, Chester A., 1140
Articles of Confederation, 21–23, 105
    discarding, 24
    federal ratio, 26
Ashcroft, John, 52
association, right of, 82

B

bail, right to, 101–102
Baker v. Carr, 57
Barron v. Baltimore, 77
Batson v. Kentucky, 98
Beacon Theatres Inc. v. Westover, 100
Beale, Robert, 89
bicameral, 24
Bill of Rights, 14, 30–31, 111, 142
    Anti-Federalists for, 72–73
    arguments over, 72–74
    call for, 74–75
    common law and, 90
    as condition of ratification, 74
    demand for, 71–72
    Eighth Amendment, 101–102
    Federalists opposing, 72
    Fifth Amendment, 92–96
    First Amendment, 77–85
    Fourth Amendment, 89–91
    Madison backing, 75
    Ninth Amendment, 103–104
    ratifying, 75–76
    Second Amendment, 86–87
    Seventh Amendment, 100
    Sixth Amendment, 97–99
    Tenth Amendment, 105–107
    Third Amendment, 88
    U.S. Constitution without, 71
Bill of Rights: Creation and Reconstruction, The (Amar), 149
Bill of Rights: Original Meaning and Current Understanding, The (Hickok), 149
Bill of Rights Web site, 150
bills of attainder, 46
Black, Hugo L., 104
Black Codes, 118
Blackmun, Harry, 96

Blackstone, William, 86
Boerne v. Flora, 80
Bonham's Case, 57
Bork, Robert, 52
Boutwell, George S., 124
Brady Handgun Violence Prevention Act, 107
Breedlove v. Sattles, 138
Brennan, William J., Jr., 46, 79, 82, 104
bribery, 53
British Bill of Rights of 1689, 84
British Constitution, 7
British monarchy, 9, 14, 15
British political theorists, 14
Brown v. Board of Education, 57
Brown v. Gilnes, 84
Brown v. Mississippi, 93
Buckley v. American Constitutional Law Foundation, 84
Burch v. Louisiana, 98
Burger, Warren E., 79
Burns, Harry, 131
Burr, Aaron, 50, 115
Bush, George, 52
Bush, George W., 50, 51, 52, 115, 126

C

cabinet, 53
California v. LaRue, 134
Cameron, Simon, 124
Cardozo, Benjamin N., 78
Carlson v. Landon, 101
Carroll v. United States, 90, 134
cases in equity, 100
cases in law, 100
Cases v. United States, 87
Causby v. United States, 94
census, 41
Champion v. Ames, 106
Charter of The London Company, 8
Chase, Salmon P., 46
Chase, Samuel P., 53
checks and balances, 43
Chimel v. California, 89
Chisholm v. Georgia, 113
Cicero, 86
Circuit Court of Appeals, 55
citizen militia, 15
civil libertarians, 46
civil rights, 82–83, 122, 141
Civil Rights Act of 1866, 118, 119, 121

Civil Rights Act of 1957, 125
Civil Rights Act of 1960, 125
Civil Rights Act of 1964, 118, 125
Civil Rights Cases, 118, 119
Civil War, 60, 117, 122
Civil War Amendments, 1, 125
Cleveland, Grover, 50
Clinton, Bill, 46, 51, 53, 136
Coke, Edward, 57
colonial government, 9, 15
colonies, 7–10, 14–15
colonists, 9, 82
Commerce Clause, 44–45
Commissioner v. Glenshaw Glass Co., 127
Committee of Detail, 33
Committee of Five, 9, 10, 15
Committee of Style, 33
Committee to Defend Martin Luther
    King, 82
Common Sense (Paine), 9
Communications Decency Act
    (CDA), 81
*Complete Bill of Rights: The Drafts,
    Debates, Sources and Origins, The*
    (Cogan), 149
condemnation, 94
conditional amendments, 30
Confederacy, 116, 121
Confederation Congress, 27
Congress, 40–41
    and amendment process, 61
    armed forces, 45
    beginning term of office, 133
    bicameral, 24
    effects of New Deal, 44
    enumerated powers, 43
    implied powers, 43
    legislation, 42–43
    limitations on power of, 45–46
    necessary and proper laws, 45
    pay raises, 142
    power to impose and collect
        taxes, 127
    powers of, 43, 45
    racial discrimination, 44–45
    regulating commerce, 43–44
    representatives in, 24
    rules of, 42–43
Congressional Record, 42
Connecticut, 21–23, 30
Connecticut colony, 8
conscience, freedom of, 78
*Constitution: A Documentary and Narra-
    tive History, The* (Smith), 150
Constitutional Convention, 23–25, 44,
    100, 103, 127
Constitutional Essays Web site, 150
constitutionality, deciding, 56–57

constitutions. *See also* U.S. Constitution
    differences in states', 23
    drafting of, 21
    state, 23–23
Continental Association, 14
Continental Congress, 21–22
Cooper v. Aaron, 57
copyright, 45
Copyright Clause, 74
Corfield v. Coryell, 60
Cornwallis, Lord, 21
Coxe, Tench, 25
Cramer v. United States, 56
crimes, 46–47, 60
cruel and unusual punishment, 102

D

Daily Advertiser, 29
Davis, Barrett, 122
Davis v. Beason, 79
Declaration of Independence, 7, 21,
    34, 84, 88
    colonial legislatures, 15
    Committee of Five, 9
    criticism of slavery, 15
    documents based on, 10
    drafting committee for, 9
    English precedents to, 7
    grievances against King George, 15
    influence of, 10
    Lincoln on, 10
    opposing tyranny, 10
    Preamble, 10, 14
    protecting people from foreign and
        domestic attack, 15
    reflecting ideas and complaints of
        colonists, 9
    right of people to overthrow
        tyranny, 14
    right to trial by jury, 15
    taxation without representation, 15
    text, 11–13
    upholding equality, 10
    ways war was made on colonies, 15
Declaration of Independence Web
    site, 150
Declaration of Rights and Grievances, 9
Declaration of Rights of 1689, 7
defamation, 81–82
defense, 43
Delaware, 21, 23, 30
democracy, 30
Democratic Federalist, A, 74
Democratic National Convention, 83
Democratic-Republican party, 50
Democrats, 117, 123, 124, 125
denial of equal rights, 14
Dillon v. Gloss, 61
direct taxes, 127

discrimination, 14, 57–58
disenfranchising voters, 121–122
District Courts, 55
District of Columbia, 45, 137
dividing states into confederations, 22
divine right, 15
domestic responsibilities, 34
domestic tranquility, 34
Dominion of New England, 8
double jeopardy, 93–94
Douglas, William O., 53, 102, 104, 138
Douglass, Frederick, 2
Dred Scott v. Sandford, 118
due process, 95–96, 98, 121–122
Duer, William, 28

E

ecclesiastical courts, 92
economic problems and Continental
    Congress, 21–22
educated people in eighteenth century, 9
Edwards v. Aguillard, 79
Edwards v. South Carolina, 84
Eighteenth Amendment, 129
Eighth Amendment, 101–102
Eisenhower, Dwight D., 136
Eisenstadt v. Baird, 104
Eisner v. Macomber, 127
Electoral College, 25, 40, 50–51,
    115, 137
Eleventh Amendment, 113
Elks' Lodge v. Ingraham, 134
Emancipation Proclamation, 116–117
eminent domain, 94–95
Employment Division v. Smith, 79–80
End to Obscenity, The, 81
Enforcement Act, 125
Engel v. Vitale, 79
England, 7–9
    boycotting shipping proposal, 14
    right against self-incrimination, 92
English Bill of Rights in 1689, 88,
    101–102
English precedents to Declaration of
    Independence, 7
English Quartering Act, 88
Enlightenment, 78
Equal Employment Opportunity
    Commission (EEOC), 52
equal protection under the law, 121–122
equal rights, denial of, 14
Equal Rights Amendment, 111–112
equality, 10, 14
Escobedo v. Illinois, 98
Establishment Clause, 78–79
Euclid v. Ambler Realty Co., 94
*Everson v. Board of Education of Ewing
    Township,* 78

ex post facto laws, 46
excessive fines, 101–102
exclusionary rule, 90
executive branch, 21, 24–25, 52–53
expression, freedom of, 80–81

F

factionalism, 30
failed amendments, 111–112
fair market value, 94
Fay v. Noia, 46
Federal Aviation Administration, 53
Federal Communications
    Commission, 53
Federal Elections Bill, 125
federal government
    branches of, 24–25
    checks and balances, 43
    legislative branch, 40–47
    purposes for, 34
    raising revenue for, 42
    status of, 60
federal ratio, 26
Federal Trade Commission, 53
*Federal Trade Commission v. Ruberoid
    Company,* 53
Federalist, The, 28–30, 31, 33, 60, 72
Federalist Farmer, The, 74
Federalist No. 10, 115
Federalist No. 39, 105
Federalist No. 43, 62
Federalist No. 69, 136
Federalist No. 80, 56, 60
Federalist No. 86, 86
Federalist Republican, A, 74
Federalists, 27–30, 71–72, 75, 105
felonies, 60
Field, Stephen J., 60
Fifteenth Amendment, 123–126
Fifth Amendment, 92–96
First Amendment, 77–85
First Continental Congress, 9, 14
Fitzsimmons, Thomas, 30
Florida Supreme Court, 50
Foner, Eric, 2
Food and Drug Administration, 53
Ford, Gerald R., 53, 140
formal declaration of independence,
    9, 15
*Founding Fathers: Brief Lives of the
    Framers of the United States
    Constitution* (Bradford), 149
Fourteenth Amendment, 121–122
Fourth Amendment, 89–91
franchise, 123
Frankfurter, Felix, 95
Franklin, Benjamin, 8–9, 24–27, 25
Free Exercise Clause, 78, 79–80

free people, relationship of government
    with, 14–15
*Freedom and the Court: Civil Rights and
    Liberties in the United States*
    (Abraham and Perry), 149
freedom of
    conscience, 78
    expression, 80–81
    movement, hindrances to, 15
    press, 80
    religion, 78–80
    speech, 80
French, confederation for mutual
    defense against, 8
French Declaration of Rights of
    1789, 10
Fry v. United States, 106
Furman v. Georgia, 102

G

*Garcia v. San Antonio Metropolitan
    Transit Authority,* 106
Garfield, James, 140
gender and right to vote, 130–131
general warrants, 89
George III, King of England,
    2, 7, 9–10, 14–15, 100
Georgia, 23, 30
Gerry, Elbridge, 27, 72
Gibbons v. Ogden, 44
gifts from foreign states, 46–47
Gitlow v. New York, 77
Glorious Revolution, 8
Gore, Al, 50, 115, 126
government
    based on consent of governed, 15
    branches of, 24–25
    creation of nation government, 21
    deriving power from governed, 14
    domestic responsibilities, 34
    domestic tranquility, 34
    establishing new, 15
    executive branch, 24–25
    international responsibilities, 34
    judicial branch, 24–25
    justice, 34
    lack of executive branch, 21
    legislative branch, 24–25
    national defense, 34
    organization under Articles of
        Confederation, 21
    power without consent of people,
        14–15
    purposes for, 34
    relationship with free people, 14–15
    securing liberty, 35
    securing rights of people, 14
Grand Council, 8
Grant, Ulysses S., 124, 125

Grayson, William, 72, 75
Great Charter, 7
Great Depression, 44
Great Writ, 46
Gregg v. Georgia, 102
Griffin v. California, 93
Griswold v. Connecticut, 83, 96, 103–104
gun regulations, 87

H

Habeas Corpus, Writ of, 46
*Hague v. Congress of Industrial
    Organizations,* 83
Hamilton, Alexander, 28–29, 31, 33, 45,
    56, 60, 72, 73, 105, 113, 136
Harper v. Virginia Board of Elections, 138
Harris v. New York, 93
Harrison, Benjamin, 50, 115
Harrison, William Henry, 51
Hayes, Rutherford B., 50, 115
Heart of Atlanta Motel v. United States,
    44, 118–119
Helvering v. Bruun, 127
Henry, Patrick, 30, 31, 34, 50, 71, 73,
    74, 76, 86
Herrera v. Collins, 46
High Commission against Puritans, 89
Hill, Anita, 52
Hodges v. United States, 118
Hollingsworth v. Virginia, 61
Holmes, Oliver Wendell, Jr., 80, 94, 96
House of Representatives, 40–43, 50
Howard, Jacob, 60
Hylton v. United States, 127

I

illegal quartering, 88
illegal search and seizure, 89–91
Illinois v. Perkins, 93
immigration, interfering with, 15
impeachment, 53, 55
in re Winship, 98
incorporation doctrine, 78
Independent Journal, 28
indirect taxes, 127
individual liberties, 28
Ingraham v. Wright, 95
initiatives, 84
injustice, 34
institutionalizing slavery, 26
intellectual brilliance, 9–10
international responsibilities, 34
Internet, 81
interstate commerce, 44
intrastate commerce, 44

J

Jackson, Andrew, 50, 57, 118
Jackson, Robert H., 53
Jackson, William, 24
Jacobson v. Massachusetts, 34
James II, King of England, 7
Jamestown Colony, 8
Jay, John, 22, 28, 29, 33, 72, 113
Jay Treaty, 52
J.E.B. v. Alabama ex rel. T.B., 98
Jefferson, Thomas, 2, 9–10, 14, 15, 45, 46, 50, 57, 71, 73, 76, 105, 115
Jefferson in Paris (film), 150
Jim Crow laws, 125
John, King of England, 7
Johnson, Andrew, 53, 117, 118, 121, 122, 123
Johnson, Lyndon B., 140
Johnson v. Zerbst, 98
Joint Anti-Fascist Committee v. McGrath, 95
Joint Committee on Reconstruction, 121
Jones v. Alfred H. Mayer, 119
judicial activism, 57, 58
judicial branch, 24–25, 45
judicial process, preventing independence of, 15
judicial restraint, 57, 58
judicial review, 56–57
jury, 55
justice, establishment of, 34

K

Kaiser Aetna v. United States, 94
Katz v. United States, 90
Katzenbach v. McClung, 119
keep and bear arms, right to, 86–87
Kennedy, Anthony, 93
Kennedy, John F., 140
Kent State University, 83
Keysaar, Alexander, 124
kings
    colonial charters and, 8
    divine right, 15
    limits on authority of, 7
Ku Klux Klan, 46, 124, 125

L

labor unions, 82
laissez-faire capitalism, 96
laws, 46–47
    authority to enforce federal laws, 52–53
    constitutionality of, 56–57

due process of, 95–96
governing relationship between ruler and subjects, 7
necessary and proper, 45
religion conflicting with, 79–80
secular legislative purpose, 78
striking down federal and state laws, 57
supreme law of the land, 63
Lee, Richard Henry, 9, 72, 75
Lee, Robert E., 117
legal counsel, right of, 98–99
legislation, 42–43
legislative branch, 24–25, 40–47
Lemon v. Kurtzman, 78
Leser v. Garnett, 61
Lewinsky, Monica, 53
Lexington, Massachusetts, 9
liberty, 34, 95
Lilburne, John, 92
Lincoln, Abraham, 2, 10, 51, 57, 116–117
Livingston, Robert R., 9
Lochner v. New York, 96
Locke, John, 14, 25, 86
Lodge, Henry Cabot, 125
Los Angeles Police Department, 93–94
lower federal courts, 45
loyal opposition, 81
Loyalists, 8

M

Madison, James, 2, 10, 22, 24, 26, 28, 30, 33, 45, 60, 62, 72, 74, 75, 76, 78, 86, 88, 89, 92, 95, 101, 103–104, 105, 113, 115, 142
Magna Carta, 7, 84, 89, 95
Magna Carta Web site, 150
Marbury v. Madison, 56, 57
Marshall, John, 56, 105, 106, 118
Marshall, Thurgood, 52, 80
Martin, Luther, 24, 57
Mary of Orange, Queen of England, 7, 8
Maryland, 21, 23, 31
Maryland colony, 8
Mason, George, 2, 10, 25, 27, 30–31, 61, 71–73, 101
Massachusetts, 9, 22–23, 31
Massachusetts Act of 1692, 95
Massachusetts Bay colony, 8
Massachusetts v. Sheppard, 90
Mayflower, 7
Mayflower Compact, 7
McCarthy v. Arndstein, 93
McCulloch v. Maryland, 45, 106
McDonald v. Santa Fe Trail Transportation Co., 119

McIntyre v. Ohio Elections Commission, 84
McKinley, William, 51
McLean, Andrew, 29
McLean, John, 29
Michigan v. Tucker, 93
militia, 15, 45, 86–87
Miller, William Lee, 118
Miller v. California, 81
Milton, John, 80
minimum voting age, 141
Minnesota v. Kickerson, 89–90
Minor v. Happersett, 130
Miranda v. Arizona, 93, 98
Miranda warnings, 93, 98
Montesquieu, 29
Moorhead v. New York ex rel. Tipaldo, 96
Morris, Gouverneur, 28, 33, 127
Mott, Lucretia, 130
Murray's Lessee v. Hoboken Land & Improvement Co., 95

N

NAACP v. Alabama, 83
National Archives and Records Administration Web site, 150
national bank, 45
National Constitution Center (NCC) Web site, 150
national courts, 21
national defense, 34
National Endowment for the Arts (NEA), 81
national government, 21–22
National Guard, 45
National Labor Relations Act, 44
National League of Cities v. Usery, 106
National Park Service Web site, 150
National Prohibition Cases, 61, 129
National Rifle Association, 87
National Treasury Employees Union v. von Raab, 90
National Women's Party, 131
National Women's Suffrage Association, 131
Native Americans, 8, 41
naturalization, 43
navy, 43, 45
Necessary and Proper Clause, 45
Necessary Evil? Slavery and the Debate Over the Constitution, A, (Keysaar), 149
Nectow v. City of Cambridge, 94
New Deal, effects of, 44
New England Confederation, 8, 9
New Hampshire, 22–23, 31
New Hampshire colony, 8

New Haven colony, 8
New Jersey, 21, 23
New Jersey colony, 8
New Jersey Plan, 24
New York, 23, 31
New York colony, 8
New York Journal, 29
New York Packet, 29
New York Times, The, 82
New York Times v. Sullivan, 82
New York v. Quarles, 93
Nineteenth Amendment, 130–131
Ninth Amendment, 103–104
Nix v. Williams, 90
Nixon, Richard M., 53, 136, 140
Nixon v. Condon, 125
Nixon v. Herndon, 125
*Nollan v. California Coastal
    Commission,* 94
non-capital crimes, 101
North American continent, 7
North Briton No. 45, The, 89
North Carolina, 23, 31

O

Olmstead v. United States, 134
opposing tyranny, 10
Oregon v. Mitchell, 141
original jurisdiction, 55

P

Paine, Thomas, 9, 85
Palko v. Connecticut, 78
Paterson, William, 24
peaceable assembly, right of, 82–83
pen names, 28
Pendleton, Edmond, 31
Pennsylvania, 21, 23, 30
Pennsylvania Abolition Society, 25
Pennsylvania Coal Co. v. Mahon, 94
Pennsylvania colony, 8
Pennsylvania Gazette, 10
*People's History of the Supreme Court:
    The Men and Women Whose Cases
    and Decisions Have Shaped Our
    Constitution, A* (Irons), 149
personal freedoms, protecting, 46
personal rights, 121
petition, right to, 84–85
Petition of Right, 88
Pilgrims, 7, 78
placemen, 28
Plymouth colony, 8
pocket veto, 43
political protesters, 82–83
Polk, James, 51

poll taxes, 138
Pollack v. Farmers' Loan and Trust Co., 127
popular support for war against
    England, 9
Powell v. Alabama, 98
*Practical Companion to the Constitution:
    How the Supreme Court Has Ruled
    on Issues from Abortion to Zoning,
    A* (Lieberman), 149
Preamble to the U.S. Constitution,
    33–35
president, 25, 47, 50–51
    additional powers and responsibilities,
        52–53
    beginning term of office, 133
    cabinet, 53
    clashes with Senate, 52
    disability of, 140
    filling vacancies, 52
    impeachment, 53
    limiting terms of, 136
    powers of, 51–52
    separate ballot for, 115
press, freedom of, 80
Presser, Herman, 87
Presser v. Illinois, 87
Prinz v. United States, 107
prior restraint, 82
privacy, right of, 83, 89–91
private property, 94–95
private sexual behavior, 104
Privilege and Immunities Clause, 60
prohibition, 129, 134–135
protecting
    people from foreign and domestic
        attack, 15
    personal freedoms, 46
pseudonyms, 28
Publius Valerius, 28, 29
Purnell v. McCormack, 57

Q

Quakers, 14
quartering, 88
Quebec, Roman system of law in, 15
Quilici v. Village of Morton Grove, 87
quorum, 21

R

racial discrimination, 44–45
Radical Republicans, 123
*Radicalism of the American Revolution:
    How a Revolution Transformed a
    Monarchical Society into a Democ-
    ratic One Unlike Any that Had
    Ever Existed, The* (Wood), 150

Randolph, Edmund, 24, 27
rationalism, 78
Reagan, Ronald, 52, 136, 140
recall of elected officials or judges, 84
*Recapturing the Constitution: Race,
    Religion and Abortion Reconsidered*
    (Presser), 150
recommended amendments, 30
reconstructing states, 117
Reconstruction Act of 1867, 123
Redemption Movement, 125
redress of grievances, 84–85
regulating commerce, 43–44
regulating interstate commerce,
    134–135
Rehnquist, William H., 96, 107
religion, 78–80
Religious Freedom Restoration Act
    (RFRA), 80
religious tests, 63
Rembar, Charles, 81
Reno v. ACLU, 81
repeal of prohibition, 135
representatives
    compensation, 42
    election of, 42
Republican Form of Government, 123
republican government, 60
Republicans, 117, 121, 124, 125
retaining rights, 103–104
Revolutionary War, 9, 14, 22
Reynolds v. United States, 79
Rhode Island, 21, 22, 23, 30, 31
Rhode Island colony, 8
right against self-incrimination, 92–93
right of
    association, 82
    eminent domain, 94–95
    legal counsel, 98–99
    peaceable assembly, 82–83
    privacy, 83, 89–91
    trial by jury, 100
right to
    bail, 101–102
    call and confront witnesses, 98
    keep and bear arms, 86–87
    petition, 84–85
    speedy and public trial, 97
    trial by jury, 15
    vote, 122, 123–126, 130–131, 138
rights
    enumeration of, 103
    personal, 121
    reserved for state and the people,
        105–107
    retaining, 103–104
Rockefeller, Nelson A., 140
Roe v. Wade, 96, 104
Roman system of law in Quebec, 15

Roosevelt, Franklin D., 44, 57, 136, 140
Roots of the Republic: American Founding Documents Interpreted (Schecter), 150
Rosenberger v. University of Virginia, 79
Rotary International v. Rotary Club of Duarte, 83
Runyon v. McCrary, 119
Rutledge, John, 52

S

Sacred File of Liberty: James Madison and the Founding of the Federal Republic, The (Banning), 149
Saenz v. Roe, 60
Santosky v. Kramer, 95
Scalia, Antonin, 80, 107
Schall v. Martin, 101
Schib v. Kuebel, 101
Scott, Dred, 118
Scottsboro Boys, 98
Seasoned Judgments: The American Constitution, Rights and History (Levy), 149
Second Amendment, 86–87
Second Continental Congress, 9
    Articles of Confederation, 21–23
    criticism of slavery, 15
    drafting constitution, 21
    opening American ports to foreign commerce, 14
Securities and Exchange Commission, 53
self-government by Pilgrims, 7
self-incrimination, right against, 92–93
Senate, 40, 43
    founding of, 41–42
    presidential clashes with, 52
    Supreme Court nominees, 52
    vice president, 42
    vice president winner, 50
Senate Judiciary Committee, 52
senators, 42, 128
Seneca Falls Convention, 10
Seneca Falls Declaration of Sentiments and Resolution, 130
separation between church and state, 63, 78
separatists, 7
1776 (film), 150
Seventeenth Amendment, 128
Seventh Amendment, 100
Shays, Daniel, Captain, 22
Shays Rebellion, 22–23
Sherbert v. Verner, 79
Sherman, Roger, 9, 72
Sixteenth Amendment, 127
Sixth Amendment, 97–99
slander, 81–82

Slaughterhouse Cases, 60
slavery
    abolition of, 14, 25
    attempts to abolish, 14
    Constitution, 25–27
    criticism of, 15
    economic dependence on, 14
    endorsement of, 46
    federal ratio, 26
    indirect references to, 26
    institutionalizing, 26
    limiting tax on, 26
    perpetuating, 60
    preventing Congress from prohibiting, 26
    prohibition of, 116–119
    renewal of slave trade by Americans, 14
    runaway slaves, 26
    states, 25
    U.S. Supreme Court and, 118
slaves, 41
    denial of equal rights, 14
    equality and, 14
    importation of, 46
    payment for loss of, 122
Smith v. Allwright, 125
South Carolina, 23, 31
speech, freedom of, 80
speedy and public trial, right to, 97
Speedy Trial Act, 97
Springer v. United States, 127
Stack v. Boyle, 101
Stanton, Elizabeth Cady, 130
State Board v. Young's Market, 134
state constitutions. *See* constitutions; states
state courts, 55
state governments, establishment of, 9
state legislators, 41–42
state legislatures
    delegates to Continental Congress, 21
    election of senators and representatives, 42
    taxes, 22
states
    admitting new, 60
    conditional ratification, 30
    conflicts between, 21
    constitutions, 23–24
    Declaration of Rights, 77
    differences in constitutions, 23
    dividing into confederations, 22
    favoring sovereignty of, 28
    freedom to trade with foreign nations, 22
    honoring other state's acts, records, and judicial proceedings, 60
    ineffectiveness to manage affairs, 22–23
    lack of cooperation among, 34

limitations on, 47
loose confederation of, 21
passing legislation, 21
ratification of amendments, 25
ratification of Constitution, 27, 30–32
regulating interstate commerce, 134–135
relinquishing power to federal government, 25
representation by population, 41
representatives in Congress, 24
respecting sovereignty of, 77
slavery, 25
sovereignty and independence of, 113
supreme over Continental Congress, 21
uniformity and consistency between, 60
Steven, John Paul, 107
Stewart, Potter, 102
Stone, Harlan Fiske, 106
Stone v. Graham, 79
Stone v. Powell, 46
Story of American Freedom, The, 2
Stuart monarchy, 8
subpoena, 98
suffrage, 123
Sullivan, L.B., 82
suppressing insurrection or rebellion, 122
Supreme Court. *See* U.S. Supreme Court
symbolic speech, 82

T

Taft, William Howard, 127
Takings Clause, 94
Talley v. California, 84
Taney, Roger, 118
taxation without representation, 9, 15
taxes, 42, 46–47
    Continental Congress, 22
    imposing and collecting, 43
    power to impose and collect, 127
    state legislatures, 22
Tenth Amendment, 105–107
Terry v. Adams, 125
Texas v. Johnson, 82
Third Amendment, 88
Thirteenth Amendment, 14, 116–119
Thomas, Clarence, 52
Thornhill v. Alabama, 84
Three-Fifths Clause, 117
Tilden, Samuel J., 50
titles, 46
trade with foreign nations, 22
treason, 53, 55–56, 60
treaties, 63

trial by jury, right of, 55, 97–98, 100
trial court, 55
Trop v. Dulles, 102
Truman, Harry S., 51, 53, 1140
Twelfth Amendment, 115
Twentieth Amendment, 133
Twenty-Fifth Amendment, 140
Twenty-First Amendment, 134–135
Twenty-Fourth Amendment, 138
Twenty-Second Amendment, 136
Twenty-Seventh Amendment, 142
Twenty-Sixth Amendment, 141
Twenty-Third Amendment, 137
tyranny, 10, 14

U

unalienable rights, 103–104
unification of colonies, 8–9
United Colonies of New England, 8
United States of America, 34
    See also America
United States v. Calandra, 90
United States v. Darby Lumber Co., 106
United States v. Grace, 84
United States v. Havens, 90
United States v. Lanza, 134
United States v. Leon, 90
United States v. Lopez, 106–107
United States v. Miller, 87
upholding equality, 10
U.S. Constitution, 14, 105
    amendments, 25, 61–62
    Article I, 40–47
    Article II, 50–53
    Article III, 55–58
    Article IV, 60
    Article V, 61–62
    Article VI, 63
    Article VII, 65
    without Bill of Rights, 71
    Committee of Detail, 33
    Committee of Style, 33
    comprehensive defense of, 28
    conditional amendments, 30
    continuing establishment of, 34
    creation of, 24–25
    Federalists, 27–30
    final draft, 26
    indirect references to slavery, 26
    oath to support, 63

organizing and drafting final text, 33
permanence and continuity of, 34
Preamble, 33–35
ratification of amendments, 25
ratification process, 27, 61–62, 65
recommendary amendments, 30
recommended amendments, 30
slavery, 25–27
state ratification of, 30–32
as supreme law of the land, 56, 63
Three-Fifths clause, 26
valid debts and contracts, 63
U.S. Supreme Court, 50
    appellate jurisdiction, 55
    Civil War Amendments, 125
    deciding constitutionality, 56–57
    discrimination, 57–58
    guidelines, 57
    jurisdiction, 100, 113
    Necessary and Proper Clause, 45
    nominees, 52
    original jurisdiction, 55
    powers of, 55
    Second Amendment and, 87
    slavery and, 118
    striking down federal and state
        laws, 57

V

valid debts and contracts, 63
Vermont, 23
Vernonia School District v. Acton, 90
veto, 42
vice president
    beginning term of office, 133
    election of, 50
    senate, 42
    separate ballot for, 115
    vacancy of office, 140
Vietnam War, 82–83, 141
Virginia, 21, 23, 31
Virginia Constitution, 10, 92
Virginia Declaration of Rights, 10, 71,
    72, 92, 101
Virginia Plan, 24
vote, right to, 123–126, 130–131, 138
voting, minimum age for, 141
Voting Rights Act Amendment
    of 1970, 141
Voting Rights Act of 1965,
    125–126, 141

W

*Walters v. National Association of
    Radiation Survivors,* 84
war
    colonies and, 9–10
    declaring, 45
War of Independence, 9–10, 21
warrants, 89
Warren, Earl, 46, 104
Washington, Bushrod, 60
Washington, D.C., 45
Washington, George, 14, 21–22, 31, 50,
    51, 52, 71, 105, 136, 140
Washington Post, The, 82
Watergate scandal, 53
We the People: Foundations
    (Ackerman), 149
We the People: Transformations
    (Ackerman), 149
Weeks v. United States, 90
Weems v. United States, 102
well-regulated militia, 86–87
White, Byron, 96, 102
White, Ronnie, 52
Whitehall, Robert, 74
Wickersham Commission, 93
Widmar v. Vincent, 79
William of Orange, King of England,
    7, 8
Williams, Roger, 78
Wilson, Henry, 124
Wilson, James, 73, 113
Wilson, Woodrow, 52
Wisconsin v. Yoder, 79
Witherspoon v. Illinois, 97
witnesses, right to call and confront, 98
Wolf v. Colorado, 90
women's suffrage, 130–131
Woodward, Charlotte, 130
World Trade Organization (Seattle), 83
Writ of Habeas Corpus, 46
Wythe, George, 31

Y

Yates v. United States, 83
*Youngstown Sheet and Tube Company v.
    Sawyer,* 53

Notes

APPENDIX

President George W. Bush
ADDRESS TO A JOINT SESSION OF CONGRESS AND THE AMERICAN PEOPLE
September 20, 2001

Commentary by Marcus A. Stadelmann, PhD
Associate Professor of Political Science
at the University of Texas at Tyler

Address to a Joint Session of Congress and the American People

America's most recent and compelling words of freedom come in the wake of the calamity that the United States—the entire world—experienced on September 11, 2001. On that fateful day in American history, the face of terrorism evoked precisely what it did not intend to: It rallied the American people to a spirit of unprecedented unity and patriotism as families across the nation sat down to dinner and discussed the price of freedom. Instead of creating panic, the terrorist acts achieved the opposite: America rallied around its flag and its president.

President Bush opened his arms wide and comforted his country and its people, vowing in a speech delivered before the U.S. Congress on September 20, 2001, that the voices of all Americans — of all freedom-loving people throughout the world — would ring true and deliver us from the scourge of terrorism. Bolstered by the sense of a noble and just cause and steeled with a steadfast determination, President Bush faced terrorism head on and resolutely proclaimed, "Whether we bring our enemies to justice, or bring justice to our enemies, justice will be done."

September 20, 2001

Mr. Speaker, Mr. President Pro Tempore, members of Congress, and fellow Americans:

In the normal course of events, Presidents come to this chamber to report on the state of the Union. Tonight, no such report is needed. It has already been delivered by the American people.

We have seen it in the courage of passengers who rushed terrorists to save others on the ground—passengers like an exceptional man named Todd Beamer. And would you please help me to welcome his wife, Lisa Beamer, here tonight.

We have seen the state of our Union in the endurance of rescuers, working past exhaustion. We have seen the unfurling of flags, the lighting of candles, the giving of blood, the saying of prayers—in English, Hebrew, and Arabic. We have seen the decency of a loving and giving people who have made the grief of strangers their own.

NOTES

Mr. Speaker: refers to the Speaker of the House, the presiding officer of the House of Representatives, elected by the majority party.

Mr. President Pro Tempore: In the U.S. Senate, usually the senior member of the majority party who presides over the Senate in the absence of the vice president.

My fellow citizens, for the last nine days, the entire world has seen for itself the state of our Union—and it is strong.

Tonight we are a country awakened to danger and called to defend freedom. Our grief has turned to anger, and anger to resolution. Whether we bring our enemies to justice, or bring justice to our enemies, justice will be done.

I thank the Congress for its leadership at such an important time. All of America was touched on the evening of the tragedy to see Republicans and Democrats joined together on the steps of this **Capitol**, singing **"God Bless America."** And you did more than sing; you acted, by delivering $40 billion to rebuild our communities and meet the needs of our military.

Speaker Hastert, Minority Leader Gephardt, Majority Leader Daschle, and **Senator Lott**, I thank you for your friendship, for your leadership and for your service to our country.

And on behalf of the American people, I thank the world for its outpouring of support. America will never forget the sounds of our National Anthem playing at **Buckingham Palace**, on the streets of Paris, and at Berlin's **Brandenburg Gate**.

We will not forget South Korean children gathering to pray outside our embassy in **Seoul**, or the prayers of sympathy offered at a mosque in **Cairo**. We will not forget moments of silence and days of mourning in Australia and Africa and Latin America.

Nor will we forget the citizens of 80 other nations who died with our own: dozens of Pakistanis; more than 130 Israelis; more than 250 citizens of India; men and women from El Salvador, Iran, Mexico, and Japan; and hundreds of British citizens. America has no truer friend than Great Britain. Once again, we are joined together in a great cause—so honored the **British Prime Minister** has crossed an ocean to show his unity of purpose with America. Thank you for coming, friend.

On September the 11th, enemies of freedom committed an act of war against our country. Americans have known wars—but for the past 136 years, they have been wars on foreign soil, except

Capitol: the building in Washington, D.C. where the U.S. Congress meets.

God Bless America: a song written by Irving Berlin in 1918, later revised, recorded, and released to the public in 1938.

Speaker Hastert: J. Dennis Hastert, a Republican from Illinois: the *Speaker of the House* is elected by the majority party to be the presiding officer of the House of Representatives.

Minority Leader Gephardt: Richard A. Gephardt, a Democrat from Missouri: the *minority leader* is elected by members of the minority party in the House of Representatives to expedite legislative business and to keep the party united.

Majority Leader Daschle: Tom Daschle, a Democratic senator from South Dakota; the *majority leader* of the U.S. Senate is the presiding officer who sets the agenda for Senate business.

Senator Lott: Trent Lott, a Republican senator from Mississippi, the minority leader of the Senate.

Buckingham Palace: residence of the British royal family in London, England.

Brandenburg Gate: a gate built in the 18th century in the German capital of Berlin. Near several government buildings and foreign embassies, the gate has been a popular rallying place, though it was in the inaccessible area between East and West Berlin from 1961 until 1989.

Seoul: the capital of South Korea.

Cairo: the capital of Egypt.

British Prime Minister: Tony Blair, leader of the Labour Party, elected to serve as the chief officer of the British Parliament in 1997.

for **one Sunday in 1941**. Americans have known the casualties of war—but not at the center of a great city on a peaceful morning. Americans have known surprise attacks—but never before on thousands of civilians. All of this was brought upon us in a single day—and night fell on a different world, a world where freedom itself is under attack.

Americans have many questions tonight. Americans are asking: Who attacked our country? The evidence we have gathered all points to a collection of loosely affiliated terrorist organizations known as **al Qaeda**. They are the same murderers indicted for **bombing American embassies in Tanzania and Kenya**, and responsible for bombing the **USS Cole**.

Al Qaeda is to terror what the mafia is to crime. But its goal is not making money; its goal is remaking the world—and imposing its radical beliefs on people everywhere.

The terrorists practice a fringe form of Islamic extremism that has been rejected by Muslim scholars and the vast majority of Muslim clerics—a fringe movement that perverts the peaceful teachings of Islam. The terrorists' directive commands them to kill Christians and Jews, to kill all Americans, and make no distinction among military and civilians, including women and children.

This group and its leader—a person named **Osama bin Laden**—are linked to many other organizations in different countries, including the **Egyptian Islamic Jihad** and the **Islamic Movement of Uzbekistan.** There are thousands of these terrorists in more than 60 countries. They are recruited from their own nations and neighborhoods and brought to camps in places like Afghanistan, where they are trained in the tactics of terror. They are sent back to their homes or sent to hide in countries around the world to plot evil and destruction.

The leadership of al Qaeda has great influence in Afghanistan and supports the **Taliban** regime in controlling most of that country. In Afghanistan, we see al Qaeda's vision for the world.

one Sunday in 1941: On Sunday, December 7, 1941, Japanese pilots attacked the U.S. military base at Pearl Harbor, Hawaii, prompting U.S. entry into World War II.

al Qaeda: the network of Islamic extremists organized by Osama bin Laden.

bombing American embassies in Tanzania and Kenya: the U.S. embassies in Dar es Salaam, Tanzania, and Nairobi, Kenya, were bombed by terrorists tied to Osama bin Laden on August 7, 1998.

USS Cole: terrorists tied to Osama bin Laden bombed this U.S. naval warship as it was refueling in Aden, Yemen, on October 12, 2000.

Osama bin Laden: considered the world's foremost terrorist, bin Laden is implicated in the airplane hijackings of September 11, 2001 that resulted in the destruction of the World Trade Center in New York City and of part of the Pentagon in Arlington, Virginia, and the combined loss of more than 6,000 lives.

Egyptian Islamic Jihad: a terrorist organization in Egypt whose goal is to overthrow the government of Egyptian President Hosni Mubarak and replace it with an Islamic state.

Islamic Movement of Uzbekistan: an organization publicly committed to the violent overthrow of the government of Uzbekistan.

Taliban: an organization of "holy warriors" or "freedom fighters" formed in 1979 to fight the Soviet occupation in Afghanistan, now the ruling faction in that country.

Afghanistan's people have been brutalized—many are starving and many have fled. Women are not allowed to attend school. You can be jailed for owning a television. Religion can be practiced only as their leaders dictate. A man can be jailed in Afghanistan if his beard is not long enough.

The United States respects the people of Afghanistan—after all, we are currently its largest source of humanitarian aid—but we condemn the Taliban regime. It is not only repressing its own people, it is threatening people everywhere by sponsoring and sheltering and supplying terrorists. By aiding and abetting murder, the Taliban regime is committing murder.

And tonight, the United States of America makes the following demands on the Taliban: Deliver to United States authorities all the leaders of al Qaeda who hide in your land. Release all foreign nationals, including American citizens, you have unjustly imprisoned. Protect foreign journalists, diplomats, and aid workers in your country. Close immediately and permanently every terrorist training camp in Afghanistan, and hand over every terrorist, and every person in their support structure, to appropriate authorities. Give the United States full access to terrorist training camps, so we can make sure they are no longer operating.

These demands are not open to negotiation or discussion. The Taliban must act, and act immediately. They will hand over the terrorists, or they will share in their fate.

I also want to speak tonight directly to **Muslims** throughout the world. We respect your faith. It's practiced freely by many millions of Americans, and by millions more in countries that America counts as friends. Its teachings are good and peaceful, and those who commit evil in the name of Allah blaspheme the name of Allah. The terrorists are traitors to their own faith, trying, in effect, to hijack **Islam** itself. The enemy of America is not our many Muslim friends; it is not our many Arab friends. Our enemy is a radical network of terrorists, and every government that supports them.

Muslims: followers of Islam.

Islam: a religion whose supreme being is Allah and whose main prophet and founder is Mohammed.

Our war on terror begins with al Qaeda, but it does not end there. It will not end until every terrorist group of global reach has been found, stopped, and defeated.

Americans are asking, why do they hate us? They hate what we see right here in this chamber—a democratically elected government. Their leaders are self-appointed. They hate our freedoms—our freedom of religion, our freedom of speech, our freedom to vote and assemble and disagree with each other.

They want to overthrow existing governments in many Muslim countries, such as Egypt, Saudi Arabia, and Jordan. They want to drive Israel out of the Middle East. They want to drive Christians and Jews out of vast regions of Asia and Africa.

These terrorists kill not merely to end lives, but to disrupt and end a way of life. With every **atrocity**, they hope that America grows fearful, retreating from the world and forsaking our friends. They stand against us, because we stand in their way.

atrocity: very cruel, evil act.

We are not deceived by their pretenses to piety. We have seen their kind before. They are the heirs of all the murderous ideologies of the 20th century. By sacrificing human life to serve their radical visions—by abandoning every value except the will to power—they follow in the path of **fascism**, and **Nazism**, and **totalitarianism**. And they will follow that path all the way, to where it ends: in history's unmarked grave of discarded lies.

fascism: system of government characterized by rigid one-party dictatorship, forcible suppression of opposition, private economic enterprise under centralized governmental control, belligerent nationalism, racism, and militarism.

Americans are asking: How will we fight and win this war? We will direct every resource at our command—every means of diplomacy, every tool of intelligence, every instrument of law enforcement, every financial influence, and every necessary weapon of war—to the disruption and to the defeat of the global terror network.

Nazism: political movement born of the German fascist political party (*National Socialist German Workers' Party*), which, under the leadership of Adolf Hitler, seized control of Germany in 1933, systematically eliminated opposition and initiated a program of nationalism, rearmament, political aggression, and racism (especially anti-Semitism).

This war will not be like the war against Iraq a decade ago, with a decisive liberation of territory and a swift conclusion. It will not look like the air war above **Kosovo** two years ago, where no ground troops were used and not a single American was lost in combat.

Totalitarianism: a system of government in which one political party or group maintains complete control under a dictatorship and bans all others.

Kosovo: a province in Serbia, Yugoslavia, where NATO launched a prolonged air strike in 1999 in an attempt to restore peace after years of civil unrest.

Our response involves far more than instant retaliation and isolated strikes. Americans should not expect one battle, but a lengthy campaign, unlike any other we have ever seen. It may include dramatic strikes, visible on TV, and covert operations, secret even in success. We will starve terrorists of funding, turn them one against another, drive them from place to place, until there is no refuge or no rest. And we will pursue nations that provide aid or safe haven to terrorism. Every nation, in every region, now has a decision to make. Either you are with us, or you are with the terrorists. From this day forward, any nation that continues to harbor or support terrorism will be regarded by the United States as a hostile regime.

Our nation has been put on notice: We are not immune from attack. We will take defensive measures against terrorism to protect Americans. Today, dozens of federal departments and agencies, as well as state and local governments, have responsibilities affecting homeland security. These efforts must be coordinated at the highest level. So tonight I announce the creation of a Cabinet-level position reporting directly to me—the Office of Homeland Security.

And tonight I also announce a distinguished American to lead this effort, to strengthen American security: a military veteran, an effective governor, a true patriot, a trusted friend—Pennsylvania's Tom Ridge. He will lead, oversee, and coordinate a comprehensive national strategy to safeguard our country against terrorism and respond to any attacks that may come.

These measures are essential. But the only way to defeat terrorism as a threat to our way of life is to stop it, eliminate it, and destroy it where it grows.

Many will be involved in this effort, from FBI agents to intelligence operatives to the **reservists** we have called to active duty. All deserve our thanks, and all have our prayers. And tonight, a few miles from the damaged Pentagon, I have a message for our military: Be ready. I've called the Armed Forces to alert, and there is a reason. The hour is coming when America will act, and you will make us proud.

reservists: military people or units not on active duty but subject to being called to serve.

This is not, however, just America's fight. And what is at stake is not just America's freedom. This is the world's fight. This is civilization's fight. This is the fight of all who believe in progress and pluralism, tolerance and freedom.

We ask every nation to join us. We will ask, and we will need, the help of police forces, intelligence services, and banking systems around the world. The United States is grateful that many nations and many international organizations have already responded—with sympathy and with support. Nations from Latin America, to Asia, to Africa, to Europe, to the Islamic world. Perhaps the **NATO** Charter reflects best the attitude of the world: An attack on one is an attack on all.

NATO: the North Atlantic Treaty Organization was formed in 1949 to mount a collective defense of member countries against aggressors.

The civilized world is rallying to America's side. They understand that if this terror goes unpunished, their own cities, their own citizens may be next. Terror, unanswered, can not only bring down buildings, it can threaten the stability of legitimate governments. And you know what—we're not going to allow it.

Americans are asking: What is expected of us? I ask you to live your lives, and hug your children. I know many citizens have fears tonight, and I ask you to be calm and resolute, even in the face of a continuing threat.

I ask you to uphold the values of America, and remember why so many have come here. We are in a fight for our principles, and our first responsibility is to live by them. No one should be singled out for unfair treatment or unkind words because of their ethnic background or religious faith.

I ask you to continue to support the victims of this tragedy with your contributions. Those who want to give can go to a central source of information, libertyunites.org, to find the names of groups providing direct help in New York, Pennsylvania, and Virginia.

The thousands of FBI agents who are now at work in this investigation may need your cooperation, and I ask you to give it.

I ask for your patience, with the delays and inconveniences that may accompany tighter security; and for your patience in what will be a long struggle.

I ask your continued participation and confidence in the American economy. Terrorists attacked a symbol of American prosperity. They did not touch its source. America is successful because of the hard work, and creativity, and enterprise of our people. These were the true strengths of our economy before September 11th, and they are our strengths today.

And, finally, please continue praying for the victims of terror and their families, for those in uniform, and for our great country. Prayer has comforted us in sorrow, and will help strengthen us for the journey ahead.

Tonight I thank my fellow Americans for what you have already done and for what you will do. And ladies and gentlemen of the Congress, I thank you, their representatives, for what you have already done and for what we will do together.

Tonight, we face new and sudden national challenges. We will come together to improve air safety, to dramatically expand the number of air marshals on domestic flights, and take new measures to prevent hijacking. We will come together to promote stability and keep our airlines flying, with direct assistance during this emergency.

We will come together to give law enforcement the additional tools it needs to track down terror here at home. We will come together to strengthen our intelligence capabilities to know the plans of terrorists before they act, and find them before they strike.

We will come together to take active steps that strengthen America's economy, and put our people back to work.

Tonight we welcome two leaders who embody the extraordinary spirit of all New Yorkers: Governor George Pataki, and Mayor Rudolph Giuliani. As a symbol of America's resolve, my administration will work with Congress, and these two leaders, to show the world that we will rebuild New York City.

After all that has just passed—all the lives taken, and all the possibilities and hopes that died with them—it is natural to wonder if America's future is one of fear. Some speak of an age of terror. I know there are struggles ahead, and dangers to face. But this country will define our times, not be defined by them. As long as the United States of America is determined and strong, this will not be an age of terror; this will be an age of liberty, here and across the world.

Great harm has been done to us. We have suffered great loss. And in our grief and anger we have found our mission and our moment. Freedom and fear are at war. The advance of human freedom—the great achievement of our time, and the great hope of every time—now depends on us. Our nation—this generation—will lift a dark threat of violence from our people and our future. We will rally the world to this cause by our efforts, by our courage. We will not tire, we will not falter, and we will not fail.

It is my hope that in the months and years ahead, life will return almost to normal. We'll go back to our lives and routines, and that is good. Even grief recedes with time and grace. But our resolve must not pass. Each of us will remember what happened that day, and to whom it happened. We'll remember the moment the news came—where we were and what we were doing. Some will remember an image of a fire, or a story of rescue. Some will carry memories of a face and a voice gone forever.

And I will carry this: It is the police shield of a man named George Howard, who died at the World Trade Center trying to save others. It was given to me by his mom, Arlene, as a proud memorial to her son. This is my reminder of lives that ended, and a task that does not end.

I will not forget this wound to our country or those who inflicted it. I will not yield; I will not rest; I will not relent in waging this struggle for freedom and security for the American people.

The course of this conflict is not known, yet its outcome is certain. Freedom and fear, justice and cruelty, have always been at war, and we know that God is not neutral between them.

Fellow citizens, we'll meet violence with patient justice—assured of the rightness of our cause, and confident of the victories to come. In all that lies before us, may God grant us wisdom, and may He watch over the United States of America.

Thank you.

COMMENTARY

On the morning of September 11, 2001, tragedy struck the United States. Two commercial airliners, hijacked by Islamic fundamentalists, crashed into the World Trade Center. The two towers of the World Trade Center, a symbol of U.S. ingenuity and international business activity, collapsed. At press time, more than 500 people were confirmed dead and nearly 5,000 more were missing and presumed dead. Hundreds of firefighters and police officers attempting to evacuate the World Trade Center were among the casualties. The attack constituted the worst terrorist attack, not just in U.S. history, but in the history of the free, democratic world. Almost three times as many U.S. citizens died in the attack on the World Trade Center as did in the Japanese surprise attack on Pearl Harbor in 1941.

Another hijacked airliner crashed into the Pentagon minutes later, inflicting close to 200 casualties. The strike severely damaged the Pentagon, a symbol of U.S. military strength. A fourth plane crashed in Pennsylvania before it could hit its target. The heroic acts of the passengers, who sacrificed their lives to save thousands of others, brought the plane down.

The unimaginable happened. Terrorism struck the U.S. mainland. Suddenly, the United States found itself in the same boat as Israel, Northern Ireland, and Russia, where terrorist acts are commonplace. The U.S. public, even though in a state of shock, came together to do whatever it could to help. Whether they donated blood, gave money, or flew the flag, millions of U.S. citizens somehow participated in the rescue effort. Instead of creating panic, the terrorist acts achieved the opposite: The U.S. public rallied around the flag and President Bush.

Some Americans opposed the idea of military strikes in retaliation, however, and reawakened the peace movement. Opposition to military retaliation was particularly strong on college campuses.

On September 20, 2001, President Bush addressed both Houses of Congress, the U.S. public, and the world community. In his speech, he attempted to achieve a number of objectives.

* First, he tried to reassure the U.S. citizens that they were safe and that the country needed to return to normalcy.

* Second, he had to explain to the public who was behind the vicious attacks and what he planned to do about them.

* Third, he needed to reassure the Islamic world that it was not the target or the enemy of the United States.

* Finally, he had to create support within the international community for whatever actions the United States planned against the terrorists and the nations harboring them.

Bush's speech begins by thanking Congress and its leaders. He praises them for their support and for passing a bill delivering $40 billion to help rebuild New York and retaliate against those responsible. Most important, he thanks them for their support of the military. Bush refers to resolutions passed by the House and the Senate authorizing him to use whatever force is necessary to punish aggression. Under the War Powers Act of 1973, the president can commit troops to a hostile situation for only 60 days. After that, Congress has the power to recall military personnel if it chooses to do so. By having both houses of Congress pass resolutions authorizing him to use force to strike back at the terrorists, Bush abides by the War Powers Act and doesn't have to worry about Congress withdrawing its support in the future. The resolutions provide him with the long-term backing of Congress for whatever military actions he deems necessary. Unlike many previous presidents, including Ford, Carter, and Reagan, President Bush is not engaging in unilateral actions against aggression, but instead is asking for Congress to support his agenda—a smart move for any long-term military action.

Gathering International Support

In the next section, Bush expresses his gratitude for all the international support the United States received. He singles out some of the most important allies in the upcoming war against terrorism. These include Great Britain, which already pledged military support, as well as France and Germany—the other great European powers that Bush wants to involve in possible military action. More importantly, he singles out Egypt, the major U.S. ally in the Middle East. He knows that support from Egypt is necessary to garner support from other Middle Eastern countries.

The speech continues by highlighting the fact that more than 600 foreign citizens perished in the attack on the World Trade Center. President Bush makes the point that the attacks impacted the international community, and he appeals to the international community for support in punishing those responsible. He clearly doesn't want to punish the terrorists alone. Like his father, President George Herbert Walker Bush, did in the war in the Persian Gulf in 1991, George W. Bush is attempting to establish an international alliance against terrorism, providing the United States with worldwide support. This support doesn't need to be military, but should involve sharing intelligence and sanctions against those countries harboring terrorists.

Placing Blame

Bush continues his speech by explaining who was behind the attack, which he calls an act of war. This designation allows him to strike back at the sources of aggression under international law. He distinguishes between attacks on military targets and attacks on civilians. For the first time in U.S. history, civilians on the U.S. mainland were the intended target of aggression, not the U.S. military.

In this section of the speech, Bush answers the big question on everybody's mind: Who was responsible for these atrocious acts? Bush puts blame on a terrorist organization named *al Qaeda* (also spelled "al Qaida"). Al Qaeda, which means "the base," is an umbrella organization for militant Islamic associations with about 10,000 members worldwide.

Al Qaeda trains its followers in terrorist strategies—mostly in Afghanistan and Sudan—and then exports these terrorists throughout the world. Al Qaeda members are stationed in about 60 mainly Muslim countries and members have been found in Europe, in Bosnia and Chechnya, and even in Latin America.

Al Qaeda is responsible for the 1998 bombings of U.S. embassies in Tanzania and Kenya and the bombing of the World Trade Center in 1993. It also committed the bombings of U.S. military barracks in Saudi Arabia and of the U.S. navy warship U.S.S. Cole in Yemen last year.

Bin Laden and al Qaeda's History and Mission

A Saudi multimillionaire, Osama bin Laden became a radical after the Soviet invasion of Afghanistan in 1979. He not only funded the Afghan freedom fighters in the 1980s, but also joined in the fighting. After the Soviets left Afghanistan in 1988, bin Laden stayed and participated in the ensuing civil war. By 1994, the Taliban—a fundamentalist Muslim sect—took over the country and bin Laden became not only a guest of the government, but contributed heavily to financing the Taliban regime. Since 1996, he has used Afghanistan as a place to train his terrorist followers.

According to Bush, al Qaeda is not interested in money, but rather the establishment of a radical Muslim state throughout the world. Bush is very careful to distinguish between radical Islamic fundamentalism and mainstream Islam. He mentions that mainstream Muslim scholars and religious leaders, as well as all Muslim countries in the Middle East, reject what al Qaeda stands for—killing Christians and Jews, especially U.S. citizens, without distinguishing between military and civilian targets.

Besides the terrorist activities mentioned by the president, bin Laden is also accused of masterminding the killing of U.S. soldiers in Somalia and the aborted assassination attempts of U.S. President Bill Clinton and Pope John Paul II, head of the Roman Catholic Church.

These terrorists, according to the president, operate in many countries and are linked to many other radical organizations—the Egyptian Islamic Jihad and the Islamic Movement of Uzbekistan, for example. Overall, al Qaeda operates in more than 60 countries. However, in most of these countries, terrorist movements are illegal and governments try to shut them down. On the other hand, a few countries allow them to operate openly.

The headquarters of al Qaeda is in Afghanistan, where the ruling Taliban regime openly identifies with al Qaeda's goals. The Afghani government itself, according to Bush, brutalizes its own people, punishing people for owning a television, women for appearing unescorted or unveiled in public, and men for not having long-enough beards.

Distinguishing between Afghanis and the Taliban

In one of the most important parts of the speech, Bush makes the distinction between the innocent people of Afghanistan and the ruling Taliban regime. He makes it clear that the United States harbors no ill will toward the people of Afghanistan. On the contrary, Bush points out that the United States is the major source of humanitarian aid for the Afghanis.

President Bush does condemn the Taliban regime for spreading terrorism throughout the world and for repressing its own people. He also lets it be known that in the U.S. view, it doesn't matter whether you commit a terrorist act or harbor terrorists. According to Bush: "By aiding and abetting murder, the Taliban regime is committing murder." Implied is that the punishment for terrorists and for nations harboring terrorists will be the same: The United States will not distinguish between terrorism and nations allowing terrorists to operate within their borders.

Making Demands of the Taliban

In a savvy move, Bush then makes several demands of the Taliban. He, of course, knows that the Taliban will refuse many of his demands, which allows the United States to justify a military strike against the Taliban regime. His demands of the Taliban include:

* Handing over the leadership of al Qaeda, and releasing all foreign nationals who have been unjustly imprisoned.
* Protecting all foreign citizens in Afghanistan, including diplomats and aid workers.
* Closing all terrorist camps, handing over every terrorist, and allowing the United States to inspect terrorist camps.

Bush states that there will be no negotiation and no compromise. If the Taliban refuses to meet the demands, the United States will punish them in a fashion similar to the terrorists.

Reassuring Muslims and the Arab World

Bush continues to reassure Muslims all over the world that the United States in not targeting their faith or the Islamic world. He tells the world that the United States respects Islam and that millions of U.S. citizens are Muslims. He criticizes the terrorists for subverting a peaceful religion, going so far as calling the terrorists traitors to their own faith. The United States respects Islam and the many Muslim nations where the religion is practiced peacefully. At the same time, the people who subvert Islam, namely the terrorists and the countries supporting them, are the only enemies of the United States.

Bush has to walk a fine line here. He wants the support of the moderate Arab nations, such as Egypt, Saudi Arabia, and Pakistan, in upcoming military action against Afghanistan. He further needs to reassure hundreds of millions of Muslims throughout the world that the United States is not an enemy of Islam. (Islam is the fastest growing religion in the world, having over one billion followers.) Bush needs to make sure that a strike against the terrorists and Afghanistan will not become a holy war between Christianity and Islam. This can be accomplished only if the leaders of moderate Islamic nations and their clergy side with the United States, or at least remain neutral. The last thing the president wants to do is to subvert some of the United States's moderate Arab allies in the Middle East by encouraging anti-American sentiment in these nations.

Setting Forth the Reason for the Attacks

Bush moves on to explain his thinking on why the terrorists attacked U.S. citizens. He states that these terrorists hate the democratic way of life. They oppose the democratic system of government whose leaders are accountable to the people. Bush explains that the leaders of terrorist organizations and governments are self-appointed and maintain themselves in power by brute force. They especially oppose the freedoms we enjoy. Bush states that these renegades hate the freedom granted U.S. citizens by the Bill of Rights—freedom of speech, freedom to criticize the government, and, most important, freedom to practice any religion one chooses. For these extremists, their way is the only way, and their religion is the only one acceptable. Everything else is not acceptable and must be destroyed.

Bin Laden and his followers believe that Christians and Jews poison the Islamic world and are infidels who must be destroyed in a *jihad,* or holy war. Among these infidels they count all the Middle Eastern governments that collaborate with the United States.

Bin Laden and his followers especially hate the United States because U.S. troops are in Saudi Arabia, close to the holy cities of Mecca and Medina. This, according to bin Laden, desecrates the Holy Land. To purge the Middle East of the U.S. presence, bin Laden advocates using whatever means are necessary to accomplish those objectives, including terrorism. In 1998, bin Laden called for the killing of all U.S. citizens.

According to Bush, these terrorists oppose pro-American governments, such as Saudi Arabia, Egypt, and Jordan and do their best to undermine and overthrow these allied governments. Bush

then proceeds to talk about Israel. For these terrorists, Israel is the major enemy. They want to
destroy the state and drive all Jews out of the
Middle East. But they won't stop there. Next, they
will drive Christians out of Asia and Africa. They
target the United States because the United
States stands by Israel. With these terrorist
attacks, they hope to undermine U.S. resolve and
to stop the United States from supporting its
friends abroad. They will not succeed.

Making Historical Comparisons

In a powerful part of the speech, Bush com-
pares the terrorists and their ideas to failed ideologies, or worldviews, of the early twentieth
century. He mentions fascism and totalitarianism
as examples, and asserts that, like these failed
ideologies, the extremist views the terrorists hold
will be defeated and perish from the earth. Interestingly, Bush leaves out communism in his list of
failed ideologies. Of course, he is counting on
Russian support against the war on terrorism and
he doesn't want to offend Russia.

Preparing the United States and the World
for a War on Terrorism

Bush continues his speech trying to prepare
the U.S. public for sacrifices. He tells the public
that the United States will use all the tools available to it, from diplomacy to economic sanctions,
to the use of force. The public needs to be prepared for hardships, including U.S. casualties.
Unlike the war in Iraq or the strike against
Yugoslavia, the war on terrorism promises to be
lengthy. It will consist of military strikes, secret
operations, and economic warfare, such as freez-
ing funds that terrorist organizations have in
Western bank accounts.

The war on terrorism targets not just the terrorists, but also every nation that supports them.

The world has to make a decision: Either stand
with the United States in its war on terrorism or
be counted as an enemy. A nation that harbors
terrorists will be considered a hostile regime and
must expect action against it.

The war on terrorism needs to be fought not
just abroad but also at home. The U.S. government
will take any defensive measures necessary to
protect the U.S. public. Bush announces the creation of a new cabinet position, the office of
Homeland Security. The person in charge of this
new cabinet position is Bush's old friend, Tom
Ridge, the Republican governor of Pennsylvania.
The function of the department is to coordinate
local, state, and federal agencies in their mission
to fight terrorism. A comprehensive national strategy to defend the country against terrorist attacks
will be put in place. Here, Bush is reacting to critics who stated that a lack of coordination among
agencies allowed such an attack to take place in
the first place.

Punishing the Guilty

The next section in Bush's speech addresses
the question of punishment. Many in the United
States want quick punishment for the terrorists
and Bush proclaims that the hour is coming when
the United States will strike back. The United
States will not strike back by itself, though. For
Bush, the war on terrorism is an international war,
and he invites everybody in the civilized world to
join in the fight.

Bush thanks the countries that already pledged
support. He singles out the countries that are part
of the North Atlantic Treaty Organization, or NATO.
Soon after the attack, NATO invoked Article 5 of
its charter—the clause that drives NATO as a
defensive alliance. It states that an attack against
any one member equals an attack against all fifteen members. In turn, all fifteen members will

strike back against the aggression committed. By invoking the clause, the other fourteen NATO members pledged their support in the war against terrorism, including the use of military force if required. This marks the first time since its creation in 1949—after the end of World War II—that NATO has invoked Article 5.

Bush makes the point that an attack such as the one on the World Trade Center can occur in any country, and that it is in the interest of the free world to make sure that it doesn't occur again.

Reassuring the Public

Bush now turns to the U.S. public. He asks them to be calm and resolute and not to panic, saying that panic only plays into the hands of the terrorists. At the same time, continuing to adhere to American values is of utmost importance. Here he appeals to the public not to single out, discriminate against, or harm people because of their ethnic or religious background. His intent here is to protect American Muslims and others with different religious beliefs and ethnicities from attacks by angry citizens.

He continues his speech, asking the U.S. people to help in whatever way they can. They can give money, cooperate with local and federal authorities, and not complain about tighter security, the resulting delays, and other inconveniences. Bush than asks the public to help preserve the economy. In subsequent statements, the president urges people to have confidence in the economy and to help prevent a recession by continuing to spend money.

Bush reaches a point in his speech where he thanks the U.S. public and the members of Congress for all they have already done. He outlines specific proposals to increase security in the United States. The president proposes to put air marshals on domestic flights to improve security, and to make sure that law enforcement agencies receive additional funds and tools to be more effective against future terrorist strikes. Bush realizes that he has to reassure the public that the U.S. government will do everything in its power to prevent another strike.

He promises economic aid to New York City and presents the Governor of New York, George Pataki, and the Mayor of New York City, Rudolph Giuliani, as exemplary Americans who embody the spirit of this country.

Bush then concludes his speech proclaiming that freedom and fear are at war. He implores the U.S. public not to give in to fear, despite the horrific losses, but to return to normal life. He states that nobody will ever forget this tragedy, especially him, and that he will dedicate the rest of his administration to punishing those responsible. As president, Bush promises not to rest or relent until the terrorists are brought to justice. The outcome of the tragedy is clear for Bush. "Freedom and fear, justice and cruelty have always been at war, and we know that God is not neutral between them." In the end, the United States will prevail and justice will be done.

Reaction to the Speech

After President Bush delivered the address, the consensus of pundits and opinion polls was that he did an exemplary job. Commentators compared his speech to President Roosevelt's declaration of war speech given in 1941. His approval rating hit an unheard-of 90 percent—a first for a peacetime president. Members of Congress, including Democrats, applauded the speech, interrupting it more than 20 times with standing ovations, and endorsed Bush's handling of the crisis. Even his most vocal critics praised the president.

In the days after the speech, it became clear that Bush accomplished his first objective: The U.S. public returned to their normal lives, although with the attack always on their minds. Support continues to pour in to the victims of the attack and New York City. The government took new measures to ensure the safety of air travel, and the average person accepts delays and additional checks without complaining. The airline industry, hurt badly in the attack, received government aid to weather the crisis. After an initial downturn, the stock market recovered. The attempt to interrupt and change the life of U.S. citizens failed. On the contrary, the country rallied around the president and the flag and the United States seemed stronger than ever.

Bush's explanation of the events and the reason behind the attack clarified the picture for the average person. A majority of citizens polled—over 80 percent—demand punishment of the terrorists. Bush convinced them that a swift reaction is not possible and that the punishment will take time—possibly years. According to polls, most U.S. citizens also expect sacrifices, even military casualties, in the war on terrorism and are prepared to accept this.

Bush also accomplished his third objective—to reassure the Islamic world that any U.S. strike is not an attack on Islam. Most moderate Middle Eastern countries condemned the attack and have offered assistance to the United States. Islamic clergy throughout the world declare that such an attack goes against the core beliefs of Islam. Even countries usually considered hostile to the United States, such as Iran and Syria, condemned the attack, and in turn, the Afghan government. After some members of the PLO (Palestine Liberation Organization) initially praised the attack, the head of the organization, Yassir Arafat, put a stop to this and even donated blood to help the victims of the attack. Not one Muslim country in the world applauded the attack or condemned the idea that the United States strike back against the Muslim terrorists.

In the United States, fear in the aftermath of the terrorist strike resulted in blatant discrimination and even some attacks against Arab-Americans. The government, especially President Bush, forcefully responded to these incidents, and the attacks abated. Bush went out of his way to reassure the U.S. public that Arab-Americans are not to blame for the attacks.

Bush's final objective was to create international support for upcoming military actions against the terrorists. He was especially successful in this area. NATO has pledged full support in the war against terrorism. The major European powers, such as Great Britain, France, and Germany reassured the United States that they would fight by its side. Even Italy announced that it would support the United States militarily. The European Union condemned the attack and stated that that it will support the United States. Already, most European countries are participating in the attempt to freeze financial assets held by the terrorists. To the surprise of many, Russia, the former Cold War enemy, announced that it will support the United States and offered the use of their military bases close to Afghanistan.

Nearly all of the Middle Eastern countries pledged their support. Saudi Arabia, one of the few countries to recognize the Taliban government in Afghanistan as legitimate, severed all diplomatic ties with the country. Major central Asian countries, such as Kazakhstan and Uzbekistan, which border Afghanistan, offered their air space and bases to the United States. All the countries bordering Afghanistan, even China and Iran, closed their borders to make it impossible for the terrorists to leave Afghanistan. Finally, Pakistan, which also recognized the Taliban as the legitimate government of Afghanistan and helped them come to power, agreed to let the United States use its country as a base for military action, though it refused to participate in any action itself. For the United States, the support of Pakistan, a nuclear power with a strong Muslim fundamentalist movement itself, was necessary in order to succeed in the war against terrorism. In the case of Pakistan, President Bush used not only diplomatic pressure, but also economic pressure. Bush lifted sanctions against the country, which is run by a military regime, and delivered much needed economic aid to Pakistan.

In conclusion, President Bush achieved the objectives he set out in his speech. He emerged not only as a national leader, but also an international leader. Like his father during the Gulf War, he is bringing an international alliance together to punish aggression. The horrible acts of September 11, 2001 brought out the best, not just in a country, but also in a relatively new president.

Freedom in Action
A Special Monthly
Give-Away for Educators

Through an exciting monthly give-away, we will do our part to get *American Words of Freedom* into America's classrooms.

Beginning in January 2002, we will select one educator per month to receive 24 free copies of *American Words of Freedom* for his or her classroom.

How to Enter:

1. **Complete the form below (or fill out a 3 x 5 card with complete information) and mail to:**

   Webster's New World American Words of Freedom
   Attn: Melisa Duffy, Marketing
   10475 Crosspoint Blvd
   Indianapolis, IN 46256

Webster's New World American Words of Freedom
Educator Give-Away

Name _____

School _____

Address _____

Daytime Phone _____

E-mail _____

Grade(s) and/or Subject(s)taught _____

Details:

No purchase necessary. One entry per month per educator. The winner will be chosen the last business day of the month and notified via phone within 10 business days. Void where prohibited by law. All submissions become the exclusive property of Hungry Minds, Inc. Hungry Minds is not responsible for lost, late, illegible, or incomplete entries or postage-due, damaged, or separated mail. Monthly give-away ends December 31, 2002.